OTIS!

ALSO BY SCOTT FREEMAN

Midnight Riders: The Story of the Allman Brothers Band

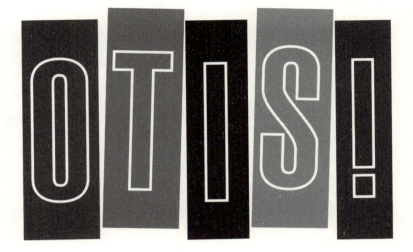

The Otis Redding Story

SCOTT FREEMAN

ST. MARTIN'S PRESS ≈ NEW YORK

www.stmartins.com

Book design by Tim Hall

Library of Congress Cataloging-in-Publication Data

Freeman, Scott.
    Otis! : the Otis Redding story / Scott Freeman.
        p.   cm.
    ISBN 0-312-26217-5
    1. Redding, Otis, d. 1967.   2. Soul musicians—United States—Biography.   I. Title:
Otis Redding story.   II. Title.

ML420.R295 F74 2001
782.421644'092—dc21
[B]   2001041976

First Edition: December 2001

10 9 8 7 6 5 4 3 2 1

For Carrolle M. King
and
Hewell "Chank" Middleton

CONTENTS

I've Got Dreams to Remember

Terrell County, Georgia, is about as far away from the spotlight as one can get, a sleepy little farming community right in the heart of the peanut belt and just twenty miles south of Plains, the hometown of Jimmy Carter. Coming out of the Depression, the entire local economy revolved around peanuts and cotton—from the acres of lush, green farmland to the sweltering mills where peanuts were shelled and cotton was ginned. For the white landowners and farmers, it was an existence that hearkened back to the big plantations before the Civil War. For the Negroes who worked the land, it also carried a familiarity. Virtually all of them sharecropped—a hard way to make a living, sometimes an impossible one.

Sharecropping had essentially replaced slavery in much of the South in the aftermath of the war. Whites still owned plantations, but they no longer owned slaves to supply the labor and lacked the money to hire free Negroes. Many of them divided their land into parcels of thirty or forty acres and rented out the plots to Negroes; the owners would supply the land and a place for a family to live, along with tools and seed and livestock. In return, the sharecropper would provide the labor and turn over a large percentage of his harvest to the landowner, selling what was left on the market. It was a grueling life that many considered little more than legalized slavery. At the very least, it could perpetuate a cycle of poverty—whenever sharecroppers were short on cash, they would have no choice but to borrow from the landowner against the next crop. It could lead them so deeply into a financial hole that they were essentially bound to the landowner for life.

Otis Redding, Sr., was a sharecropper for a prominent Terrell County farmer named W. G. "Will" Lang who grew peanuts and cotton, and also raised cattle and hogs on a fifteen-hundred-acre spread that was adjacent to his brother's fifteen-hundred-acre spread. Mr. Redding was married to Fannie Mae Redding and by 1940 had three daughters: Louise (four), Christie (three), and Darlene (one). His first son came on September 9, 1941, and he was named Otis Ray Redding, Jr. Young Otis was born in a little sharecropper house on the Lang farm that sat next to Highway 55 about eight miles south of Dawson, the biggest town in the county.

The Reddings were surrounded by family. Otis's grandmother on his mother's side, Lizzie Roseman, lived just down the road. And his grandfather on his father's side, Monroe Mack, also lived in the same neighborhood. So did an uncle and an aunt. They were all involved in farming in one way or another, mostly sharecropping or working their own modest plots of land or hiring out to work in the fields.

Two things distinguished Mr. Redding from the other sharecroppers around Terrell County: his religious fervor and his ambition. He longed to be a preacher just as he longed for a better life. And to a young Negro family in south Georgia, a better life meant moving 120 miles northeast to Macon. It was close enough to maintain family ties back home, but large enough to offer the chance for a life that simply wasn't possible laboring on a sweat-drenched farm. Just as Memphis and Chicago acted as magnets for blacks from the Mississippi Delta migrating north, Macon was a destination point for poor rural families from the farms of south Georgia. A strong and bustling city, Macon had jobs waiting to be filled whether you were white or black. It boasted a strong industrial base—textiles, ceramics, cotton, and lumber—that thrived off the area's abundant natural resources. Downtown Macon rests on a dividing line near what was once the shoreline of the Atlantic Ocean. The land north of the city is marked by gentle hills and soil rich with red clay, which lured several large brick and ceramics companies to Macon. The Coastal Plain begins just south of the city; the terrain quickly turns flat and the soil turns sandy and white. There are acres upon acres of pine trees south of Macon, making lumber a prime industry. The area also holds 60 percent of the world's purest kaolin reserves. Known to locals as "white gold," kaolin is a chalky underground clay and the key ingredient of hundreds of products, ranging from toothpaste and antacid tablets to china and chemicals. As the industries grew, Macon also developed into a railroad hub—home of eleven different rail lines and a distribution point for produce and cotton.

At its heart, the city was still very much Old South. Country. Simple values, simple times. People were gracious and genteel. Because Macon was isolated in the center of the largest state east of the Mississippi and a hundred miles away from the nearest city, it was essentially allowed to grow into a comfortable entity unto itself. Through the years, Macon developed its own unique rhythm of life, symbolized by the dozens of antebellum homes that still grace the city. The outside world could seem far, far away; often it didn't seem to really matter at all.

Macon also boasted a large and vibrant Negro community—people of color have steadily constituted nearly 45 percent of the city's population ever since Reconstruction. The two communities existed under an uneasy truce. The dynamic was set in place during the days of slavery; whites expected to be accepted as caring despots ruling the city and blacks were expected to submissively acquiesce, to go along to get along. But because their large population gave Negroes a significant power base, the relations between the races were particularly polarized. More than fifty years after the fact, whites still bristled that former slaves had dared to seek, and *win*, elected positions of power during Reconstruction.

In a 1922 special edition celebrating the city's centennial, the *Macon News* wrote:

For a time, the Negroes, carpetbaggers and scalawags made themselves politically very obnoxious. Pulaski Holt, a Negro merchant who bore the same name as a prominent white citizen, was elected an alderman. Ed Woodliff, a Negro barber, was also elected to the council. Jeff Long, a Negro tailor, was elected to Congress. When President Grant appointed H. M. Turner, a Negro preacher, postmaster of Macon, a wave of indignation swept over the city. A delegation went to Washington to protest. Turner was later implicated in a stolen bank note scheme. The evidence was not sufficient, but the hearing developed gross immorality on his part and his removal followed. His tenure of office did not exceed two weeks.

In truth, Henry McNeal Turner was run out of office because he was every white person's nightmare—an articulate and charismatic black man who demanded his rights, a forerunner of the militancy of Elijah Muhammad and Malcolm X. Known as "the Black Moses," Henry Turner was the grandson of an enslaved African prince and grew up as a Free Negro. He received an education, and was elected to the Georgia General Assembly in the first postwar elections along with thirty-one other Negroes. As soon as they were seated, the white-dominated legislature expelled them using the rather novel grounds that the state constitution never guaranteed that the right to vote also included the right to hold elected office.

"I will not beg for my rights," Turner said in a famed protest speech. "I come here to demand my rights, and to hurl thunderbolts at the men who would dare to cross the threshold of my manhood. You may think you are doing yourselves honor by expelling us from this house; but when we go, we will light a torch of truth that will never be extinguished." Turner later left Georgia to become the national leader of the African Methodist Episcopal (A.M.E.) Church, growing so pessimistic about race relations in the United States that he urged Negroes to return to their motherland of Africa. "There is no hope that prejudice will diminish," he said. "It is instilled into the minds of the son by the father, and that son in turn will hand it down."

Those words often seemed especially prophetic in Macon. The two races had remained separate and apart for generations, rarely interacting beyond white housewives conversing with their Negro maids. Black families gravitated to the humble neighborhoods that sprang up after the Civil War—Pleasant Hill just north of downtown, Unionville just west of downtown, Fort Hill in east Macon, Tybee in southwest Macon, and Bellevue on the western fringes of the city. So long as the Negroes were discreet about what they did and didn't commit crimes against white people, the black communities were pretty much left to themselves. However, if they strayed from those boundaries, the punishment could be swift and merciless. In the 1920s a

Negro man dared to kill a white deputy sheriff who came to arrest him at a downtown pool hall on Broadway; a few hours later he was spotted by deputies north of Macon and gunned down. His body was then brought back, tied with rope to the fender of a car, and dragged down Broadway for all to see. The body was left in front of the Douglass Theatre, the Negro movie house.

By the time the Redding family moved to Macon in 1942, the black population was beginning to make small strides. The first public high school for Negroes, Hudson Industrial School, was built in 1922. There were a handful of physicians and one Negro hospital. There were even two small black business districts in downtown. But Negroes held little sway politically or socially. "That was segregation at its greatest," said David Tharpe, who grew up in Bellevue and pursued a singing career before becoming a pastor. "Back in that era, they said people knew their place. It was hard for black people because you had no rights. The police could beat you up; you were a citizen without rights. There were very few whites who were sympathetic to the black man and his plight. A lot of black men, if a white person came to the door, they'd say, 'Tell 'em I ain't home.' My father was not a man who was afraid; he always went to the door and he always taught us to look a man in the eye."

The Redding family settled in a federal housing project called Tindall Heights west of downtown. It was sparkling new, the second in a series of housing projects that sprang up in the city in the aftermath of the Depression. There were nearly four hundred units built with the efficient look of an Army base—rows upon rows of two-story red brick buildings set up like a series of flat dominoes. The Reddings' apartment was number 97-B in the western portion of the complex, just off Plant Street. Their building housed five other apartments and sat up on a little hill overlooking the campus of Mercer University, the stately white Methodist college.

All the apartments at Tindall Heights were laid out essentially the same way—small kitchen and living room on the bottom floor, bedrooms and bathroom upstairs. For the people who moved there when it first opened, Tindall Heights must have seemed exotic and luxurious beyond description. Most were more accustomed to shanty houses that boasted few amenities beyond the roof over their heads. Some had electricity; many didn't. To go to the bathroom meant going to the outhouse. Hot water was often produced on the top of a wood-burning stove. Electric refrigerators were still a novelty. Tindall Heights offered the kind of modern amenities that most of its tenants had never known before. A press release announcing the opening of the complex giddily boasted of apartments with electric refrigerators, automatic hot-water heaters, gas ranges, built-in kitchen cabinets, gas heat, and "a complete bathroom indoors."

Like most housing projects, the bright and shining veneer of Tindall Heights quickly evaporated. It had all the warmth of a prison, and the life there was just about as hard. Dignity and respect were often in short supply. There was no sense of community because the residents were so transient. The street corners became hangouts for kids who had no jobs, no hope, and no future. Youth gangs began to organize. Crime was often a primary means of support. Outsiders avoided going there after the sun went down. One essential truth quickly made itself evident: Tindall Heights was no place to call home; it was a place to escape.

Mr. Redding found work as a laborer and maintenance man at Robins Field (now Robins Air Force Base), an Air Force depot about sixteen miles south of Macon that opened in 1943 to service the bombers flying missions in World War II. By then, the family had grown to eight members with the birth of a sixth child, Luther Rodgers, and the new dream became saving enough money to buy their very own house. The family hustled for money, squirreling away whatever they could for the future. Mrs. Redding began working as a maid at the Woolworth's department store on Cherry Street in downtown Macon and sold Avon on the side. Mr. Redding picked up extra cash by farming a patch of land out on Rivoli Road. Both Otis and his brother were expected to help their father farm, and maybe that's when his family came to realize that Otis was different. He was always the mischievous and playful one, the one who'd get into trouble in an instant and then get himself out of it with a flash of his smile. "When we would go out to the farm, Otis would play," Luther Rodgers said. "He would sing all the way out there, while he was there, and then all the way back. We finally just stopped carrying him out there."

Otis was enchanted by music. Like most of the other musicians who came from the South, the spark was kindled by the impassioned and soaring hymns he heard in church as a child. By the time he was ten, he had picked up a habit that would remain with him for life—constantly pounding out a backbeat on whatever happened to be in front of him. "In elementary school, he was crazy about drums," said Luther Rodgers. "Every time you'd see him he was beating on something—spoons, pencils, just riding in the car and beating out a rhythm on the dash."

Otis sang with the choir at Vineville Baptist Church, and eventually played drums behind a gospel group that had a local Sunday-morning radio show. For a seventh-grade talent show at the B. S. Ingram School, Otis wanted to both sing *and* play a drum solo. "I remember when he had his tonsils taken out," said Luther Rodgers. "Oh, boy, he was pitiful. I remember him saying, 'Will I be able to sing again?' And my father said, 'Sure, probably you'll be able to sing better.'" By the eighth grade, Otis was messing with the piano. He'd bang on the school piano every chance he could, and if a friend's family happened to own one, Otis would invariably show up and maneuver his way over to the bench and find an excuse to start playing.

Just after Otis turned fourteen in November of 1955, the family escaped Tindall Heights and moved to the Bellevue section of Macon. By then, there was a baby sister in the family, Deborah, and Mr. Redding bought a little four-room house on Pike Street. It was like most of the others in the neighborhood—small and cheap, built from planks of wood that sometimes fit and sometimes didn't. Years later, Otis would talk about his mother stuffing rags into cracks in the walls to keep out the cold during the winter. The neighborhood was a step above the projects, especially for the kids, but it was still far from paradise. "Bellevue was a tough area, but Tindall Heights was tougher," said Luther Rodgers. "You didn't have to fight every day in Bellevue, but you had to be strong to live there."

The house sat up on a high patch of land that locals called "Sugar Hill," and that's where Otis met many of the Bellevue kids who would become his lifelong friends. Living next door was a kid named George "Bubba" Howard who started playing with Otis. Bubba Howard introduced Otis to his cousin, who also, improbably, carried the nickname of "Bubba"—Willie "Bubba" Sailor. "Otis was about a year older than me," said Bubba Sailor. "I used to go up on that hill to see my cousin. We'd all play football and softball. Pike Street was country at the time; it was a dirt road. There were about six houses together up there and that was it."

Later they began trekking through the woods, taking a shortcut through the cemetery over to an area known as "the Bottom" where two brothers named Benny and Charles Davis lived. And just a stone's throw away from the Davis brothers was a kid named Sylvester Huckaby, whose father worked for the railroad. "Huck" would quickly become Otis's closest friend. "There were eight of us in the family, and he was born next-to-last," said Juanita Huckaby, his older sister. "When he was eight months old, we had a scare and took him to the hospital and he stayed there for a month. When he came back from the hospital, we were so glad he was alive that he was spoiled after that. He was a mama's boy. He and his daddy didn't have the greatest relationship. He'd listen to his mama. He was always telling her about the things he was going to buy for her after he was a man."

For Huck, life was one grand adventure. He was always exploring, always getting into trouble. A little branch next to his house fed into Durr's Lake, a big recreation area for white people on Log Cabin Drive. There was a skating rink, a floating dock out in the lake for diving, and a big slide. One time he tried to dam up the branch just to see if he could do it. Another time when it rose after a hard rain, he got one of his mother's tubs and was going to float downstream to the lake; she caught him just as he was climbing aboard the makeshift boat.

They were all rough-and-tumble kids. There was a big field down at the Bottom where they would play football nearly every afternoon. The games were always competitive and physical—they didn't play "touch," they played full-contact tackle, and Otis was the chief trash-talker of the group. He was a good athlete, tall and lean and quick. Huck was a little taller than Otis, stocky and strong. Charles Davis was the biggest kid of them all and he'd often drag Otis and other would-be tacklers down the field, simply refusing to go down. During one game Otis came flying into him with a bone-jarring hit. Charles landed on his thigh and couldn't walk for two or three weeks.

In many ways, Bellevue was a great place to be a boy growing up. The landscape was thick with woods for exploring and hunting and playing. In the fall, they'd congregate under the big pecan trees near Otis's house and stuff paper bags full of pecans, then take them home for their mothers to bake buttery-sweet pies. In the summer they'd sneak over to Durr's Lake; the fact they were all forbidden from going there only served to inspire them to sneak through the woods at every opportunity and try to sneak in a swim. Nearly every inch of the lake was visible from the main buildings, and most of the time it was too crowded to swim without detection, but sometimes they could sneak into a little corner at the back of the lake and delight in swimming in the same water as the white folks.

Their main swimming hole as kids was a spot they called "the Big Rock," just a little place along the branch where the water pooled around a large boulder. As they grew older, they began going down to the huge rock quarry on Georgia Industrial Highway about a mile away from the Bottom. It was about two acres wide and immeasurably deep—a hole carved into the ground that was fed by underground streams and rainfall. The water inside was pristine and there were huge cliffs rising 150 feet and more along the western edge. The bravest souls climbed the cliffs for diving; the less adventurous dived from shorter cliffs along the northern side and waded in on the side with a shallow bank.

Folks from Bellevue claimed the rock quarry as their own; the white people who owned the land thought otherwise. They lived about a half mile away in a big white-columned house that sat on a high hill overlooking the quarry. Whenever they'd spy the Negro kids swimming on their land, the white folks would jump into pickup trucks and go racing over to the quarry to chase them away. It was a never-ending game of cat and mouse: Just as the white folks could see the kids swimming, the kids could see the white folks gathering their forces for an assault. They would gleefully watch the frenzy over at the mansion, then scamper off into the woods as soon as the pickup trucks hit the road. Hidden away, the kids would wait until the white people grew impatient and went back home; then, before long, the quarry would again be filled with kids swimming as if nothing had ever happened.

But things in Bellevue weren't always so benign. The issue of race was a constant, from the separate drinking fountains downtown to stories of brutality that were in constant circulation in the Negro community. One day, Benny Davis was walking through the woods on his way home. He turned a corner, looked up, and saw a black man dangling from the limb of a tree, a rope's noose tight around his neck. Benny ran away as fast as his legs would take him, and he never walked through those woods again.

Bellevue was a close-knit community. People looked out for one another and everyone seemed to know everyone else's business. The Redding family made an immediate impression on the people in their new neighborhood, especially Mr. Redding, who had become a lay preacher and carried himself with the dignity and bearing of a man of the cloth. And he always was impeccably dressed. "When that black man got dressed, brother, he was somebody!" the Reverend Moses Dumas, a longtime family friend, said with a laugh. "He was sharp."

"Mr. Redding was respected just about everywhere; he was just that type of person," said Bubba Sailor. "He was quiet; he was a minister. People respected him because of the way he handled himself. Otis's momma was one of the sweetest people you'd ever want to know. I don't know if you know his brother or his sisters, but you can tell by them that they were raised right. Everybody was laid-back, except Otis. Otis was kind of the wild one."

Like a lot of the black kids from Macon, Otis worshiped Little Richard and James Brown—both rose to stardom from Macon. Little Richard had grown up in Pleasant Hill, just a couple of miles away from Bellevue, and that alone was proof enough to fuel the dreams of every aspiring singer and musician in town. In fact, just two weeks before "Long Tall Sally" hit #1, Little Richard was playing at the Elk's Club in downtown Macon and it cost just a buck to get in. If Richard Penniman, the son of a Macon bootlegger, could make it out of Pleasant Hill, why couldn't Otis Redding make it out of Bellevue? As soon as he heard Little Richard, Otis knew he was going to be a singer. It was that simple. Nothing less would do. His focus was set. He wore out a copy of "Long Tall Sally," not listening to it so much as studying it and learning every nuance of Little Richard's voice, from the hoarse holler to the out-of-nowhere falsettos. "One of these days, I'm going to be just like Little Richard," Otis would tell his friends over and over. "You'll see, one of these days."

From the moment Otis brought Little Richard records into the house, his father began to despair. Mr. Redding was very old-fashioned. To him, that kind of music sprang from the devil. It wasn't healthy. It wasn't right. Especially for a man of the cloth. "If you was a preacher, you had to live with that pressure," said the Reverend Moses Dumas. "Back in that day, to be a preacher—and especially if you're trying to come up—you're scuffling; you didn't want somebody to say: 'Here he is trying to tell us what to do and he can't tell his own son.' He just did what the average parent in that day would do. He didn't want his son in that rock 'n' roll field. He believed in the Bible and the Lord, and he felt like that was just wrong."

Then Mr. Redding found out something that just made him absolutely sick with worry: Otis was sneaking out of his bedroom window on Sunday nights, going over to a Bellevue nightclub called Hillview Springs to sing rock and roll. Mr. Redding couldn't understand it. All his other children were solid and rooted; Otis Jr. was his problem child. Mr. Redding was worried to death. His son was barely fifteen years old and going to a nightclub? A *nightclub*! He confronted Otis, bluntly told him that he was a disgrace, that nightclubs were houses of sin, and that he was sinning by going to them. "You ain't never gonna amount to nothing," Mr. Redding informed his son. "Nothing."

Sweet Soul Music

You couldn't find a more improbable launching pad for stardom than the Hillview Springs Social Club. It was tucked away in the woods off a snaking dirt road, the kind of place you had to know about to get to. And unless you lived in Bellevue or had friends there, you might not know about it at all. Near the front door, there was a pine tree with a Philip Morris advertising tin nailed to the trunk; it showed two white men smoking cigarettes and the standing joke was that those were the only white people who'd ever been to Hillview Springs.

The clubhouse sat near a spacious fishing pond called Clay's Lake. In good weather you could usually find guys from around the neighborhood hoping to hook a catfish for supper. A dozen or more picnic tables sat by on the banks of the lake in the shade of tall pine trees, making Hillview Springs a popular spot for daytime family excursions and company barbecues. The clubhouse itself was a squat rectangular concrete-block building. Walk inside, and you faced a hazy bar. The concrete floor was painted maroon, which made the place seem even darker than it was. The radio was usually on, always tuned to the sweaty R&B music of Ray Charles, Hank Ballard and the Midnighters, Fats Domino, Joe Turner, the Drifters. A piano was pushed over in the left corner near the bathrooms, an area that also served as the bandstand. At one of the tables off to the right, there was usually a card game in progress and there was a place in the back where you could get drinks a little stronger than RC Cola or NuGrape soda.

In the fall of 1956, the Gladys Williams Band began playing every Sunday night at Hillview Springs and it became *the* place to be: Everyone knew that when Gladys Williams was in the house, the house was guaranteed to rock. She was one of the original blues divas, sultry and glamorous and salty. Her publicity photo shows her peering seductively at the camera, wearing a flashy evening gown that bares her mocha-colored shoulder. Her long, luxuriant hair is brushed over and draped across her left shoulder, topped off with one small lock curling up her forehead. Her band was versatile enough to perform square-dance music at the white V.F.W. clubs, then head over to a black club for some steaming, get-down blues. "Gladys could play that piano, man," said Jessie Hancock. "And sing like a bird. She could sing them blues and then turn right around and play a waltz or sing a song like 'Stardust.' And Gladys, she had a talent for cussing and drinking that liquor. She'd get drunk. But the drunker she got, the more she could play."

She was a master of the art of getting a crowd on its feet, jumping and hollering as if they were going into a heated religious fervor and joyfully testifying. Gladys would stoke things up with her piano-playing; then she'd send her horn players out into the crowd to play long solos. They called it "walkin' the floor." Inevitably, if the weather was good, they would step out the front door and go strolling up the street as they played, taking much of the audience with them while the rhythm section stayed inside laying down a simmering backbeat until the horn players finally came back to fire things up for one final chorus.

Gladys was known around Macon for taking young musicians under her wing, and at Hillview Springs she hosted a talent contest halfway through her set that offered a $5 first prize. She would give practically anyone a chance, but she had one iron-clad rule that she made sure everyone understood up front: Step up on *her* bandstand and you'd better have the stuff. Otherwise she'd usher you right off, and if she'd had a few drinks—which was often the case—she might go out of her way to insult you in the process. Gladys Williams didn't suffer fools easily.

It was a chilly October night when she was confronted by a lanky kid who looked like he was being pushed forward by a couple of friends. He was handsome, big almond-shaped brown eyes and a smile that wouldn't stop. He was bustling with energy, bouncing on his toes and blurting out that he wanted to enter her talent show.

"What's your name?" she asked.

"Otis Redding, Miz Gladys," he shyly replied.

"How old are you, boy?"

"Fifteen."

"What do you do?"

"I try to sing, Miz Gladys; I try to sing."

"Okay, what you want to sing?"

"I want to sing 'Long Tall Sally.' "

"Okay, sing it."

He hesitated for a moment, then began softly singing. She doodled around the piano until she figured out which key he was singing in. She motioned for him to stop, then turned to the crowd. "Okay, everyone; Mr. Otis Redding is gonna sing, 'Long Tall Sally.' " She turned to the band, told them to play in the key of A, and counted off the song. Otis jumped in late, trying to sing just the way he remembered Little Richard doing it on his record player. Problem was, as soon as he began belting out the song, his voice changed keys. The musicians were playing in the key of A and Otis was now singing somewhere up around the key of C-sharp. He also had no understanding of keeping musical time. Sometimes he was a beat or two *ahead* of the band. Other times he was a beat or two *behind* them. But seldom was Otis actually *with* them. He had simply closed his eyes and was lost in his own world, completely oblivious to everybody else. He thought he was doing great.

Gladys called an immediate halt to things. "Goddammit, boy, you ain't got no time!" she scolded him, unceremoniously shooing Otis off the bandstand.

Jessie Hancock and Percy Welch were playing in Gladys's band that night and they cornered Otis a few minutes later and tried to console him; they told him they thought he had a nice voice, he just had to learn how to harness it. "Look, man, listen to the band," Jessie told him. "Just try to keep up with us."

Otis was embarrassed, but he wasn't discouraged. He used the fiasco as motivation. He paid heed to what Jessie and Percy had told him. He also paid close attention to Miss Gladys, how she wrapped her voice around the music and how she engaged the crowd with her banter or with just one perfectly timed sly smile. Otis went home and went to work, practicing incessantly to apply what he'd been taught. Little Richard had just released a new single, "Heebie Jeebies," and Otis quickly learned it, singing it over and over until he was sure he was ready to go back to Hillview Springs. And this time he tore the place up. He was amateurish and sometimes inept, but there clearly was a spark of dazzling talent. The crowd cheered him on and Otis won the $5 first prize. Then he came back the following week and won again. His confidence grew with each week. Miz Gladys would introduce him and Otis would strut up to the microphone, swaying to the backbeat and flashing all thirty-two in a huge grin that made his joy feel contagious to everyone in the room.

"That song ["Heebie Jeebies"] really inspired me to start singing because I won the talent show with it," Otis later told writer Stanley Booth. "I remember it went, 'My bad luck baby put the jinx on me.' I won for fifteen Sunday nights straight with that song. And then they wouldn't let me sing no more, wouldn't let me win that five dollars anymore."

It's impossible to explain how little Macon, Georgia, became an epicenter of influence on modern pop music. There were cities that produced more successful musicians but, aside from Memphis, it would be difficult to find one city that has produced more groundbreaking musical figures in the last fifty years. Every single star who rose out of Macon was a visionary, someone who changed the basic equation and redefined the way people looked at popular music. If Little Richard didn't create rock 'n' roll, he certainly joined Chuck Berry and Elvis Presley in setting the parameters. James Brown soon followed him and created what became known as funk. And Otis would become the third member of that triumvirate, a singer who came to embody the very essence of soul music. Then, as if to prove it was no fluke, a few years later the city produced the Allman Brothers Band, which emerged out of Macon with a fusion of blues and rock and jazz and country that opened up completely new possibilities in rock music.

"Why Macon? I used to say it was the water, something in the water," shrugged Hamp "King Bee" Swain, who was a guiding force behind the R&B scene in Macon. As a bandleader, Swain gave Little Richard one of his first full-time singing jobs. As Macon's most popular disc jockey, he introduced James Brown to the world and then, later, Otis Redding. "I think it had to do with religion and gospel music, which had a lot of influence on Otis; the same with James and the same with Richard."

Yet gospel music was the influence all over the South, and Macon was the place where the roads converged. Somehow all the elements were set in place and the exact right people showed up at the exact right time to take advantage of them. The city's transformation into a musical greenhouse can be traced back to the turn of the century, when a wealthy black businessman named Charles Douglass opened a theater for the black community in downtown Macon on Broadway. Local lore has it that Douglass was inspired to build the theater when he took his wife to a show at Macon's stately Grand Opera House and was forced to enter through a rear door, then climb a rickety set of spiral stairs to the third balcony.

The Douglass Theatre was conceived as a more compact, intimate version of the Grand Opera House. It offered less seating capacity, but Charles Douglass made sure that his theater exuded elegance and class. Even the seats were customized with the initials "CD" in fancy type molded in iron at the end of each row. The theater opened its doors in 1921, offering a blend of vaudeville shows and silent movies with an in-house pianist providing the soundtrack. It wasn't long before the Douglass became one of the most prestigious black music venues in the South. Duke Ellington and Cab Calloway performed there. So did Ma Rainey and Ida Cox and the comedy act of Butterbeans and Susie. Bessie Smith played the Douglass so often that she eventually adopted an orphaned boy from Macon as her son.

The Douglass's musical prominence was eventually superseded when a promoter named Clint Brantley somehow convinced city officials during the height of segregation to let him use the 4,000-seat City Auditorium for black-oriented entertainment. Brantley was a light-skinned Negro who wore glasses with thick black frames and was known for cussing up a storm. He moved to Macon in 1922 as a semi-professional musician and opened a barbershop. By the late 1930's, he ran a little club on Fifth Street called the Two-Spot. Just a block away from the Douglass, the Two-Spot featured live bands and served as Brantley's apprenticeship in the music business. He had the vision to recognize the market for live music and eventually expanded his operation to the Auditorium. From there, Brantley became a local power, booking the hottest R&B acts in the business—everyone from Fats Waller and Ray Charles to Louis Jordan and Sam Cooke. Unlike the Douglass, whites were allowed inside the Auditorium for the "race" shows. But they were restricted to the balcony where a string was usually placed at stage center—whites would sit on one side of the string, blacks on the other. "Man, them white people would be *jumping* upstairs," chuckled Jessie Hancock. "They'd be *dancing* up there; I didn't know they could dance like that!"

The decades of high-quality shows at the Douglass and the City Auditorium fostered a hungry appetite for live music in the black community. With the Two-Spot packing in the crowds every weekend, it wasn't long before juke joints featuring live music were opening up all over Macon. City officials took a hands-off approach to the black clubs; it was pretty much "anything goes" so long as it didn't spill out on the sidewalk where their white constituents might see it.

"At that time, they had what they called 'party houses' down on Fifth Street," said Jessie Hancock. "You know about party houses— prostitutes and gambling and stuff. It was just like it was up in Memphis and Kansas City, right here in Macon. Everybody was making money, even the police because they were being paid off. The police wouldn't bother you about nothing. They had gambling houses down on Broadway and the police would be sitting up there gambling. The musicians had it made; if you wanted to play, you could get in a band. Just to show you how musicians think, we'd start at about one o'clock in the afternoon at a jam session at Adam's Lounge in East Macon; people would come all the way from Athens and Atlanta to jam and we'd just play all day. After that, we'd take about an hour or two break and then play for our money that night from nine to one. We'd finish, pack up, and then go out to Bellevue to an all-night club and jam all night. We loved it just that much."

Like most of the good musicians from Macon, Jessie Hancock got his start playing with Gladys Williams. He was a child when he first heard her perform, he received his first musical instruction from her saxophone player for 50 cents per lesson, and then he joined her band when he grew up. Dozens of other musicians could tell the same story. Gladys Williams was the driving wheel behind the local music scene, founding her band prior to the Depression and turning it into the premier group of the area.

"Unfortunately, Gladys came along when female musicians and bandleaders were rare; otherwise she would have really been a big, big, big star," said Hamp Swain, who played alto saxophone with her group. "For Jessie and myself and a lot of others, she was kind of like a momma figure. She kept everybody straight, and she would lay out a few choice words at times. But she took care of us and taught us a lot, not only about music but about life itself. She had been around and she could tell some stories; if you didn't learn something from her, well, then, shame on you."

Gladys Williams had the musical ability to combine substance with all her stage flash. She'd studied music at the Hampton Institute in Virginia—courtesy of a scholarship from an anonymous white benefactor. In addition to her band work, she also played piano for three different churches and two funeral homes and put on programs in the schools. She recognized raw talent and enjoyed nurturing it, acting as a mentor for a long list of local musicians that included Lena Horne and Little Richard. And she loved performing enough to have a career that stretched over four decades, taking her from posh white country clubs to little Negro dives that had no electricity and pianos that had more beer stains than working keys. "We played some real joints, some tough jobs," said Jessie Hancock. "That's all you had. It was play that or play nothing. We played in this little country town one night and when we got there, we saw the sheriff standing out in the parking lot and leaning on his car. I thought, 'Uh-oh, we're going to have trouble tonight.' But he was out there selling liquor; if you wanted a drink, you went outside to see the sheriff. And the band sounded so good that he went home and got his wife and brought her back and went to dancing with her. [Gladys Williams] was known all over Georgia; she turned down a record contract because she didn't want to get on the road and follow no record. She stayed right here in Macon and made her living—a good living, too. Clint, most of the time, was booking her. Between Gladys Williams and Clint Brantley, they were everything in Macon. Everything."

It seems fitting that someone as flamboyant as Little Richard didn't sit around waiting for fate to find him; he went out and tracked it down. He was twelve years old when Clint Brantley promoted a show starring a popular gospel singer named Sister Rosetta Stone at the City Auditorium. Before the show, Richard found Brantley in the lobby and marched right up to him. "Mr. Clint," he proclaimed, "Sister Rosetta said I could open the program."

Brantley chuckled at the kid, then dismissed him. "Boy, go on," he said. "You can't open no program."

When the curtains opened an hour later, Brantley was shocked to see the kid standing in the spotlight. "There he was, singing like hell!" Brantley said. "And I thought, 'Well, shit, this damned boy can *sing*.' "

Richard Penniman was born in 1935 and grew up in the Pleasant Hill neighborhood of Macon, one of twelve children. There was always something odd about him, something radically different from the other kids he grew up with. In high school, he was prissy and feminine to the point that he'd show up for class wearing girls' pedal-pusher pants. He'd visit friends at Tindall Heights and be chased out by a gang of mocking boys. Richard began his show-business career singing with Gladys Williams. Eventually he put together a group with Percy Welch, the drummer from Gladys's band, and they worked the "chitlin' circuit" all over the Southeast. One night he saw a singer named Billy Wright walk onstage at the Royal Peacock Club in Atlanta wearing wild, brightly colored clothes and hair stacked in a pompadour. Richard looked at Billy Wright and saw a vision for himself. He came back home, adopted the look, and then took it to the extreme. He'd walk into a joint in Macon in his full regalia—pancake makeup, feather boa, flashy suit—and people would stop in their tracks and stare. See Little Richard once and you never forgot him.

By 1953, Richard's persona was in full bloom. Clint Brantley was his manager and he had hooked up with Hamp Swain, singing with the Hamp Tones all over the Southeast. Everywhere they went, Little Richard shocked and dazzled the crowds. "If you played a place once, a city once, and the audience saw him, if you advertised that you were coming back then they would be there six on a horse," said Hamp. "They didn't want to miss that show. He was a showman; he was *quite* a showman. All the guys around Macon, they knew him and knew what to expect. But go to a strange city and Little Richard would shake 'em up, man."

Richard's hottest tune was a wild jumper called "Tutti Frutti" that he'd played around Macon for a couple of years. It brilliantly captured the essence of Little Richard—brimming with youthful energy and verve, racing at a breakaway pace, and featuring what are still some of the raunchiest lyrics ever conceived in rock 'n' roll: "Tutti Frutti / Good booty . . . Miss Lucy / Is juicy . . . Miss Tight / Is all right . . . You can grease it / Make it easy . . . Awop-bop-a-loo-mop-awop-god-damn!" You didn't even have to understand *why* it was dirty to understand that it *was* dirty, and it never failed to drive an audience into a frenzy. They wouldn't know whether to laugh at the words or be offended, whether to stare at the crazy fool singing them or dance to the irresistible beat. And, usually, they wound up doing some odd combination of all four.

In 1955, Richard caught the ear of Art Rupe at Specialty Records— the home of such R&B stars as Lloyd Price, Guitar Slim, Art Neville, and Roy Milton—and went to New Orleans to record a record. Legend has it that the first session was a study in frustration; nothing Richard sang caught their ear. Everyone broke for lunch and headed to a place called the Dew Drop Inn to eat. Richard spied a piano in the corner and performed an impromptu version of "Tutti Frutti." They weren't sure what it was, but they were sure that it was a hit. A local songwriter was commissioned to clean up the lyrics and Richard was brought back into the studio to record the new "cleaner" version.

A tape of the song made its way to John R. (Richbourg), the famed late-night disc jockey at Nashville's WLAC, a 50,000-watt AM radio powerhouse that could be heard up and down the Eastern Seaboard once the sun went down. Not long after the recording sessions, Percy Welch was driving Richard to a gig and the radio was tuned to WLAC. "Here's a young man you ain't never heard before," they heard John R. announce. "I don't know what he's sayin' and I don't know what the song's about. But you listen to it and you tell me. Call me if you like it." With that introduction, John R. cued up "Tutti Frutti." As soon as Little Richard heard his own voice singing on the radio, he began bouncing up and down in his car seat like someone having a seizure. "O-oo my head! O-oo my head!" he shouted over and over in his high-pitched effeminate voice. "My record! It's on the radio! O-oo, I'm gonna get me a Cadillac! I betcha I get me a Cadillac! My record, man! It's on the radio!"

By the time "Tutti Frutti" finished playing, the switchboard at WLAC was lit up with callers and John R. wound up playing the song eight times in a row. "Tutti Frutti" hit the R&B charts in late 1955 and rose to #2. It was soon followed by "Long Tall Sally," which shot up the R&B charts to #1. "Little Richard started rock 'n' roll," said Jessie Hancock. "I don't care what nobody says; he started rock 'n' roll. I know because I was there and I saw it. Nobody else was doin' that but Little Richard."

As Little Richard reached for stardom, Hamp Swain hung up his saxophone and was sitting behind the microphone at WBML, a meager 1,000-watt radio station in Macon that shifted down to a virtually invisible 250 watts after sundown and could hardly be heard a couple of miles away beyond the tower. Hamp was a natural for radio, musically hip with a rich and deep voice that resonated over the airwaves. Two hundred and fifty watts or not, Hamp "The King Bee" Swain's *Night Rider Show* quickly became the hottest thing going in Macon; during one ratings period he was pulling in over 59 percent of the total local radio audience, white and black. Those kinds of numbers gave him an incredible sway over the R&B scene, both in the city and beyond—when the King Bee pushed a new record, the impact could be measured far outside the range of his radio tower. Which is why Clint Brantley brought him a record cut in late 1955 by a twenty-two-year-old kid just out of reform school. His name was James Brown.

Born in Barnwell, South Carolina, in 1933, James Brown had dropped out of school in the seventh grade to perform with gospel groups and a little R&B combo. He quickly gained a local reputation as a dynamic singer who also played the drums and piano. But there wasn't much money in that, so James depended on theft and burglary to supplement his income. He was caught breaking into a car at the age of sixteen and sentenced to hard labor at a juvenile work farm in Toccoa, a Georgia mountain town about a hundred miles north of Augusta. When he was released in 1952, he began singing in a gospel quartet called the Gospel Starlighters that eventually changed its name to the Flames when the group began performing R&B music. Like Little Richard, James Brown was never one to sit back and wait for fate to come to him. When Richard went to Toccoa in early 1955 to perform at a joint called Bill's Rendezvous Club, the Flames showed up and took over the stage during an intermission. Nobody invited them—they just walked up and began their show. They impressed Richard's road manager, Luke "Fats" Gardner, who gave them Brantley's address and phone number and told them to get in touch.

"That Saturday, four or five little niggers walked through the door, little country boys," Brantley said in his characteristically colorful language. "I had partied the night before; I'd drank a little whiskey and I wasn't feeling good. One of them did the talking, Johnny Terry. He said, 'Mr. Brantley, we is the Flames. We're from Toccoa. We sing and we're looking for someone to manage us.' And I said, 'Well, I don't want to.' I had some little niggers out of Jacksonville, the Speeds. They'd come up to Macon and I'd recorded them and then I never did hear no more from them. So I didn't want to be bothered; I thought it was another bunch of Speeds."

Something hit Brantley as the kids turned to leave. Maybe it was the look of disappointment etched on their faces, the distance they'd traveled for nothing. Or maybe it was instinct. But as they reached the door, he asked them to come back. "What do y'all sing?" he asked.

"We sing rock 'n' roll; we sing blues; we can also sing spirituals," Johnny Terry replied.

"Sing me a good spiritual," Brantley said. "I don't feel good this morning. It might pick me up." The Flames huddled for a moment, then began singing a song called "Looking for My Mother."

"Goddamn, man, them son-of-a-bitches, they looked for her, too," Brantley said with a deep laugh. "All under the tables, all under the damned seats. Everywhere. When they got through, I said, 'Boys, y'all can sing!' James was the leader. I got their address and their phone number and two weeks later, I had them back down here. They tore Macon up."

Their signature song was called, "Please, Please, Please," a mid-tempo ballad based loosely on the Muddy Waters classic "Baby, Please Don't Go." The lyrics were almost nonexistent; the essence of the song was James Brown singing the word "please" over and over and over again, emoting and pleading and begging with greater and greater passion on every go-round. The band eventually cut a demo of the song, which made its way over to Hamp Swain at WBML; he gave it a listen, then cued it up. "It was one of those acetates like we used to cut commercials, and it played from the inside out," Hamp said. "I put it on the air and we got a tremendous reaction. Immediately. The phone lines just lit up."

"Please, Please, Please" was a hit single, but James Brown would continue to bounce around Macon for another two years before achieving true national stardom. His arrival was a godsend for Clint Brantley, who was about to have a major falling-out with Little Richard. "Richard, he was gonna fuck with you," Brantley said. "That's the difference between he and James Brown. I told James one time that I needed two thousand dollars; I owed it to a cracker. And a few days later, that two thousand dollars was here. That's how he would do. James did everything he could for me; I didn't have to ask him to do it, he did it. Richard didn't ever do a damned thing. All I got out of Richard, I took it."

Brantley was known around Macon as a nice guy, a slick talker who knew the entertainment business inside out and knew how to play the angles. But he also wasn't somebody to cross. He usually had two or three huge bodyguard types hanging around with him to provide muscle when he needed it. When he split with Little Richard, Brantley used a lawyer to get a court order to collect $1,200 Richard owed him from advances. Days later, at a concert in Augusta, Georgia, Richard was served papers that repossessed his new El Dorado to pay off the debt. Initially Richard ignored the deputy sheriffs and wouldn't accept the papers. After the show, they confronted him in an alley behind the auditorium and demanded the car keys. Richard refused. When he saw a deputy pick up a brick to break a side window on the locked El Dorado, Richard lost it. He started screaming and ran over and kicked the cop in the ass, an almost comical gesture that resulted in Richard getting pummeled by the sheriffs with fists and blackjacks. "They beat the shit out of him; they liked to have killed him," Brantley said with a slight chuckle. "A lot of folks have said that I did it, but I was home in bed."

About a year after that, Little Richard would survive a crash scare on an airplane during a tour of Australia and announce his intentions to give up his music career to enroll in the seminary. When a member of his band voiced skepticism, Richard tossed four diamond rings, valued at $8,000, into the Hunter River in Sydney to prove his sincerity. "If you want to live for the Lord," Richard told reporters, "you can't rock 'n' roll, too. God doesn't like it." In October of 1957, he flew home to Los Angeles to be baptized as a Seventh-Day Adventist and to "prepare for the end of the world."

He would never again be a force in rock 'n' roll.

While Little Richard and James Brown were scorching the charts with their hit records, Otis Redding was sweating in the hot sun digging wells and roofing houses around Bellevue. Even with his success at the Hillview Springs talent show, Otis had to put his dreams on hold when a doctor diagnosed his father with tuberculosis, a bacterial infection of the lungs that usually took at least a year to fully cure. The timing couldn't have been worse: the family had just moved into their new home and owed a monthly mortgage of $50. "Everyone was just flat broke," said Luther Rodgers Redding. "My father was ill, he was in the hospital more than he was at home, my mother was working, and it was just a burden."

Otis was the oldest son in the family, and it was his responsibility to help see the family through the crisis. He dropped out of Ballard-Hudson High School and found work drilling wells. "It was a pretty easy job," Otis said. "It sounds hard but it's pretty easy. The hardest thing about it is when you have to change bits. They have big iron bits that weigh 250 pounds and we'd have to change them, put them on the stem so we could drill. That was the hardest part about it."

The only good thing about the job was that he was able to work with Bubba Howard and Bubba Sailor. "He enjoyed that because he was with his friends," said Bubba Sailor. "Now, Bubba Howard ran the rig, and Otis didn't have to do nothing but sit down. They'd drill the hole and when they'd clean it out, all he'd have to do was wait for the bell to come out and swing it over. And then sit back down."

Otis Redding was fifteen years old and poised to become just another kid from the projects—uneducated, poor, and working manual labor for the rest of his life. He began a pattern of bouncing from job to job. He roofed houses with Charles and Benny Davis. He was a the delivery boy for a grocery store. One time he found a job on a construction crew and was put to work operating an air hammer. Bubba Sailor gave him a ride on his first day. "Come pick me up about four-thirty," Otis said as he got out of the car that morning. Around lunchtime, Bubba's phone rang. "Come get me," Otis said. "I quit."

Music was his lifeline. He never stopped singing; he never stopped dreaming. Not long after the talent shows, it looked as if Otis had received the break of a lifetime. Someone from the Upsetters, Little Richard's old backup band, heard him sing at Hillview Springs. When Otis was invited to go on the road with the group, he jumped at the chance and was soon sending home $25 a week. On the surface, it was a natural pairing. But Otis was in way over his head. His talent was raw and and untamed. He wasn't ready for life on the road. He was naive, a teenage kid a long ways from home. Otis stayed with the Upsetters for only a few weeks; he wound up stranded in Florida and came home to Bellevue to go back to roofing houses with the Davis brothers. He used to amaze them, up on top of a house in the hot Macon sun singing his lungs out all day long. "Otis just sung, sung, sung, all the time," said Charles Davis. "He'd never give out. I didn't see how he could do it."

Otis and Benny Davis used to fight all the time. Benny was shorter than Otis, but he could push him around because he was stocky and Otis was skinny. "Then he started gaining weight, so we didn't fight no more after that," Benny said with a laugh. "After that, we played music together." The Davis brothers were budding musicians—their oldest brother, Richard Russell Davis, had played drums for Little Richard. Charles Davis was learning the drums and Benny Davis was showing quite a flair as a guitar player, so they became the rhythm section for Otis's very first band. They had a friend named Charles Smith who could play Little Richard note for note on the piano, and the combo was rounded out by a saxophone player named Ishmael "Ish" Mosley. Ish had grown up just a couple of blocks away and was the only real musician of the group; he'd taken up the saxophone in the Army, had played with the first black-based military parade band back in 1947, and then went out on the road with Little Richard. He was the oldest, already married and raising children.

Charles and Benny's mother was a street preacher known as Sister Brantley; on Sunday mornings she hosted Sunday school and church in their little house in Bellevue. As soon as the services were over, Ish and Charles Smith and Otis would show up, gather around her piano, and jam all afternoon. Charles Davis didn't even own a drum kit; he'd just beat away on buckets and chairs, anything that might make a percussive sound. Charles Smith amazed them all with his piano-playing, especially because he'd lost his thumb in an accident. He was a sensitive, brooding kid who would eventually kill himself playing Russian roulette.

Aside from Sunday afternoons jamming with the Davis brothers, Otis would go out at night looking for chances to sing. Sometimes he would show up at a Gladys Williams gig and perform a couple of songs. Other times, he and Bubba Sailor would make the rounds of clubs around Bellevue that featured live music. As soon as the band took a break, Otis would bop up to the musicians and try to hustle his way onstage.

One night they went over to Porter Stadium to see their high-school team, the Ballard-Hudson Maroon Tigers, play football. Bubba's parents gave him enough money to get both of them in, but Otis decided they should jump the fence and save the cash for later. They picked an out-of-the-way spot under the bleachers and climbed inside. Almost immediately, they ran into some other stragglers who knew Otis. "Come on, man," they said. "Sing a song." Otis wasn't the least bit shy. He began belting out Little Richard—*loud*, at the top of his lungs, closing his eyes and moving his body to a beat that only he could hear. Never mind that he'd just crawled over a fence, snuck into Porter Stadium, and was supposed to be down under the bleachers hiding out. The cops heard him singing and he'd barely finished the first chorus when they came down and threw them all out. "I was mad because I tore up a pair of new blue jeans climbing over that fence," said Bubba Sailor. "But Otis, he loved to sing. Anywhere. Anywhere at all. If you asked him to sing, you never had to ask twice."

Mr. Redding was scandalized by his son and felt helpless to stop him. Otis just wouldn't listen to reason. Mr. Redding was still sick and eventually was sent to a tuberculosis hospital in Rome, Georgia, about 170 miles northwest of Macon, where he would stay for weeks and maybe months. One of the last things he did before he left was write letters to every single preacher he knew. He told them how worried he was about his son, how Otis had climbed out of his bedroom window to go sing at Hillview Springs, and how he was spending all his time in nightclubs and wasting his life away on foolishness. "Please, talk to my son and pray for him; pray *hard* for him," Mr. Redding wrote. "Keep him out of those nightclubs."

By then, it was too late. Otis was already long gone.

In January of 1958, WIBB-AM pulled off a coup and lured Hamp Swain away from WBML. WIBB was a 5,000-watt, white-owned station that already had two black DJs, Big Saul and Satellite Poppa. Both carried significant weight in the R&B community—Satellite Poppa was a singer who performed all over the Southeast under his real name, Ray Brown; Big Saul had supervised the recording of James Brown's "Please, Please, Please," which was cut right in the WIBB studio. As soon as Hamp arrived at his new job, the station manager called him into his office with the news that WIBB was going to sponsor a local version of the Apollo Theatre's amateur talent contest and asked him to host the show with Satellite Poppa. Once that was settled, the station moved quickly to get the show off and running. They secured a movie house called the Roxy Theatre on Hazel Street and hired a band led by Roye Mathis—the pianist and organist from Hamp's old group—to provide the musical backup. *The Teenage Party* debuted on February 8, a Thursday night. The featured act was Macon's hottest young band, Pat Teacake and His Mighty Panthers. Admission was 35 cents.

The talent show proved popular from the very beginning, although there were some early kinks to work out. To begin with, Thursday was a horrible night to hold a "teen party"—it was a school night and most parents weren't going to let their kids out of the house that late.

And WIBB couldn't broadcast the show because the station signed off the air at sundown. Some of the problems were solved in late March when the show moved to Saturday mornings at eleven A.M., with a live broadcast starting thirty minutes later. Hamp and Satellite Poppa and Big Saul hyped the show incessantly and there was usually a line of people waiting to get in when the doors opened. Still, the Roxy was strictly low-rent. It was a Quonset hut and looked as if someone had split a giant oil drum in half, laid it flat on its side, and stuck some seats inside; it looked like it belonged on an Army base. It also was in a very tough neighborhood called Tybee where outsiders were not welcome. The Tybee kids were fiercely protective of their turf. To discourage outsiders from coming to the Roxy to see movies, they were known to pull out switchblades as soon as the lights went down and slice up the seats to make the theater seem run-down and threatening.

One of the initial *Teenage Party* shows was held in the Douglass, and that's where everyone wanted it to be on a full-time basis. The stately old theater would lend instant class and credibility to the talent show, give it an air of elegance and importance. After a three-month stand at the Roxy, a deal was finally struck and *The Teenage Party* moved permanently to the Douglass Theatre, where it quickly began taking on whole new dimensions.

The line of kids waiting every Saturday morning to get inside kept getting longer and longer, stretching around the building and up Broadway to Cherry Street, then on up Cherry Street. The contestants would show up early and go backstage to sign up for the show on a first-come, first-served basis. Someone would ask them what they wanted to sing and they'd huddle with the band to figure out what key to play in. Or a singer could bring their own musicians to accompany them.

For a small town like Macon, *The Teenage Party* was a major production. The house band kicked off a hot R&B instrumental with Hamp playing saxophone to start the show. Then the lights would dim and Satellite Poppa would rappel from the ceiling with a rope, firing a battery-powered pistol that shot off long streams of sparks and dressed in a custom-made silver space suit that was complete with a glow-in-the-dark helmet and "satellite" prongs sticking out of it. The gimmick never failed to drive the kids absolutely crazy. Hamp and the band would shift into a dirty blues riff and Satellite Poppa would step up to the microphone and sing a song. By the time the show went on the air at eleven-thirty A.M., the crowd at the Douglass would be at a fevered pitch, and Hamp and Satellite Poppa would begin bringing out the contestants. Judging was easy: When the crowd approved, they cheered. When they didn't, they would mercilessly boo the unfortunate contestant off the stage, and they did it with such relish that it quickly became an essential part of the show. Losers seldom came back twice; it could be that brutal.

Otis spent his Saturday mornings roofing houses and listening to *The Teenage Party*. Winning the talent show became his obsession; the trick was in getting off work in time to go. At first he decided to work twice as fast so he could leave early; that ended when he strained his back trying to carry two trays of tile up the ladder. After that, he enlisted his baby brother, Luther Rodgers, to come help out. Otis left work in time to go put on his dress clothes and make it to the show and enter the contest.

His debut at the talent show wasn't as humbling as his debut at Hillview Springs with Gladys Williams, but it was close enough. Otis never meshed with the backup band, never got into a groove. His musical time was out of sync; every note he sang seemed awkward and out of place. Afterwards, a guy named Johnny Jenkins walked up to him. Otis knew Johnny from the clubs around Bellevue—he played guitar for Pat Teacake and His Mighty Panthers and had caused quite a stir around town. "You should let me play behind you," Johnny told him. "I can make you sound good." They stood and talked for a long time. Johnny thought Otis had obvious talent but told him that he needed to work on his timing. "If you're willing to give up some of your spare time when you ain't working on houses, we're playing out at Club 15 every weekend," Johnny said. "Come out and we'll work a little."

Otis nodded his head. "Yeah," he said. "I'll be there."

He showed up at their next gig, got up to sing a Little Richard tune, and with Johnny playing behind him, Otis effortlessly fell into the groove. "You can take a man that can't sing and if you put the right kind of music behind him, he'll sound good," said Johnny. "A guitar player can make a singer sound good. And with me, Otis found out that he could sound better than he thought he could sound. And he didn't want to sing with nobody but Johnny Jenkins. There was a lot of talent going on down at the Douglass. When I played behind him, he started winning."

The next time Otis showed up at *The Teenage Party*, he was fully rehearsed with Johnny and the rest of the band. He waited to the side of the stage, nervously bouncing on his feet and flexing his shoulders like a boxer waiting for the bell to sound. And when they called his name, he bounded up onstage with a smile that carried such joy it seemed intoxicating. He glanced at Johnny, who counted off the song, and then Otis started singing his heart out, doing his best Little Richard in a voice that was raw and gruff and full of pure emotion.

For Otis, standing on that stage at the Douglass Theatre that morning was like catching a glimpse of his dreams in detail so vivid that they must have seemed real enough to touch. This wasn't some backwoods joint in Bellevue. It wasn't some dive down on Cotton Avenue. Close your eyes and blink, and it could be the stage at the Apollo. Every single seat from the front row to the back of the balcony was filled with kids. They were clapping for him. Calling out his name. Screaming for one more song. It was in those moments that Otis Redding began his transformation into a star. The light was faint and many didn't recognize it at first. But for others, it was too obvious to miss. "I already knew he could sing because I'd been following him around to the different clubs where he was singing," said Bubba Sailor. "But when he walked out there at the Douglass, man, he just had no fear. None. That's when I knew Otis could make it as a singer."

Johnny Jenkins made the difference. Once Otis hooked up with Johnny, everything began to click into place.

Johnny "Guitar" Jenkins had "star" written all over him. He was tall, light-skinned and Hollywood handsome, flamboyant, and by far the best guitar player in Macon. Offstage he was quiet and soft-spoken. Put a guitar in his hands and it was like flipping a switch. He'd walk out wearing wild clothing, a bandanna wrapped around his long hair. He'd dance and gyrate, and then amaze a crowd with his lightning-fast playing. He'd throw his guitar behind his back and hardly miss a beat. He'd hold it behind his head, playing meaty blues licks. He'd raise the guitar up to his mouth and pick the strings with his teeth and tongue. He'd hump his guitar, or play while doing a cheerleader's split. The fact that he was left-handed made him seem even more exotic because he didn't restring his guitar for a lefty; instead he simply played a regular guitar turned upside down.

If all that sounds reminiscent of Jimi Hendrix, there's a reason. As a teenager, Hendrix spent a summer in Macon with relatives living in Fort Hill and went to hear Pat Teacake's band at a place called Sawyer's Lake. The young Hendrix was transfixed by Johnny Jenkins who, like Jimi, was left-handed. It was obvious, later, that Johnny had made a strong impression on Hendrix. Johnny has no recollection of ever meeting him at Sawyer's Lake, but they did run into each other over a decade later in New York City. "We were late meeting each other," said Johnny. "Years later, I was playing a place called The Scene. He remembered me and he came in. And my guitar was stolen. I'd just bought it; it cost me $2,000. He was there and seen that I was in need and gave me one of his custom guitars—he was left-handed, too. I didn't know he was watching me at Sawyer's Lake. He was just another fan out there. They all knew Jimi Hendrix because he got famous with his style, but they didn't really know where it came from. They'd never seen Johnny. Nobody'd seen me but Jimi."

Johnny Jenkins grew up in a tiny country community called Swift Creek just southeast of Macon that was big enough for one little store and not much else. His house had no electricity and the only light at night came from kerosene lamps; every day or so, Johnny would go trudging through the woods to the store to pick up the kerosene. Folks from Swift Creek gathered most Sundays for a neighborhood fish fry. "I was too young to go but I used to sneak down there and peek through the bushes and see them frolicking," Johnny said. "They'd be down there drinking stump liquor and frying catfish. A guy would be playing guitar and another guy blowing harmonica. There wasn't a drum to beat on; somebody'd take a drink crate and use it for a drum to time themselves. And I followed the guy playing the guitar home. I'd sit in his backyard and got to know him real good and respected him. He seen where I was interested in the guitar and he'd sit around and let me watch him play."

Johnny's first guitar was handmade. He used a cigar box, thumb-tacks, and two kinds of rubber bands: "Big fat ones like they use to tie collard greens for the bass strings, and little ones like they use with newspapers on the lead strings." It wasn't nearly enough to sat-isfy his appetite. Johnny's older sister was dating a guy who watched him struggling to master the unmasterable contraption. Maybe he was trying to score points with Johnny's sister or maybe he recognized the kid's hunger and it touched him, but he took Johnny to a pawn shop in Macon and bought him a used Gibson electric guitar.

You seldom saw Johnny Jenkins without that guitar. "I used to go through the woods to get to the store and I never did go alone," he said. "I'd go through there with my guitar, playing and singing. And I'd look up and the birds would be following me. I'd walk twenty or thirty yards; the birds would leave where they were and go right up to where I was at. They'd be up in the top of the pine trees, singing along and following me through the woods." He began calling his new friends "the pinetoppers."

His musical education came primarily from his radio, which was powered by a huge battery the size of a car battery and always tuned to WBML. Johnny taught himself guitar by playing along with the songs he heard on the radio, and he quickly became good enough that he could listen to a record one or two times and then repeat it note for note on the guitar. Johnny never considered making money playing music—by the time he was a teenager, he had done every-thing from pulp-wooding and logging to digging wells and working on cars. Anything to scrape together a buck. Then he met a drummer named Pat Teacake who was putting together a band and needed a guitar player. Pat Teacake's real name was Charles Abrams and he was another Tindall Heights kid, given his unforgettable nickname because of his love of flapjacks. The lineup changed often but the core band was "Cake," Johnny, a sax player named Sonny "Hip" Goss (who had played with Little Richard), and vocalist Bill Jones, a sweet-voiced kid from Tindall Heights who idolized Little Willie John so much that he called himself "Little Willie" Jones.

Pat Teacake and His Mighty Panthers began playing around Macon in the summer of 1957, debuting at the R.Y.A. Club downtown on Poplar Street. The band worked hard, scrounging up gigs wherever they could find them, and soon established themselves as the best young R&B band in town. Sundays were one of the most popular nights for live music because all the local bands would be back in Macon from their out-of-town weekend gigs. The Panthers often pulled a double shift on Sundays—playing at the V.F.W. Club on Poplar Street from eight-thirty P.M. to eleven-thirty, then heading out Gray Highway to Club 15 where they went on right after midnight and played until the wee hours of the morning.

"Sunday night was a hot night in Macon," said Hamp Swain. "They used to do a thing at 12:01 A.M. at Club 15. See, you couldn't sell alcoholic beverages on Sunday; so 12:01 was technically Monday morning. Friday, Saturday, Sunday—all these joints were jumping. They were open during the week and selling a few beers. But the real thing was on the weekend. They'd have live bands, food, and just tremendous crowds."

By the time they began backing up Otis at the Douglass shows, Pat Teacake's group was a veteran of the talent contests. They were a featured act when *The Teenage Party* first debuted at the Roxy, often hired as the show's house band. Once Otis began sitting in with the Panthers at Club 15, it gave him a natural advantage over the other contestants at *The Teenage Party*. His sound was more rehearsed, more prepared and tested. And just like at Hillview Springs, he began a long win streak. Otis would come jumping onstage and sing a letter-perfect Little Richard song over Johnny's sharp guitar licks while the kids screamed as if it was Little Richard himself onstage. Otis's chief rival was a singer from South Macon named Oscar Mack, who won many of the early contests. Oscar had a high, soaring voice like Sam Cooke and he was a natural showman.

Hamp Swain was one of many who thought that if a major talent ever emerged from the *Teenage Party* shows, it would prove to be Oscar Mack. Everyone appreciated Otis, but his entire repertoire consisted of Little Richard songs. The world already had one Little Richard and didn't need another. Besides, a singer had to do dance steps to entertain, and Otis couldn't dance to save his life. "At the time, I thought Oscar Mack was *the* talent over Otis," Hamp said, shaking his head and laughing. "But Otis wanted to be a singer. That was obvious. He really wanted to be a big singer. He was willing to work hard, learning as much about music as he could. Otis just started winning every week. He was always the number one singer. I guess he kind of surprised everybody. Otis actually had a little more talent than a lot of us gave him credit for having."

Hard to Handle

By the time Otis turned seventeen, all of Mr. Redding's fears for his son seemed to be coming true, and more. Otis had grown wild. He seldom came home early; some nights he didn't come home at all. And it wasn't just music and nightclubs; it also was the company Otis was keeping. Mr. Redding felt disgraced, telling friends how wonderful all of his children were except for his oldest son. "Otis's the worst child I have," Mr. Redding would lament. "He worries me to death because he ain't never going to amount to nothing."

Despite his father's best intentions, Otis was a child of Bellevue. He hung out with kids from the street, not kids from the church. There was Bubba Sailor and Bubba Howard, the Davis brothers, and a handful of others. Foremost was Huck, who was already a legendary character around Bellevue. The stories abound. When he lived in a little one-room cottage behind his parents' house, Huck made sure no one could ever sneak up on him. He rigged it up so that a red light began flashing inside as soon as someone stepped on the first step. When they hit the second step, a telephone bell began ringing loudly inside. He kept a big bowl of loose change on a table inside and he'd warn neighborhood kids not to touch it, telling them there was 20,000 volts of electricity running through it. Huck's abundance of caution was a by-product of his occupation as one of Macon's main suppliers of stump whiskey, bootleg liquor, and drugs. Later, when he lived in a tiny duplex on Mumford Road and needed a hiding place for his stash, Huck chiseled through the concrete floor and excavated a large hole. He stashed the contraband in the hole, hiding it beneath a throwaway rug and a television set. In his bathroom was another hidden compartment, which he reached by pulling the soap dish off the wall.

Huck loved to read and research and figure things out. He even invented odd contraptions. One time, he motorized his sister's hand-cranked ice-cream maker but not before an early prototype slung icy milk all over the walls. When Huck moved into a second-floor apartment and decided he didn't like climbing the stairs, he built a home-made, motorized elevator to take him up and down. People at once admired him and feared him. Huck could talk all day long and hold you in rapt attention, telling spellbinding and often hilarious tall tales with the rhythm of a master storyteller. Get on his bad side and his easygoing persona quickly evaporated. His reputation preceded him. Everybody knew Huck showed no mercy when he got into a fight; he'd beat people up and wouldn't stop until he decided he'd delivered a very explicit message.

A perfect example happened when a guy nicknamed "Quick Check" tried to stiff Huck on a debt. There was a regular hangout in Bellevue, a shot house up on Hollingsworth Road where people congregated to shoot craps and sip bootleg whiskey from baby-food jars for fifty cents a slug. Quick Check showed up one afternoon and as he walked in, all activity slowly came to a halt. Every eye in the room focused on the series of knots that were raised up all across Quick Check's forehead and face. Nobody said a word as he gulped down a shot of liquor from the baby-food jar. Then, in voices no louder than a whisper, a chant began and every single person in the house joined in: "Huck, Huck, Huck, Huck." Quick Check started trembling. He smashed his shot glass on the fireplace, and everyone lit out of there like they were running from a ghost.

"Otis was here all the time to see Ves," said Juanita Huckaby, using the family nickname for Huck. "He was the muscles that did the fighting. I don't know whether Otis could fight like Ves. Ves was mean. If anything got out of hand, Ves could handle it."

While Huck usually kept Otis out of the line of fire, Otis himself was quite capable with his fists. "Oh yeah, he could be dangerous," said Bubba Sailor. "The man was six feet tall—he was big and he could fight if he had to. But you really had to push him 'cause he'd just run his mouth and talk as long as you wanted to do that. Whenever Otis got into trouble, it'd be because of my brother-in-law, Bubba Howard; he'd run his mouth and he was quick to pull out a gun."

Bubba Howard was definitely the loose cannon in Otis's group of friends, a guy who was always ready for a fight. Like the time a kid from the neighborhood attacked his ten-year-old brother. Bubba Howard called together all of his brother's friends. He told them all to go home, get their bows and arrows, and then tie nails around the points of all their arrows. That night, he met the kids just down the street from the attacker's wood-frame house. Bubba Howard tore up a bunch of rags, soaked them in kerosene, and methodically wrapped them around the tips of the arrows. Then he set the rags on fire and dispatched his assault team down the street on their wobbly bicycles, shooting the flaming arrows at the house. The attacker's mother happened to be sitting out on the front porch; as the arrows came flying, she didn't begin screaming so much as she began hysterically yelping. She finally regained her composure long enough to put out the fires while Bubba Howard and his band of kids escaped through the darkness. "Bubba Howard would start trouble; man, he was something else," said Bubba Sailor. "I've seen him want to do things and Otis talked him out of it. He'd listen to Otis sometimes. But if he was mad about something, he wouldn't listen to nobody. He wouldn't even listen to his own daddy; Bubba'd fight his daddy, too."

Bubba Howard acted as the peacekeeper when the Davis brothers rented an old abandoned service station in Bellevue for $30 a month and opened up their own juke joint. They outfitted it with a jukebox, set up a grill for hamburgers, and sold soft drinks. "Sometimes we'd play and Otis would sing," said Charles Davis. "It was a little small place and we'd pack 'em in. One night we were jamming in there about two o'clock in the morning and some ministers called the cops. They came in and said, 'Turn it down now or we'll pull your license off the wall.' Well, there were about a thousand licenses hanging up on the wall, but wasn't none of them ours! I was seventeen years old and didn't know anything about having to have licenses. It hit us so bad that we didn't open it up no more. It was getting a little wild anyway. There would be a line outside and you couldn't move inside because of all the people. We were afraid some people might get hurt, too, that some fights might break out, but they never did. We had Bubba Howard hanging around, and Otis, he could hold his own, too. So that kept everybody quiet."

They were all street kids, in and out of trouble. Otis was the leader—the one with the charisma, the one with the ideas. They looked out for one another. Pick a fight with one, you picked a fight with all. One day, Otis showed up all beaten up. He told them he'd been in East Macon and was jumped by about fifteen guys. "We all got together, and we were gonna go over there and fight," said Charles Davis. "That's when we found out it was just one guy; it wasn't no fifteen guys. They were playing basketball and Otis really had competitive spirit and they got into it. We went over there and he wanted to put a little scare into everybody over there in East Macon, which we did—we were some pretty tough guys."

"We hung together," said Benny Davis. "We had our little band, or gang. . . . You know what I mean. If you messed with one of us, hey, you've got to come after all of us. We used to have rock fights. We never played with guns much, except just one time. I never have shot nobody. Guns, we respected them more at that time than they do now."

Even in the late 1950s, youth gangs were common around Macon. It was a way of protecting yourself in a tough neighborhood—safety in numbers. And it also was a way of feeling you belonged to something. There were a handful of gangs within Bellevue; sometimes they'd fight among themselves but they'd usually band together to protect their neighborhood turf. It wasn't just the Tybee kids putting the Roxy Theatre off-limits. It was the Mudcats over in East Macon. It was Unionville and Hudson. It was Tindall Heights and Bellevue. Downtown Macon, where the Douglass stood, was neutral territory. But for an outsider to venture into a black neighborhood, it could get dangerous. "You didn't go over to Tindall Heights if they didn't know you," said Bubba Sailor. "You had to be known because they would whistle a warning. Everybody knew that whistle. There was too many guys over there and they'd all grew up together. Man, they just had that place sewed up and strangers couldn't go in there. Otis, everybody knew him over there so didn't nobody bother him."

Because of the Douglass shows, Otis was becoming a popular figure all around Macon, a local celebrity. He could usually move freely from one neighborhood to another with impunity. People liked hanging out with him. He could sing. He always had a smile on his face.

He could talk jive with the best of them. He was hyper, always wanting to do something and always wanting to keep moving. He also was
discovering one of the fringe benefits of being a singer—women. All
the girls were crazy about Otis. They flocked to him. He was tall,
good-looking, and confident, smoking Salem cigarettes with a smooth
sophistication. "I smoked Kents and he got me to smoking Salems,"
said Bubba Sailor. "He'd say, 'Kents? That's your momma's cigarette,
man.'"

When Bubba Sailor bought a car as soon as he turned sixteen, he
and Otis became familiar figures cruising around Bellevue on the
prowl for chicks and hanging out with friends. Bubba had just begun
seeing his first girlfriend. Her parents wouldn't let her date, so he
went over to her house. They spent the evening sitting pristinely on
the sofa, watching television with her parents. Bubba got home
around ten o'clock and called Otis to check in.

"Man, where you been?" Otis asked.

"At my girlfriend's house," said Bubba.

"Get any pussy?"

"Naw."

"What'd you do?"

"We watched TV."

Otis rolled with laughter. "Come on, man," he said. "You let *her*
stay on the sofa and watch TV. All this pussy out here? Come get me.
Me and you goin' out."

Before long, Bubba had forgotten all about his first girlfriend; he
was too busy keeping up with Otis. There were times he nailed one
girl in the afternoon and then got a different one that night. Bubba
didn't have to do anything, just be with Otis. "I was young and I didn't
have a conversation for a girl; Otis had the conversation," said Bubba
Sailor. "And like Little Richard said, you didn't get no pussy unless
you had a car or you could sing. So we had a combination: I had the
car and Otis could sing. So we rolled pretty good, you know what
I'm saying?"

They all had big dreams—of driving big fancy cars and wearing
fancy clothes and having enough money to buy their freedom out of
Bellevue. For most of them, it was all smoke and mirrors, dreams so
far removed that they never really even believed in them. But Otis

was different. He had an advantage the others didn't, a possible life-line away from the streets. He'd tell anybody who'd listen how he was going to be a big star someday; they might not believe him, but he'd tell them anyway. He still refused to hold a steady job, as if he was literally forcing himself to make his living solely from singing. When he needed money, he'd usually roof houses with the Davis brothers and Huck, or land some other short-term work. For a while, he delivered firewood. Once, he and Bubba Sailor landed a job wash-ing cars. At the end of the day, the boss told Bubba to get a wheel-barrow—he was going to fill it up with black sludge from the grease trap for Bubba to haul away. Bubba didn't want the sludge to spill out and ruin his clothes, so he asked his boss to only fill the wheel-barrow halfway up. When the boss ignored him and filled it to the top with sludge, Bubba refused to push it. He was fired on the spot, told to go get his pay for the day and leave. As Bubba began walking to the office, he heard Otis call out, "Bring mine back with you."

Aside from chasing the girls, Otis's attention seldom strayed from singing. Every time he and Bubba Sailor rode together, it was the same: Otis would beat on the dashboard like a drummer, singing along with whatever song happened to be playing on the radio. "Sometimes he'd spend the night at my house," said Bubba. "My mother would always make him call his mother to let her know where he was. And he'd sing all night long. He'd sing all the way to my house. He'd sing in bed. He'd wake up singing. He would. He just sang, man. All the time."

Winning the talent shows at the Douglass was a major accomplish-ment, but it didn't come close to quenching Otis's thirst. And when he started singing professionally in the summer of 1958, he stopped competing in the talent show altogether. The Douglass shows were for amateurs, and Otis now felt above that. His first jobs singing around town were with a local group called Jazzbo Brown and the House Rockers that included saxophonist Ish Mosley. The House Rockers debuted on August 1, 1958, at the D.A.V. (Disabled American Veterans) Club on Poplar Street in downtown Macon and played a few other dates around town. But Otis didn't hang around very long.

In November, Little Willie Jones left Pat Teacake's band and, thanks to Johnny Jenkins, Otis was invited to replace him.

It was a major step up. Otis was hooking up with the city's best young R&B band. He could pick up the *Macon Telegraph* and see his name in advertisements promoting their gigs; the ads were published in the "Social and Personal News of Our Negro Community," the daily zoned two-page section of the newspaper. " 'Rocking' Otis Redding," the ads called him one week. "That House Rocking Young Man," they said the next. Then they began calling him "Otis 'Rocking Robin' Redding."

While it was tremendous local exposure, it was hardly a glamourous life. Otis was beginning a long and often mind-numbing apprenticeship on the not-so-fondly nicknamed "chitlin' circuit" of the Deep South. It wasn't really a circuit at all, and chitlin's were seldom the draw, but every black musician of a certain age could tell you about them—juke joints housed in buildings of various ill repair in the black section of town that featured hot music, cold beer, fast women, and equally fast fists. Typical was a Macon joint on Anthony Road called Almeida's; people nicknamed it "Music in the Trees" because audio speakers were hung outside from tree branches. "These were juke joints and gangsters were running them," said Jessie Hancock. "You'd go to Almeida's, you might see *anything*. People dancing or drinking liquor or gambling in the front. Police in the kitchen eating fried catfish, getting their payoff, and then leaving."

One of Otis's first initiations to life on the road came from Satellite Poppa, who also performed as Ray Brown and the Red Caps and sometimes took Pat Teacake's band to back him up. Satellite Poppa was strictly a blues singer; he took Otis with him because Otis could sing country songs and Elvis Presley songs. Satellite Poppa used that versatility as a hook to gain a competitive edge on the other bands playing the white fraternity-house circuit. Otis traveled with Satellite Poppa to the University of Georgia and Georgia Tech and other colleges around the Southeast, as far west as Mississippi and as far south as lower Florida and as far north as Tennessee. The jobs could be quite lucrative, sometimes paying $300 and $400 at a time when a weekly salary of $50 was considered a good living. Still, it was a grinding experience. "It was very, very tiring," said Satellite Poppa. "A lot of times we just had to sleep on the side of the road. Finding a motel room, that was unheard-of, man; you'd just sleep in your car or just stay at the club until daybreak if you were too far away from your home base."

In the meantime Otis became a fixture around Macon, singing with Pat Teacake. Then Little Willie Jones came back to sing with the group in March of 1959 and rather than trying to choose between him and Otis, Pat Teacake simply used both of them and billed their shows as a "Battle of the Blues" between the two singers. That didn't last long. Otis dropped out in May; a couple of months later, Johnny gave his notice, too. Each had grown frustrated playing the same old songs in the same old clubs. Johnny wanted to learn the latest hits as soon as they came on the radio to stay current and fresh. He also wanted to do his own material. "Pat Teacake, he didn't know but one beat, really," said Johnny. "Everything he played, he played with the same beat. It just made me sick. I'd say, 'When you're on one song, make it sound that way; then when you get on another song, get another style or another *something*, man.' He didn't agree with all that. He actually tried to say I thought I was better than anyone else. I said, 'It ain't that way. We all love each other. We all need to be together, doing *something*. But you're always doing the *same* something.'"

Otis was more of a willing pupil. Johnny encouraged him to expand his repertoire beyond Little Richard and worked with him to develop a sense of musical time. "Otis knew the songs, but he didn't know when to come in or when to go out or when to stop," Johnny said. "You'd count off the song—one, two, three, four—to go. And hell, he don't go! It was as simple as that. When he made a mistake, I could play so fast and quick that I could catch them and correct them through the music and nobody could ever tell. I did that to keep him from being frustrated and angry; he had a quick temper, too, and he didn't want to be bothered by nobody else except me. It was a lot of work." Johnny paused and laughed warmly. "He was a mess, man!"

By the time Johnny left Pat Teacake, he already had his new group together. Johnny called his band the Pinetoppers, named after the birds that used to follow him in the treetops whenever he walked through the woods playing his guitar. Otis, of course, was in. For drummer and saxophone player, they recruited Otis's friends from the Bottom, Charles Davis and Ish Mosley. The bass player was a guy named Samuel Davis—everybody called him "Poor Sam." He had played for a while with Pat Teacake's band after Johnny taught him the rudiments of bass. Poor Sam's chief asset was money; he had a good job as a porter at a downtown car dealership, and since he had fronted them the cash to buy equipment, he also doubled as the band's manager. Finally, Johnny held an ace up his sleeve: a smooth-talking white boy who wanted to find jobs for the new band. He was promising to get them on the frat circuit where they could make some real money, as much in one night as they would make playing a week's worth of club dates around Macon. Johnny liked him. Unlike most white folks, he didn't try to lord over black people; he treated them as equals. He even had the nerve to show up one night at Club 15 to listen to Johnny play with Pat Teacake's band, a single white face in a sea of unfriendly black ones.

The white boy's name was Phil Walden.

In these days of multiplatinum albums and corporate marketing machines and glitzy videos, it's easy to forget just how revolutionary rock 'n' roll was when it first hit in the mid-1950s. It was much more than just a musical trend. It ushered in fundamental changes in American culture, evolving into an underground language for a generation of kids rebelling against the staid mainstream conservatism of the Eisenhower era. It also provided a bridge between an entire generation of white and black kids. The two races had always been segregated in every way. They didn't go to school together. They didn't shop in the same stores. They didn't live in the same neighborhoods. They didn't even drink from the same water fountains. Nothing linked them or brought them together on a common ground.

Just as Joe Louis and Jackie Robinson and Louis Armstrong and Duke Ellington had accomplished the unthinkable—inspiring white fans to cheer for blacks—Elvis Presley had opened the door for white teens to experience their first glimpse at black culture. Elvis was the "white singer with the Negro voice" and nearly all of his early hits at Sun Records were scorching covers of R&B hits that made no effort to sugarcoat the music's underlying sexual tension. After that, there was no turning back. Pat Boone might have had a hit with a saccharine version of "Tutti Frutti," but white kids bought the record and then went scampering to find Little Richard's original version. In fact, Richard has always maintained that white kids would play Pat Boone when their parents were around, then play *his* records when the adults were gone. It was black music that inspired many white kids, especially those from the South, to begin questioning some of their very basic values. Heroes like Chuck Berry and Little Richard and Bo Diddley helped personalize Negroes. White kids began adopting the rather radical notion that the black culture might actually hold something of worth and value, something worth investigating and appreciating and embracing.

Phil Walden was one of the first wave of white kids to cross the line. Born in 1940 in Greenville, South Carolina, he grew up in Macon in a childhood typical of most Southerners. Racism was the norm and "nigger" was an acceptable and popular adjective. He was introduced to "race records" by his older brother, Clark, who religiously listened to groups such as the "5" Royales and the Midnighters and blues singers like Howlin' Wolf and Muddy Waters. One night, Phil was on his way to watch a swim meet at the YMCA when he noticed a crowd gathering across the street for an Amos Milburn concert at the City Auditorium. He was only in the ninth grade and his family would have been scandalized had they known, but Phil walked up and bought a ticket and made his way to the upper balcony where whites were allowed to sit. He wasn't very impressed with Milburn, who struck Phil as a fat guy sitting at the piano, but he was swept away by the opening act: Little Richard.

"He just destroyed me," Phil said. "At that time, he was strictly a local act. He had this microphone between his legs and he would pound that piano. He would wave to all the gay guys, all his 'sisters' in the audience. The crowd was dancing with this uninhibited joy. I was just fascinated by that music. I had never been exposed to something that *raw* in my life. When I heard 'A-womp-bomp-a-loo-momp,' I knew I didn't want to sell insurance or used cars. I wanted to be in the music business."

Even years later, Phil would retain the distinct memory of sitting at the dinner table listening to Hamp Swain on the radio and hearing

"Tutti Frutti" for the first time—he turned the volume up real loud and his daddy snarled, "Turn that goddamned thing down." Weeks later, Phil was downtown on Cherry Street and saw someone on the other side of the street, walking down the sidewalk twirling a parasol. Phil stared for a moment, then gulped when he realized it was Little Richard. When he saw Richard cross to his side of the street and walk right towards him, Phil froze. He was too scared to even say hello. As they passed, Phil finally blurted out, "Tutti Frutti." And without skipping a beat, Richard beamed and replied, "Oh rutti," and kept on walking down the sidewalk.

By the time he was a senior at Sidney Lanier High School, Phil had immersed himself in R&B music. He was a regular at the shows at the City Auditorium, often dragging along his little brother, Alan. He also became a fixture at the WIBB studios, bringing requests to Hamp Swain and just hanging out. He even forged friendships with blacks, much to his father's chagrin. To Phil, it wasn't so much music as it was a lifestyle. While most of his contemporaries in school dressed conservatively, Phil took his look straight from James Dean and Elvis Presley, wearing blue jeans slung real low and sporting a carefully coiffed ducktail haircut. To some he came across as a hood. But he knew how to use his reputation to his advantage, to accomplish what he wanted. "He projected that image as a hood, when he wanted to," said George Hart, an Atlanta businessman who went to high school with him. "Phil was always on the edge of nonconformity or hoodism, but he always had one foot planted very firmly in the mainstream. He was always the leader type. He was cool back when it was cool to be cool."

The only question for Phil wasn't *whether* he was going to be involved in music, but *how*. He couldn't sing, couldn't play a musical instrument. He discovered his niche quite by accident. Percy Welch had released a record called "Back Door Man" that became a local hit. Phil was the president of his high-school fraternity and decided to hire Percy to perform at a rush party. When he went to meet Percy, Phil treated him like a star and even made sure to get an autographed copy of the record. Then Percy showed up at the party with a pickup band and no PA system, singing through a cheap and decidedly lo-fi guitar amplifier. He told Phil he had "forgotten" to bring the PA; it's more likely he didn't own one. Listening to Percy that night, Phil realized there had to be a market for someone who booked and managed black R&B bands. He could make sure they had sharp clothes to wear, a good sound system, amplifiers that worked. He could ensure the bands were rehearsed and kept a set lineup and actually showed up when a gig was booked. And he could also make sure they were paid afterwards.

His first act was a local vocal group called the Heartbreakers, composed of two carhops and a bus-station worker. Phil rehearsed the band in the baggage room of the Greyhound bus station in Macon and when he thought they were ready began entering the group in the *Teenage Party* talent show. Every Saturday morning, Phil would drive down to the Douglass, solemnly waiting for the Heartbreakers to tear down the house. Whites weren't allowed inside, so Phil would park outside the Douglass and listen to the show on his car radio. Every single week the Heartbreakers entered the contest and every single week they lost to a Little Richard sound-alike named Otis Redding. It never occurred to Phil that he didn't need to be handling the Heartbreakers; he needed to be handling the singer who kept beating them.

After graduating from high school, Phil enrolled at Macon's Mercer University and began booking a few dates for Pat Teacake's group after Bill Jones took over as the lone vocalist. When Johnny Jenkins began talking about forming his own group, Phil encouraged him. It seemed only natural. Johnny was the guitarist and set the band's musical tone; it made no sense for him to be handling those chores in a band that carried somebody else's name. Phil told Johnny to call him if he put a new group together.

Johnny "Guitar" Jenkins and the Fabulous Pinetoppers debuted on Sunday night, July 26, 1959, at the D.A.V. Club—a little upstairs club on Poplar Street downtown. The following Sunday, the band moved down the street to the Grand Dukes Club, a popular teen R&B hangout. It became the group's first regular gig. The money was minuscule, solely dependent on the size of the crowd. They usually walked out with $10 or $15 each; Ish Mosley remembers leaving one night with 50 cents. Sometimes they didn't get paid at all. One night Charles

Davis spotted Otis out behind a nightspot after a gig, crying because the club owner had stiffed them.

When Johnny decided the group was ready for inspection, he invited Phil Walden to come hear the Pinetoppers perform at Lakeside Amusement Park, a lake and recreation area for whites in East Macon. The band came out smoking, sharpened by Johnny's demand for constant rehearsals. The rhythm section of Charles Davis and Poor Sam was tight and concise. Ish played discreet rhythm horn lines and wailing solos. And Johnny whipped the white kids into a frenzy, gyrating and bending notes. His performance was so far removed from Pat Boone and Paul Anka and even Elvis Presley that it must have seemed like something dropped down from another planet. Then out came Otis, doing his best Little Richard.

Phil was blown away. The only thing he could compare it to was the night he first heard Little Richard at the City Auditorium. He immediately recognized the singer's voice. Phil had never seen him but he knew exactly who it was: that kid who had broken his heart every week by beating the Heartbreakers at *The Teenage Party*. Phil was waiting backstage after the first set, ready to get to work booking the band. Johnny introduced Phil to Otis. They shook hands and exchanged pleasantries, neither one knowing that it was the beginning of a friendship and business partnership that would defy societal boundaries and take them further than even their wildest dreams ever imagined.

Ol' Blessed

By the time Otis turned eighteen on September 9, 1959, he had fallen madly in love with a girl from East Macon named Zelma Atwood. He first saw her at a *Teenage Party* show at the Douglass, then ran into her downtown one afternoon and immediately started laying down the smooth talk. "Hey, baby," he said with a sly smile. "What's going on?"

Zelma swatted him away. "I ain't your baby," she snapped back, stopping him cold in his tracks.

When he spotted her on a city bus a few days later, Otis tried to make another approach. This time Zelma simply ignored him, treating him as if he didn't exist. To Zelma, Otis Redding was nothing more than a kid from Bellevue with a smooth line and little else; and she didn't want to have a thing to do with him. But Otis was smitten, determined to win her over. His friends didn't understand the attraction—Otis pretty much had his pick of the women around Macon and no one considered Zelma the most attractive thing in town. She was more than a head shorter than Otis, thin and wiry and athletic and far from the voluptuous figure favored in that day. But she had big, expressive eyes and she had attitude. She also dressed well because her parents, James and Essie Atwood, made sure their daughter had the best clothes. And there was something about her that seemed solid, stable.

The sheer force of Otis's will finally melted Zelma—he simply wouldn't take no for an answer. He spied her one night a few weeks later at the Grand Dukes Club while he was singing with the Pine-toppers. This time he was polite and gentlemanly and they wound up talking nearly all night. A few days later, Otis and Bubba Sailor were out cruising around. Otis spied Zelma walking up Broadway in front of the Douglass; he made Bubba stop the car and offered Zelma a lift home to her house on Jackson Street Lane in East Macon. "He had a date with her that night and Zelma had a first cousin named Robbie, so we started double-dating," said Bubba Sailor. "After that, Otis talked about Zelma all the time. He just fell in love with her. Feeling like that, it kind of amazed him a little bit. It was the first time he'd ever acted that way. He was cooked, boy. He was *cooked*."

It happened just that fast. And within weeks, Zelma Atwood was pregnant with Otis Redding's first child.

Not long after Otis's birthday, he was out cruising with Bubba Sailor when somebody flagged them down. "Otis, get home," the man said. "Your house done burned down." Otis's eyes got big. He seemed to be fighting to hold himself together. They rushed to Sugar Hill and found nothing but smoldering ashes where the house once had stood. The family had to go back to Tindall Heights, moving into apartment 21-D. Otis began spending more and more time sleeping over at Bubba Sailor's house or crashing with other friends. He was ready to be out on his own anyway; he and his father were constantly at odds over Otis's singing career.

And it didn't help that Otis was young and common sense wasn't always his strongest suit. One night he and Johnny wanted to go up to Forsyth, a little town about twenty-five miles north of Macon. Bubba Sailor wasn't around and they had no other transportation. Otis's solution? He hot-wired his daddy's Mercury and off they went. When Mr. Redding realized his car was missing, he called the police and reported it stolen. Later that night, Otis and Johnny were pulled over by the highway patrol, taken from the car, and forced to lie facedown on the highway with shotguns aimed at the back of their heads. When the officers figured out that Otis Redding, Jr., was driving a car reported stolen by Otis Redding, Sr., they decided it had to be a mistake and let Otis and Johnny go—they never noticed there were no keys dangling from the ignition.

But that was only the beginning of Otis and Johnny's problems. On the way back home, Otis managed to grind the transmission into submission and the car locked up in reverse, refusing to go forward. Instead of calling for help, Otis looked at Johnny and said, "Well, there ain't but one way we can get back to Macon." He simply turned

the car around and backed the Mercury all the way home. Once arrived—with the engine making a good half dozen different sickly
sounds—Otis parked the car in his yard and scampered off on foot
without ever saying a word to his father. "He didn't have very much
respect for his daddy," said Johnny. "Me and him both was good for
cutting the fool. We didn't know no better. But he was more dangerous than I was because I had the sense to back off of some damned
things. He never did back off of anything; it didn't make no difference
to him what comes. He didn't know the word *dangerous*. Didn't know
the meaning of it."

Johnny wanted for the Pinetoppers what he hadn't had in Pat Teacake's group—a well-rehearsed band that kept up with the current
Hit Parade. The group practiced incessantly, sometimes out at Club
15 and sometimes at a Bellevue club called Mann's Drive-In and sometimes in the apartment of a friend who lived on Durr's Drive by the
Bottom. "The Pinetoppers, we was a tight band," said Ish Mosley. "We
was so tight that if somebody was gonna make a mistake, we could
feel it coming. And we could cover for them. And that's just how tight
we was. And there were times with new songs, we'd just get up onstage and play them without rehearsing. One musician could cover
for the other. And as good as Johnny was, he could do a lot of covering. He covered for me plenty of times."

Johnny was the driving force behind the Pinetoppers. They all
knew that. It was his band, that simple. Without him, there wouldn't
be a band. "Johnny carried the band," said Ish. "He was a nice guy;
he was a smooth guy. He had a lot of showmanship. Another thing I
can say about him, he didn't let what he could do on the guitar go to
his head. Or become sophisticated. Johnny is good people."

"Johnny was Prince before there was a Prince," said Charles Davis.
"His hair was long. He was a real hippie. He was really laid-back until
he got onstage, and then he was a wildman. A real showman. Everybody loved him, loved his playing. We called him 'Pretty Boy' Johnny
Jenkins."

They all had little nicknames, a private lingo that only they understood. Otis was "Rocking" because he rocked the house. Ish was
called "Yardbird" after jazz legend Charlie Parker. Charles Davis was

"Sticks" because he was the drummer. Sam Davis was "Poor Sam." Johnny had trouble remembering names, so he simply began calling everybody "Blessed." And someone who could really sing? Well, they could really "puke." It broke up Charles Davis the first time he heard Johnny use the term. *What? Puke?* "Yeah, ol' Blessed," Johnny replied in his smooth, deep voice. "That boy, he sure could puke."

Of all the Pinetoppers, Johnny and Ish were the only real professional-level musicians. Charles Davis was such a novice that Otis often sat down behind his drum kit and showed him riffs to play. And Poor Sam was barely a passable bass player. He only knew how to play at the root position of the neck of his bass guitar, in the keys of E and A. If a song happened to be in another key and another spot on the neck, he'd have to use a capo. "He's the only bass player that was ever known to play with a capo!" Johnny said. "That's a mess, ain't it? We had some twisted-up musicians, boy. In all kinds of ways!"

Johnny had known from the moment he heard Otis sing at the Douglass that he had the gift, the ability to sing from the heart and to convey that emotion to any audience. A lot of singers emoted on-stage and a lot of them pranced around like a rooster in heat and a lot of them were convincing Method actors. With Otis, it was real. You could feel it in every word he sang. "That was the thing, see," Johnny said. "When he'd get to singing, he'd just put his whole heart into it; he didn't just sing to be singing a song. That's the reason he couldn't lip-synch to his songs later on when he was on television. You can rehearse a song over and over until you can stand up there and sing it in your sleep. But when you sing it from the heart, it's always going to be different each time you sing it."

Johnny focused on helping Otis with his sense of time and to over-come his often stiff stage presence. He wanted Otis to learn to dance, until he figured out that Otis didn't have enough coordination to sing and dance at the same time. "When he could do the steps, he couldn't sing," Johnny said. "And when he sang, he couldn't do the steps. So I finally said, 'Well, leave the dancing alone and stick to the micro-phone.' That's why, if you see him on film, you'll see him standing right in one spot. Sweating. Moving [the trunk of his body]. That foot standing still."

The relationship between Otis and Johnny was complicated. Otis was used to leading and he wasn't always willing to do what Johnny wanted him to do. If Otis thought he had a better idea, he'd simply do it his way, damn what Johnny thought. On top of that, Johnny was beginning to develop a drinking problem that would haunt him for years, and when Johnny was drunk, he could cut the fool like nobody else. Otis didn't always appreciate what Johnny told him, or the blunt way in which he told him.

As for Johnny, he didn't like having his leadership constantly challenged. While his affection for Otis is obvious, he also won't mince words when talking about his old friend. In fact, Johnny will invite people who ask him about Otis to go elsewhere if they don't want to hear the truth. "People always want me to make him sound like a good guy and, see, I know better," he said. "I was there with him. He was a bully. He was hell to get along with. He wanted things to go his way and if they didn't, he was ready to fight. He didn't mind fighting, and he *could* fight. He was six feet three, about 215 pounds. He was big. He was that big and that mean, too. He was everything you think of concerning being hardheaded, mean, and bullified. Otis didn't pretend to be bad or a bully; that's just the way he was. It made no difference whether it was the band, a woman, a friend, a buddy, or whatever. The way he said was the way it was supposed to go. And if it didn't, he'd back it up with his fists or whatever it took."

To the others, the hierarchy was obvious—Johnny was the bandleader and Otis his chief lieutenant. They trusted the instincts of both, ready to follow where they led. "To me, Otis didn't seem hardheaded," said Charles Davis. "Otis would just do his thing. He'd say, 'Let's do it like *this*, man.' And to me, it always added something; it would always come out good. He was a little stubborn at times. The few people he didn't like, they'd catch it sometimes because he could be a tough guy. But he liked me. We'd have a few arguments, but we usually got along good. Otis was really a rocker. A strong rocker. And he had to have a drummer that could hang with him because if you couldn't, he'd play the drums himself. He'd ask me, 'Ain't you up to it tonight, Sticks? I told you, man, a strong backbeat. If you can't do it, move out of the way.' And I'd be embarrassed, but I'd do it. He made me really work. Otis, he could push you. He was business. He was all about making it."

That drive and focus to succeed was something Otis shared with Phil Walden, who had opened up an office for his fledgling booking agency on extremely familiar turf—the Macon Professional Building on Mulberry Street where WIBB and Hamp Swain were headquartered. Phil was still a student at Mercer when he rented the tiny nine- by twelve-foot room for a modest $33 monthly rent. Otis helped him paint the walls and Phil furnished it with two Army-surplus desks, a portable typewriter, and a telephone. What he lacked in accommodations and clients, he made up in verve. He was a natural, a kid crazy in love with music. He was cocky and shrewd, a hustler. When he opened up his agency, he called it Phil Walden and Associates even though he had no associates and he was booking only a couple of local acts. To create the illusion of success, he plastered publicity shots of the hottest R&B stars on the walls of his office and taped his card ("Another Fine Attraction Available from Phil Walden and Associates") over the names of the agencies that actually represented them. Whenever the telephone rang—which was seldom, if at all—Phil would answer in a high falsetto: "Hello? . . . Yes, hold on, please; Mr. Walden is on the other line." He'd put down the phone down a few seconds, then pick it up again and answer in his deepest voice.

The typical business day consisted of Phil and Otis hanging out, playing cards and shooting the breeze and trying to hustle gigs over the telephone. Phil quickly noticed that he wasn't the only one who could find the angles; Otis somehow always seemed to show up around lunchtime and a routine had discreetly fallen into place. As the clock reached noon, Phil would usually give Otis a couple of dollars and send him over to Nu-Way Wieners—a local New York–styled hot-dog joint a couple of blocks away on Cotton Avenue—to get them each a couple of dogs and sodas. Not only would Otis get a free, if modest, lunch; he'd often fail to bring back change, explaining to Phil that he'd spilled the drinks and had to go back and get two more. It didn't take Phil long to realize that Otis was so broke that he was simply pocketing the change.

Money was short for both of them and gigs were scarce. The Pinetoppers were just starting out and had to scrounge up any job they could find. The only steady work was at the Grand Dukes every

Sunday night, and the band was so hungry to play that they agreed to do two shows on Christmas Day in 1959. The first, from ten A.M. until two P.M., was billed as a Christmas party. Then they came back that night and played until well after midnight.

By that point, Otis's old buddy from Bellevue, Charles Smith, was occasionally playing piano with the group. And Bill Jones was on board as the band's second vocalist, which enabled the Pinetoppers to offer four distinct movements at every performance. The first set would be all instrumental, showing off Johnny's guitar theatrics. Then Otis would come out and sing six or seven songs, followed by a set by Bill Jones. At the end of the night, Otis and Bill would sing together, trading lines and harmonizing. It made for a rich blend—Otis's voice was husky and rough, all rock 'n' roll; Bill's was smooth and silky, the elegant bluesman. And just as Johnny pushed Otis to go beyond Little Richard, he also encouraged Bill Jones to go beyond Little Willie John. Otis had added covers of songs by Sam Cooke and the Drifters and Brook Benton to his repertoire, and Bill Jones was doing the latest B. B. King and Bobby "Blue" Bland tunes.

Still, as good as they sounded, the Pinetoppers were working sporadically, and in the late spring of 1960 Otis threw the band into sudden disarray when he announced that he was going to California. His sister was living out there and had offered him a place to stay. Otis was getting impatient; he hoped California would be his ticket to the big time. He arrived, landed work at a car wash, and quickly began singing with a group called the Shooters that had connections with a little label out of Denver called Finer Arts Records. Just weeks after arriving, Otis stepped into a recording studio for the very first time. He cut four songs and Finer Arts released two of them on a 45 single—an up-tempo rocker co-written by Otis called "She's All Right," backed with a song called "Tuff Enuff." Otis's voice was filled with youthful vigor, soaring to falsetto-sounding high notes reminiscent of the songs recorded for Sun Records by the teenage Elvis Presley before his voice matured and deepened. While the sound was raw and the songs largely forgettable, "She's All Right" also carried remarkable hints at what was to come. The song kicked off with an unexpected ascending horn line (played with, believe it or not, a flute) and featured a prominent bass line, both of which would become hallmarks of Otis's later recordings.

Despite its charms, "She's All Right" disappeared from the musical landscape almost as soon as it was released. It wasn't long before Otis decided to go home to Macon, where he had left Zelma pregnant with his child and little more than a promise he would return. "He said he was going to California and he was going to be a star and going to come back [with] all this money and we were going to get married," Zelma said. "And I'm like, *'Sure you is.'*"

Before he left for California, Otis had told Bubba Sailor to look after Zelma, an easy enough task since Bubba was still dating Zelma's cousin. "We'd go see Zelma two or three times a week, pick her up and take her out riding or whatever," Bubba said. "She never doubted he'd be back. She just missed him. She'd talk about him all the time, how she missed him. And when she found out he was coming home, she was the happiest woman alive."

The first thing Otis did when he came back to Macon was grill Bubba Sailor on Zelma's activities during his absence. "Jealous," Bubba said, laughing. "Jealous to death." He needn't have worried. Zelma was pregnant and when their first son, Dexter, was born, it thrilled Otis. He and Zelma still weren't married and weren't even living together. But he was at her house constantly, staying with her and seeing after her and playing with the baby.

Otis rejoined Johnny and the Pinetoppers as if he'd never left. His homecoming gig was August 14, 1960, at the D.A.V. Club and the ad in the local paper made sure everyone knew Otis was home from an exotic adventure: "Just back from L.A. Calif! Otis 'Rocking' Redding!" Once Otis returned, the band started making measurable progress. They still played the local gigs at D.A.V. and Club 15, but Phil also began lining up fraternity jobs on the weekends all across the Deep South. The band also underwent its first personnel change—drummer Charles Davis was out and Willie "Ploonie" Bowden was in.

Ploonie was another Bellevue kid. He had picked up his nickname as an infant when he had climbed up into a wheelbarrow and promptly fell out. They tried to calm his tears; nothing worked until someone began cooing the nonsensical *"ploonie, ploonie"* at him and he finally began squealing with laughter. After that, everybody called him "Ploonie," to the point that many of his friends today can't tell you his real name. As a child, Ploonie found himself fascinated by percussive sounds. One of his favorite hangouts was in the alley behind the Dempsey Hotel—a grand old building that dominates the city skyline. Ploonie would always find empty beer boxes stacked up against the wall, and he'd sneak back and bang on the boxes like a set of drums. After he saw Pat Teacake perform at the *Teenage Party* shows, he decided it was time to get serious. He tracked down a local jazz drummer named Buddy Lowe and began taking lessons. Ploonie knew Otis and Ish and when the drummer's chair in the Pinetoppers came open he was invited to fill it.

"Okay," Ploonie replied. "When do I start?"

"Well, you start tonight at the Grand Dukes."

Ploonie spent much of that first gig completely lost. He was young and inexperienced. His entire kit consisted of a bass drum and a snare; he didn't even have a hi-hat, much less cymbals. He didn't know any of the songs. And most of all, they played everything so *fast*. "I'd never worked with Johnny before; I'd just seen him with Pat Teacake when they did *The Teenage Party*," said Ploonie. "That first night, man, I'll tell you, it was something else. I felt *slow*. Johnny was so fast; I looked at him and said, 'Man, the rest of the guitar players around here don't play *this* fast.' "

When the band played out-of-town jobs, Poor Sam's Mercury would be loaded down like a pack mule—instruments strapped on top, trunk filled with amplifiers and and drums, and people inside the car sitting on mike stands and cords. They would usually gather in Macon on a Friday afternoon, maybe a couple of hours before Ish Mosley got off work at Robins Air Force Base. First they would run by Ish's house to pick up his saxophone and a change of clothes. Then they would head over to Perry Hills, a Bellevue barbecue joint that was one of Otis's favorite places to eat. They would fortify themselves for the trip, pick up a to-go order for Ish, and head south to Warner Robins. They'd wait for Ish by the main gate of the Air Force base, then be off—east to Athens and the University of Georgia or west to

Tuscaloosa and the University of Alabama or north to Atlanta and Georgia Tech.

Once they reached the frat house, the guys would set up in a rec room. By ten o'clock, the party would be going full-tilt, often resembling some wild scene out of *Animal House*—white kids packed inside, drinking and dancing and raising hell and trying to impress the sorority girls. The party would usually last to midnight or one in the morning, but every so often someone would have access to a house out in the country and they'd slip the band some extra money to pack up and follow the party.

One night they were in Auburn when one of kids offered the use of his father's lakefront cabin on a huge ranch. The guys packed up the gear, drove out to the cabin, unloaded, and played until the sun came up and everyone was at the edge of exhaustion. The cabin happened to be outfitted with bunks and everyone—the black musicians and the white frat boys—just collapsed into bed without even noticing they were breaking one of the strongest Southern taboos. "There was a white one here, a black one there, a white one there, and a black one here," Ish Mosley said, laughing. "And nobody said *nothing*."

Race was a constant in their lives. And it was especially dangerous for five young black kids traveling on the road in the Deep South as the civil-rights movement began to pick up steam. Negroes all over the South were galvanized in 1955 when Rosa Parks refused to give up her seat to a white rider on a city bus in Montgomery, Alabama. Her arrest and jailing proved to be the first significant moment in the movement. A young Baptist preacher named Dr. Martin Luther King, Jr., led a boycott of the bus system that lasted over a year and, before city officials finally gave in, nearly drove into bankruptcy every white business in downtown. Incidents of blacks demanding equal rights began springing up all over the South, from voter registration efforts in Mississippi to college students walking into a white lunch counter in Greensboro, North Carolina, and demanding service.

But the movement didn't become a cause célèbre with Northern liberals until the spring of 1961. On May 4, a group of thirteen blacks boarded two buses in Washington, D.C., determined to ride through the South and challenge segregation of bus stations that were considered interstate facilities and subject to federal law that mandated integration. The group, known as "the Freedom Riders," arrived in Atlanta with little fanfare. On Mother's Day they pulled out on two buses—one a Greyhound and one a Trailways—and headed west towards Alabama. That's when all hell broke loose. The Greyhound carried nine Freedom Riders and five very brave white passengers. It arrived in Anniston, Alabama, and was immediately attacked by a large mob armed with clubs, bricks, iron pipes, and knives. The driver panicked and sat still for a very long thirty seconds while the bus was pummeled before he finally threw it into reverse and made an escape. About fifty cars gave chase and just outside town they managed to shoot out the bus tires. When the Greyhound lurched to a halt, the mob attacked and set it on fire, blocking the doors to prevent the passengers from escaping before a group of Alabama state troopers came to the rescue. Meanwhile, the Trailways bus arrived in Anniston an hour later, and two passengers were beaten up before it managed to scurry away.

Despite the mayhem, the Freedom Riders were undeterred. They found new transportation and carried on, heading west and unaware that the notorious Birmingham police chief Bull Conner had cut a deal with the local Ku Klux Klan: When the Freedom Riders arrived at the bus station, the Klan would be given fifteen minutes to give them a private greeting. It was a brutal ambush, a government-sanctioned bloodbath. The protesters barely escaped death and the violence extended out into the crowd, where a white photographer from the Birmingham paper was clubbed on the head with a lead pipe and seven bystanders were injured badly enough to be hospitalized before the police finally interceded and broke things up. In the next day's paper, Chief Bull Conner blamed the whole thing on "out-of-town meddlers."

A few days later, with a full press party in tow, it happened all over again in Montgomery. The bus arrived at a seemingly deserted bus station, and John Lewis—one of the student leaders and now a U.S. congressman—stepped off to address a group of reporters. He was answering a question when he suddenly stopped midsentence and stood with a frozen look on his face. The reporters were puzzled for a moment, then turned around to see an advancing white mob armed with baseball bats, lead pipes, and bottles. Lewis and two Freedom Riders were beaten unconscious and then arrested for starting the riot. John Seigenthaler, the administrative assistant to U.S. Attorney General Robert Kennedy, witnessed the carnage from an office in a building next door and ran down to the street trying to break it up; he was felled by an iron pipe to the head. The incident generated national headlines and Kennedy was so incensed by the carnage that he sent six hundred federal marshals to Alabama to restore order.

In the midst of all that, Otis and the Pinetoppers had to drive to Alabama to play a frat gig. Everyone was on edge. They all knew about the racial troubles. They knew the white folks were stirred up like hornets. The fact they were musicians usually provided them with a safe-haven visa—unless they happened upon a particularly sadistic white cop. They arrived at the gig without incident. Everyone was hungry, so a couple of the frat brothers offered to go with them over to the bus station to get food. No one thought twice about it because it was something they'd done dozens of times.

They pulled in and their car was suddenly surrounded by a phalanx of deputies accompanied by growling German shepherds—they had unwittingly walked in on another Freedom Riders ambush. It was a harrowing moment. They all had visions of iron pipes and baseball bats and lynchings. Fortunately, a couple of the white frat boys rushed up to quickly placate the cops. "We was scared; we didn't know what was going to happen," said Charles Davis, who was filling in for Ploonie and would soon rejoin the band on a permanent basis. "Some of the white boys who drove us there, their parents were lawyers and doctors, influential people. So they let them know who we was and what it was all about. And they apologized and told us to get our food. We didn't go in, though. We let the college kids go in and get the food; we didn't want them to think we were starting anything. We was just happy to get out of there."

It was just one of many indignities they had to endure on the road. The music was the saving grace; the three or four hours they spent onstage made the long, harrowing hours out on the road seem worth the effort. They'd pass the time swapping stories, telling jokes, and singing gospel songs. "We'd sing a lot of gospel on the way to gigs,"

Charles Davis said. "That's the kind of fun we had in the car on the way. We hardly sung any rock 'n' roll songs; it was all gospel. Johnny really loved the gospel groups. So did Bill Jones."

As much as Johnny enjoyed performing, he was quickly developing an intense dislike of the road. He hated having to pile into a single car, crawling over people and equipment and trying to find a comfortable position to sit. He hated having to eat hot dogs because no other food could be had on the road, and then chasing them down with Alka-Seltzer to kill the heartburn. He hated the moments of sleep in a bouncing car that always seemed to be traveling on a bumpy road somewhere in the deep of the night. He hated stopping on the side of the road and getting out to piss because the white people wouldn't allow them in their rest rooms.

"We were going through some small town one night and we were getting some gas," he said. "And the police wanted to know whose car that was, that niggers didn't have no business in a car like that. We had to get them to call all the way back to Macon and talk to Phil. And Phil told them it was his car and we were on a job. Then they want us to get all the instruments out and play. The lot wasn't paved, it was just rocks, and you're out there beating on them damned rocks trying to convince them that you're a musician! That ain't half of what happened on that road. I hear people say the road was a lot of fun and how much they enjoyed it. Anybody sitting up and saying it was fun, they lying."

They were all lifelong veterans of dealing with suspicious white people. If a white cop hassled them, they'd often go right into a Stepin Fetchit routine and talk their way out of it: *Lawd, cap'n, we ain't doin' nothin'; we's jus' musicians.* "It'd be a bit rough sometimes," said Charles Davis. "You got a little humble out there on that highway."

Shout Bamalama

Phil Walden wasn't the only budding music entrepreneur to open an office in the Macon Professional Building. When Otis spied a new sign on a door upstairs for something called Confederate Records in late 1961, he waltzed right through the door. Inside, a lanky white man wearing thick glasses was sitting behind a desk. His name was Bobby Smith. Otis walked up to introduce himself. "My name is Otis Redding," he announced. "I'm a singer."

Bobby Smith asked Otis what he sang and his hopes dimmed when Otis mentioned Little Richard—the last thing the world needed was some neighborhood kid wanting to sing "Tutti Frutti." He asked Otis if he wrote songs. Otis smiled and nodded. "I'll sing one," he said. With no accompaniment other than the snap of his fingers, he launched into a tune he called "Shout Bamalama." It was a fast-paced rock 'n' roll song with a rather off-the-wall storyline.

Bobby had no clue what "Shout Bamalama" was about, but he was excited by what he heard. He was a fanatic about lyrics and he fell in love with the intricate wordplay in the song, the host of characters and their colorful nicknames—Nine Feet, Ten Feet, Leo the Monkey, and the Lion. The title character, Bamalama, was the name of an actual person from Macon who sported a large pompadour and played the washboard.

Otis finished singing and looked at Bobby with expectant eyes. Bobby's face broke out into a grin and he nodded his head. Pausing a moment for dramatic effect, he finally declared, "I think we can do something with it."

In actuality, Bobby Smith owned a record company that was little more than a name stenciled on a door. He was a former used-car salesman and music buff who had once spent most of his weekends driving thirty miles west to a little town called Roberta for the best rock 'n' roll in middle Georgia—a singer named Wayne Cochran who played every Saturday night at Lake Henderson in front of crowds of three hundred and more squeezed onto the dance floor. Part of Cochran's draw was the thirty-minute radio show he hosted on a little 250-watt station in nearby Thomaston. He also was a charismatic performer, tall and handsome with strong blue eyes, and sandy-haired. Wayne Cochran could turn the stage into his pulpit, rhythm and blues into his religion. He sounded so black that he would later become affectionately known as the "Blue-Eyed Soul Brother."

Like most of the other Lake Henderson regulars, Bobby Smith thought Wayne Cochran was a star, the coolest thing he'd ever seen on a stage. They became instant friends, often chatting between sets. Then Bobby had a car wreck that took his right eye and left him legally blind in the other. Wayne found out about the accident and went to Macon to visit him. Bobby was in bad shape, facing the loss of his eyesight and the knowledge that he'd never be able to hold a real job again. Wayne offered him a perfect alternative: How about going into the music business? Bobby could manage Wayne's career and get him bookings. It would give Bobby something to do once he left the hospital and also free up Wayne to concentrate on his music.

Bobby may have been a complete neophyte, but he jumped into his new role with a headstrong enthusiasm. He opened an office in the Macon Professional Building, often hanging out down in the WIBB studios with Hamp Swain and learning everything he could about the local scene. He started off small, booking Wayne's band at fraternity houses before eventually promoting dance shows himself. "Then I decided, 'There's got to be more this this; we've got to get a record,'" he said. "So I asked Wayne, 'Can you write a song?'"

Wayne had never written a song in his life. That didn't stop Bobby. He met a guy from Vidalia named Ed Perry who owned a mom-and-pop label called Gala Records that released 45s around the onion country in South Georgia. Bobby quickly set up a deal for Wayne to record for Gala and sent the band to the public television station at the University of Georgia, which had a makeshift recording studio and cheap rates. Wayne cut a couple of energetic covers of other people's hits; Gala Records put them out, but few people bought copies. Bobby quickly decided it was silly to go through a middleman when he could set up his own label and do the same basic thing himself. He called his label Confederate Records, and signed Wayne Cochran as his first artist.

Forming a record company was simple; getting an actual record in stores and on the radio proved not quite as easy. Bobby and Wayne traveled all over the state looking for airplay and shelf space for Wayne's records. They lived humbly and dreamed big—surviving on Bobby's disability checks, sustained by peanut-butter crackers washed down with RC Colas, and regularly driving up to Nashville to knock on doors that no one seemed to answer.

Bobby and Wayne soon met Phil Walden. And once Bobby expressed interest in recording Otis, their interests began to merge. "Phil would come in from Mercer about two-thirty or three o'clock and get on that phone booking shows," Bobby said. "His thing was booking, mine was in the recording end. He hustled; boy, he *hustled*."

Phil was already becoming known around Macon for his hard-edged bargaining. He not only handled bookings for Mercer's fraternities; he also began elbowing in on Clint Brantley's stranglehold on booking larger acts into town. At one point, Phil set up a deal to bring the Drifters to a fraternity house for a $5,000 fee. Clint Brantley found out and told one of his assistants (another Mercer student) to go to the fraternity and offer to do the show for $2,500. Phil lost the job and a few days later he spied Brantley's assistant in the dining hall at Mercer. Phil got right in his face. "If you ever do that again, I'll kick your ass," he snarled.

"Why wait?" the kid shot back, refusing to back down. Phil made a quick retreat.

The accepted legend is that Phil saw Otis's genius from the very start. In truth, nearly everyone agrees that Phil's focus at that point was on Johnny Jenkins. "The money wasn't behind Otis; the money was behind Johnny," said saxophonist Ish Mosley. "Phil wasn't really pushing Otis. You hear that? He was pushing Johnny Jenkins."

Johnny had just recorded and released his own single, an instrumental called "Love Twist." The record was getting heavy airplay around Macon, especially on WNEX where it was championed by a disc jockey named Frank Clark. "Love Twist" was released on a label out of Atlanta called Tifco Records, owned by a banker named James Newton who had heard Johnny perform and loved his sound. But there was no room for Otis on the record; Newton wanted instrumentals that showcased Johnny's scorching guitar. Even the B-side was an instrumental, a song called "Pinetop."

There was every reason for Phil to push Johnny. He was the bandleader. He had charisma. He cut a striking figure onstage. "Johnny was hip before his time," said drummer Charles Davis. "He got to be a real bad alcoholic and that really messed things up for him. We were playing in Augusta, playing behind Jimmy Reed at a college about the time he made 'Big Boss Man.' Jimmy Reed's chauffeur came in and said, 'Don't let Jimmy have anything to drink.' And he found something to drink and he was so drunk, when he got onstage he couldn't hardly sing. And Johnny got drunk that night and he walked through a plate-glass window. It didn't cut him, didn't hurt him. He was standing on the other side of the window with glass falling off him and he says, 'What happened, ol' Blessed?' And I told him, 'Well, ol' Blessed, looks like you just walked through a plate-glass window.' He had no idea what had happened."

"Johnny Jenkins, boy, was he a freaky guy in his day," Wayne Cochran said. "He would talk in rhymes: 'I hate to be bold but could I ask for a Red Gold?' Handsome guy. Mustache and goatee. Incredible showman. The guy could play. Left-handed guitar, upside down. He'd talk with his guitar. He'd lay his guitar down on the floor and he'd hit it with his foot and dance on it. He'd be playing it and he'd hit a string and then bend the neck forward. Phil Walden bought him a new guitar one time, a red Gibson. He played it and bent the neck forward and it snapped the whole neck off the guitar! Just cracked it off!"

"Johnny was Hollywood, man, strictly Hollywood," said Bobby Smith. "He was light-skinned and looked like a movie star. He'd wear that bandanna around his head and put that guitar down around his knees and play it and put on a show, man. His outfit might not have been worth ten dollars, but he looked like a million. He had style. He had it all going. But he was a guitar player. How many records can you sell as an instrumentalist? You can't sell that many."

To Bobby, Otis was always the one destined to be a star. And Otis held a secret weapon that tended to separate the pretenders from the contenders—he could write songs. Lots of people could sing, but only the special ones could come up with original material. Bobby championed Otis in the early days. They spent hours together hanging around Bobby's office. Otis was perpetually short of cash, often hitting up Bobby for five bucks when he stopped by. "I took a liking to him," Bobby said. "He'd wear on you like a glove."

They were all bridging deeply entrenched racial divides. It was even more remarkable considering the civil-rights movement had come to Macon and tensions were at a fevered pitch as Negroes began to push for the end of Jim Crow laws. In early 1962, fifteen young Negroes were arrested for trying sit in the front seats of the city's public buses. The bus system was then boycotted until Macon rescinded an ordinance that had forced Negroes to sit in the back of the bus. At the same time, the local NAACP was pushing for integration of white businesses. "Many of our local stores are now offering service at food counters on an integrated basis," read an advertisement published in the "Negro Community News" section of the *Macon Telegraph*. "Such cooperation is worthy of strong support. Make your buying dollars help you." There were mass meetings nearly every night in Macon at various Negro churches. The Reverend Moses Dumas was one of the more vocal ministers; so was Otis Redding, Sr., who was now pastor of his own church. "We were going from church to church every night," said Reverend Dumas. "And Reverend Redding, he was right there."

It was an often sobering time for the whites who befriended Otis and Johnny and other black musicians. "I never have been prejudiced," Bobby Smith said. "I never had a black-white issue. If I liked you, what was right was right. You would have liked Otis. He dressed nice and clean. Always bouncing. He'd talk to you and bounce. He just didn't really have nothing. I never will forget one night, Otis came knocking on the back door—not the front door—with a guy from one of these furniture companies down on Poplar Street. The guy was going to repossess his washer and dryer, and he needed twelve dollars. He and Zelma had just gotten married and they didn't have *anything*. And the first thing I told him was, 'Don't ever knock on my back door again.' And then I loaned him that twelve dollars. Anybody that wanted to run over Otis had to run over me."

Otis and Zelma had wed on August 17, 1961, just two weeks shy of Otis's twentieth birthday, with the Reverend C. J. Andrews of Tindall Heights performing the ceremony. At first the couple moved in with Zelma's grandmother, then lived in a house so dingy that Bobby could see the ground through the cracks in the floor. Not long after that, he gave Otis the money to get a duplex apartment over in East Macon near Fort Hawkins. Otis was jobless and, by most women's definitions, his future was bleak. Zelma didn't care—she believed in her husband's dreams. "Things were tough, but I always expected Otis to succeed," she said later. "I always felt he had talent. I was young when we got married. But if you marry a man and you see the direction that he wants to go in, you either support it or you get off the bandwagon." And Zelma was in for the long haul.

Bobby soon moved to get Otis on Confederate Records and set up a recording session to cut "Shout Bamalama" at the public television studio in Athens. On a Sunday morning in early spring of 1962, Bobby and Otis began to round up musicians from around Macon to make the trip. There was just one problem: Johnny Jenkins was supposed to go with them and he was nowhere to be found. Otis's relationship with the Pinetoppers was rocky through that period. He would appear with them at local clubs one month and then be missing the next—Little Willie Jones would be the featured vocalist. "Shout Bamalama" was recorded during one of the lulls; only Ish Mosley from the Pinetoppers accompanied Otis to the studio, although Johnny was supposed to be there.

"It was time for Otis to go record and Johnny's going to play guitar," Bobby said. "We had everybody except Johnny in the car and we could not find him anywhere. I had the studio set up for two o'clock. Otis knew another guitar player, Carl Guitar, Jr. [Thomas]. He was good—outside of Johnny Jenkins, he was just about the best rhythm-and-blues guitar player around. So Otis went and asked him and he jumped in the car and went with us. We had a guy who played the drums, called 'Cheyenne.' He was an Indian, had feet about fourteen or fifteen inches long."

The band was rounded out by Wayne Cochran on bass and Ish on saxophone. "When Bobby Smith took us to record 'Shout Bamalama,' the musicians was some hungry motor-scooters," said Ish. "We were broke. And they bought Otis steak! *Steak!*"

"Didn't none of us have nothing," Wayne said. "They put us in a couple of cars and we had to get money together for gas money and Pepsi-Colas and peanut-butter crackers. And that was it. We had no money. Nobody got paid. You were just excited to be recording: 'Gee, that's my bass,' you know?"

The musicians were all crowded into a single room for the recording, Ish's sax almost as loud as Otis's voice. The record began with the sounds of a loud party, voices talking and laughing. That was Otis's idea; Bobby wanted something at the front of the song and Otis said, "Well, let's just all holler." Then Otis came in and sang the first line a cappella. He paused for a brief moment before the band kicked in behind him with a fast backbeat. Behind the vocals, Wayne played a rollicking rock 'n' roll bass line and Ish blared a recurring King Curtis–styled riff. But most of all, the recording was an Otis Redding showcase: "Shout Bamalama" was his first tour de force on record. His voice carried a youthful vigor. It wrapped around you, drew you in with so much vitality and exuberance that it simply made you feel good to listen to it.

He sang those crazy-sounding lyrics at such a breakneck pace that he sounded breathless, gasping for air by the end of the first verse. "Listen to the words of that song," Wayne Cochran said with clear awe in his voice. " 'Leo the Monkey told the Lion one day / There's a bad little fellow comin' down your way' . . . Otis wrote that. Tell me, where in the world did those words come from? *Where?*"

"Shout Bamalama" was backed with a song called "Fat Gal" which, according to Wayne, was written by Little Richard and given to Otis. The record was released on Confederate Records and Hamp Swain immediately began playing "Shout Bamalama" on WIBB. It caused a local sensation, but elsewhere Bobby ran into an unexpected obstacle: Many of the R&B stations wouldn't even listen to the record;

they'd see Confederate Records on the label and pitch the 45 into the trash. The point was driven home when Otis and Bobby drove to a station in North Augusta, South Carolina. They played the song in the studio and the program director seemed to like it. "But Bobby," he finally said, "we don't like this 'Confederate' label."

Bobby soon had a new patch of records printed up under a new label, Orbit Records. He traveled with Otis all over the southeast pushing "Shout Bamalama" to program directors. One of the first places they hit was a station in Columbia, South Carolina, where former WIBB disc jockey Big Saul was working. That one was easy; Big Saul well remembered Otis from the Douglass talent shows. "I never will forget coming back from Columbia," Bobby said. "It must have been twelve o'clock at night. And in the black community, rhythm and blues was WLAC. Nashville, Tennessee. John R. We were listening to WLAC and Otis said, 'Bobby, I'd give anything if that station would play my record.' And I said, 'Well, you can't never tell.' "

Otis's comment gnawed at Bobby. Why *not* drive up to Nashville and see John R., personally take him a copy of "Shout Bamalama"? What in the world did they have to lose? Rejection? Bobby had been rejected by every rinky-dink station in Georgia; rejection didn't faze him any longer. Wayne drove him up and Phil insisted on tagging along—after all, John R. was one of his heroes. They walked into the station and somehow talked their way into saying hello to the legendary disc jockey. "He was a real nice man," said Bobby. "I was the one who did the talking. I introduced myself and told him what I had, what I was trying to do down in Macon, and that I'd appreciate anything he could do for me. He took my number and said he'd see what he could do. Well, on the way back home that night, here it came: 'Otis Redding's "Shout Bamalama." ' And it just knocked me out because I only went up there because of what Otis had said. Otis, he just couldn't believe it, man. He was walking high."

John R. played the record for several weeks, but it never caught fire. Still, Otis and Johnny Jenkins suddenly enjoyed an elevated status around Macon—both had records on the radio and Otis was being played on the vaunted WLAC. Road gigs also were more and more frequent, and Bobby began to travel on the road with Otis and Johnny whenever he could. Actually, his job was supplying the transportation; he had a nine-passenger station wagon, which always seemed to have about twelve people crammed inside on the way to gigs. The core band was still intact: Johnny, Ish, Charles Davis on drums, Poor Sam on bass. Phil would often come along, as would Huck and other friends from Bellevue.

"We were really clean-cut guys at that time, especially compared with other bands," Charles Davis said. "We were kind of like choir-boys in those days. We would wear a uniform every now and then, but we would all be in suits and ties even if we wore our individual clothes. That was one thing we had to be, clean. Otis and Phil were like that. Johnny was real clean anyway; he was the pretty boy. His hair was long. Poor Sam and Ish had processed hair. I wore my hair long. I'd play a drum solo and have my hair fall in my face and they'd go, 'Look at his hair!' "

One night they were playing in Atlanta at a club on Auburn Avenue across from the famed Royal Peacock, where Sam Cooke was head-lining. He was one of Otis's heroes and Otis had incorporated a good portion of the Sam Cooke songbook into his repertoire. When they arrived at the club and saw that the star was performing across the street, everybody told Otis: Don't sing any of those Sam Cooke songs because people can go right across the street and *see* Sam Cooke. "And he got up there and sung two or three songs and then did a Sam Cooke song," Ish said, laughing. "And everybody jumped up and went on across the street. We had a Thursday, Friday, and Saturday at that club. And they canceled us. So that weekend, we didn't make no money."

The gigs were not only more frequent; they were higher-profile. The Pinetoppers backed Jimmy Reed and R&B stars such as Arthur Alexander, Nappy Brown, and the Midnighters. "Back then, you *had* to [be able to] play," said Ish. "A club would bring in a big celebrity and then hire a local band to play behind them. They would bring their [own] music and sometimes you didn't have time to rehearse. So you had either a good ear, or they could make you feel so bad."

The Pinetoppers remained a fixture around Macon, playing every gig they could find. They sometimes played "Teenage Twist" parties in Francesca's Room at the Ricky-Dell Shopping Center on Anthony Road in the afternoons, then came back that night to play adult dances. They played Mann's Drive-In in Bellevue and the Middle Georgia Veteran's Club on Cotton Avenue. And they still were regulars out at Club 15, playing "Enjoy the Twist" parties and once opening a show for the "exotic Alice Red and her sensational dancers."

The Pinetoppers were playing at Club 15 the night of a James Brown "Homecoming Show" at the City Auditorium. Joe Tex was on the bill and took the stage determined to steal the limelight. "Joe had that showmanship," said Newton "Newt" Collier, a trumpet player from Tindall Heights who would go on to play with Sam and Dave. "One of the things he used to do, when he sang 'Skinny Legs,' he'd bring a woman onstage and he'd always make sure it was a skinny woman with a wig on. And he'd always fall down, and when he fell down he was going to snatch that wig off her head. Joe liked to keep the audience on their toes."

Joe Tex also was a masterful mimic and decided to have a little fun at James Brown's expense. James always walked out onstage wearing a colorful, regal-looking cape, and he was known for breaking down and falling to his knees during a dramatic moment in a song. On this night, Joe walked out wearing a ragged blanket around his shoulders, moth-eaten and full of holes. He did a picture-perfect imitation of a James Brown fall except that he grabbed his back as soon as he reached his knees. Then he got back up, tangled himself up in the blanket, and fought to get out while he sang, "Please, please, please . . . get me out of this cape." This was supposed to be James Brown's moment in his adopted hometown and here was Joe Tex ruining it. James wasn't in a very good mood when he showed up at Club 15 later that night.

Joe Tex was already there. James walked in armed and bullets started flying. Everybody leapt offstage. Otis dove for the crowd. Johnny dove for the men's room. Ish broke his saxophone when he tossed it in the air scrambling for cover. By the stage was a wall with a couple of draped windows. One of them—the window Poor Sam picked to dive through—happened to be boarded over. He hit it head-first and knocked himself out. Joe Tex scrambled out of the club and ran to safety under the cloak of darkness until he hid away in a cluster of trees.

"I was the last person to know what was happening," said Charles

Davis, who was sitting behind his drum kit with his eyes closed when the shooting began. "I'm playing and I'm just getting down. We were in the middle of one of our songs and people were so noisy, I really couldn't hear the shooting. By the time I figured out what had happened, everybody was on the floor—I'm up there on the stage and everybody's done left the stage, Otis and everybody else. I made my way over to a closet door and pushed my way in there. People were going out windows. Boy, it was rough!"

"Seven people got shot," Johnny Jenkins said. "They were reloading and coming back in, hiding behind pianos, the bar. And Ish and all of us had to get behind the piano. They went around later, a guy went around later, and I think he gave each one of the injured a hundred dollars apiece not to carry it no further and not to talk to the press. And that just quietened it down. Hell, I was just hoping I would survive, really. That wasn't no unusual thing—we had it all. We had incidents and stuff at the clubs up and down Poplar Street. That was just something our music carried with it. A lot of people didn't want to book us because of that: Everywhere Johnny Jenkins and the Pinetoppers go, there's a fight or there's a shoot-up. There was a lot of that stuff going on."

It didn't take long for Otis and Wayne Cochran to become close friends. Wayne helped the Pinetoppers get into some of the better clubs around the state that otherwise wouldn't have booked a Negro R&B band. Wayne was a country boy who considered himself fortunate not to have had racism shoved on him growing up. He was almost blind to it, which made hanging out with Otis an eye-opening experience. "I loved Otis Redding," he said. "He was very good to me. And he was kind. Very talented. Handsome guy. Neat. Clean as a pin. There was a pretty locally famous restaurant just off Mulberry Street. We'd go there for lunch sometimes, but Otis couldn't go in because he was black. What bothered me, you could go to a restaurant like that and sit at the counter and eat. And a white guy could sit down beside you, he'd been drunk for three days and smelled like a brewery and was filthy as a pig and cussing like a sailor, and it was all right because he was white. I'd sit there and think, something is bad wrong here."

There was the time Wayne and Otis traveled out in rural Georgia, making the rounds of radio stations. It was summertime and they decided they wanted ice cream, so Wayne pulled into a Dairy Queen. The two of them walked up to the window and ordered ice-cream cones. A woman brought them to the window. She handed Wayne his cone, and he paid her a quarter. Then she looked at Otis: "I'm sorry; I can't give you yours here. You'll have to come around to the back window."

Wayne was dumbfounded. "What do you mean? We're standing right here! What do you mean he has to go around back?"

"Well," she replied. "We can't serve colored people here. We have to serve them at the back window."

Wayne turned to Otis. "Give me your quarter." He took the coin, handed it to the clerk, took the ice-cream cone, and handed it to Otis. "I kept saying: 'This is wrong; this is idiotic; this is stupid.' You know, Otis was probably hurt and upset. But you've got to understand, he'd been treated like that forever. That was nothing new to him. And he didn't want me to get in trouble, because all this was new to me and I was ready to burn that place down. Here's a white kid, raised in Thomaston, Georgia. Redneckville. Father a cotton-miller and moonshiner. Grandfather a paid-up member of the KKK for life, until he got out of it because they got away from what they really formed to do—the KKK wasn't formed for racism in the beginning; it was vigilantism. That was an unlikely environment, but music . . . See, I would have given anything to be able to sit down beside Ray Charles. Music just takes all that away. You appreciate someone's talent and they become your idol. Who cares what color? That's dumb."

Wayne almost went out of his way to thumb his nose at racial boundaries. He'd go out to Club 15 and sit in with the Pinetoppers; he made members of his band go out there, too. And when he got up onstage, he was the blackest white man anyone could ever imagine. "He was so close to James Brown that it wasn't real," said Bobby Smith. "He would do virtually anything to get an audience's attention. He did this routine he called 'shaky legs' where his legs would go all rubbery. He'd swivel his hips. He'd go out into the crowd. He'd lay down on the floor and sing."

Not long after "Shout Bamalama" was released, Wayne and Otis shared the stage at a show Bobby booked out at Lakeside Park in East Macon in front of a packed house of white kids. It was billed as a "Battle of the Bands" between Johnny Jenkins and the Pinetoppers and Wayne Cochran and the Rockin' Capris. It turned into one of the greatest performances either Otis or Wayne ever gave. They finished with a duet on the Isley Brothers' hit, "Shout." Both were sweating, gesturing wildly to the crowd, and hamming it up with all they had. Finally, as the song slowed to a crawl, they fell to the floor and lay down still whispering the lyrics: "Little bit softer now / Shout! / Little bit softer now . . ." As the music began picking up steam like a locomotive gathering speed, Otis and Wayne began rising to their feet. The beat kept gaining momentum until the band was cranking out the music as loud and furious as they could go. "You could not get within a mile of that place," said Bobby. "They came up off the floor singing 'Shout!' And, man, those kids were going crazy!"

These Arms of Mine

Not long after he recorded "Shout Bamalama," Otis sang Bobby another tune he had written, called "These Arms of Mine." It was a slow and simmering song of passionate longing—about as different from "Bamalama" as a song could be—and Bobby liked it from the moment he heard it. But he didn't want Otis to cut another record so soon after "Bamalama"; instead he decided to give the song to a local group called Buddy Leech and the Playboys. "They were hot," said Bobby. "Teenagers were flocking out to Lakeside Park to hear them—in droves. I liked their style and gave them the song. Otis went with me to record it with them and we put it out on Confederate."

At the same time, Phil Walden was making significant headway with Johnny Jenkins. "Love Twist" had caught the ear of Joe Galkin, the southeastern representative of Atlantic Records. Galkin had picked up "Love Twist" for his own label, Gerald Records, and it wound up selling a healthy 25,000 copies. He also began hyping the record to Jerry Wexler, the vice president of Atlantic. Wexler wasn't interested in picking up "Love Twist," but he did take out an option on Johnny's next record. Galkin had come up with an angle: A group called Booker T. and the MG's had just scored a huge instrumental hit called "Green Onions" for the Memphis-based Stax Records, which was distributed by Atlantic. Given the label's success with instrumental hits, why not send Johnny Jenkins to Memphis to record at the Stax studio? Wexler thought Galkin was a hustler, but a hustler with good hunches. Galkin wanted $2,000 for Johnny Jenkins; Wexler decided to put up the cash.

Atlantic's interest was a major coup. Founded in 1947 by Ahmet Ertegun—the son of the former Turkish ambassador to the United States—and an A&R man named Herb Abramson, Atlantic Records had evolved into an R&B powerhouse. Ray Charles recorded for Atlantic. So did Ruth Brown and Joe Turner. So did the Drifters and the Coasters. Clyde McPhatter, LaVerne Baker, Ben E. King, Solomon Burke—the list of Atlantic stars seemed endless.

Joe Galkin also had taken notice of Otis and eventually set up a meeting with Bobby Smith. "I'm out doing everything I could for Otis, and Joe Galkin called me and asked me to come to Atlanta to meet him," Bobby said. "I went up there and met him in a big ol' hotel on the corner of Peachtree Street. He knew I didn't have no money. I was just getting started and doing everything I could to make it. And he said he'd like to promote 'Shout Bamalama,' that he'd take a nickel a record to promote it for me. I said that was fine. He said not to worry about it until we got things going."

With Jerry Wexler's blessings, Galkin set up Johnny's recording session and it was decided that Otis would go along and also try to record a song. Galkin would later tell a writer that he really didn't see a future for Otis; in fact, he said he told Phil that Otis was a lousy singer and that he only gave Otis the chance to record at Phil's insistence, and only then if there was time left over after Johnny finished. While that was Galkin's story, it wasn't necessarily true. Joe Galkin was, in fact, positioning himself to steal Otis Redding away from Bobby Smith. In later court documents, Galkin told the real story—that he actually was very much interested in Otis and went to Memphis that day with the intent of getting Otis a recording contract with Stax Records. Galkin said that he convinced Stax co-founder Jim Stewart to record a demo tape on Otis, which he hoped would be strong enough to convince Jim to sign Otis. Before Otis ever even recorded a song, Jim Stewart and Joe Galkin reached a quick oral agreement: If Stax signed Otis Redding, they would split in half all monies the label received from his recordings.

The session was scheduled for the afternoon of August 14, 1962. Johnny had no driver's license and Phil couldn't go because of classes at Mercer, so Otis drove him to Memphis using a station wagon he had borrowed from Bobby Smith. When Otis showed up at the studio sitting behind the wheel and carried Johnny's equipment inside and then sat in the corner without saying a word to anybody, the musicians at Stax figured he was Johnny's valet. Johnny set up his gear and began teaching an instrumental he'd written called "Pinetopper" to the MG's—organist Booker T. Jones, guitarist Steve Cropper, bassist Donald "Duck" Dunn, and drummer Al Jackson Jr. The session never took off. Johnny's song was a swinging blues and ill-suited for the R&B-entrenched MG's; his sound and their sound simply never jelled. Jim Stewart gave up after about two and a half hours, turning to Galkin and complaining, "I cannot make a record with this group."

The session shut down with about an hour of studio time left to go. And exactly what happened next depends on who you ask.

Johnny Jenkins: "I had recorded and had so much time left that I went to the guy and asked him, 'Hey, why not let Otis use the rest of my time?' They didn't want to be bothered with it. So I told them, 'If he can't record then I ain't playing no more.' The only thing I had going for me was my playing. They said, 'Well, Johnny, don't feel like that.' I said, 'That ain't the way I *feel;* that's just the way it is.' So they walked off and talked about ten minutes and said, 'Well, okay, bring him on in, Johnny.' They brought Otis in and I played behind him. Like I told you, his timing was bad. So I stayed there with him, got it right down pat, enough for them to record something. That's what that was."

Steve Cropper: "I thought Otis Redding was Johnny Jenkins's driver. He was just helping out, unloading the amps and stuff, and I didn't know he was part of the group. He just kind of sat around all day long. We'd already sent the band home and [drummer] Al Jackson came up to me and said, 'There's a guy here with Johnny, and he's been after me all day long about wanting us to hear him sing. Could you take five minutes and listen to this guy sing?' Otis sat down at the piano and said, 'I don't play anything. Can you just play me some triplets?' So I started playing and he came out [singing], 'These Arms of Mine.' Holy mackerel! We were like, 'What? Wait a minute!' Jim Stewart came in and he heard that and our mouths just dropped open. So Jim started running around, 'Where's Booker?' Everybody had gone. So we rolled the tape and cut this thing; Johnny played the guitar and I played the triplets on the piano."

Booker T. Jones: "Otis was the shoeshine boy in the band, the valet. And they let him sing sometimes. He came in and said, 'Look, I've gotta do an audition today; will you play for me?' And I said, 'Sure, what key?' I just sort of followed along as he sang 'These Arms of Mine.' "

Jim Stewart: "Everybody was fixing to go home; Joe Galkin insisted that we give Otis a listen. Some of the musicians had already left— Booker T. had already walked out. We had Steve Cropper shift from guitar over to piano and, believe me, Steve can't play piano. We did this up-tempo thing called 'Hey Hey Baby' and nobody was too excited because it sounded just like Little Richard. I told Joe I didn't think the world was waiting for another Little Richard. But Joe said [Otis] also had a ballad, and could we do that, too? I said fine. It was 'These Arms of Mine.' And there was something different about it— he really poured his soul into it. But no one was particularly impressed. Nobody was saying, 'Here's a superstar.' "

Duck Dunn: "I didn't see it immediately, no. To be honest, when we did 'These Arms of Mine,' me and Al Jackson, we both worked at clubs. I was in a hurry to get out of there that day because in those days working at a club was my main source of income. We'd been in the studio all day long. I had to be at work at nine, and I think Al had to be at work an hour later than I did. So these guys were wanting to throw this thing together about six o'clock, and I'm usually out the door by that time. So I was kind of on pins and needles because I had one of those bosses that would chew your ass out if you were late, who thought he was doing you a favor by giving you a job. My first reaction was kind of like, 'Jim, you know, you don't need another Little Richard.' See, that's how much I know."

Singer William Bell: "I was always around the studio. I had records out, but when I was home I was always in the studio. Johnny came in to do a session and at the end of the day, we needed a couple of more songs and Johnny didn't have any more. So Otis says, 'Well, I've got a little song that I've written, but I don't know if anybody will like it or not.' So he started humming. The rhythm section was sitting around, and started playing along with him and working it up. I'll never forget it; it was 'These Arms of Mine.' Johnny obviously didn't know the song, so they asked Otis if he'd get on the mike and just sing it down while the band worked it up. When they started with playback, they had a big speaker from the old theater out in the studio portion where you could listen to the playback. And they started playing it back and it was like late in the evening when all the secretaries were getting ready to get off. But everybody started coming into the studio, 'Who is that? What is that?' It was just like magic. As they say, the rest is history."

Stax Records began in 1960 as a strictly mom-and-pop operation before it quickly blossomed into a soul label that would rival Motown in influence, if not popularity. Stax was the brainchild of a brother and sister, Jim Stewart and Estelle Stewart Axton, who were born in Middleton, Tennessee. Jim's day job was working in the bonds department of the First National Bank; at night, he was a fiddle player who performed with several country bands. Estelle also was in the banking industry, working as a teller for the Union Planter's Bank. But music was her first love—she played the organ in church and listened to the radio with a passion.

Jim Stewart looked like a banker. He was a studious-looking man with thick black hair combed straight back and greased down; he wore black-frame glasses and conservative suits. But his nerdish appearance belied his fascination with music. He spent hours setting up a small studio in his garage, playing with the equipment, and learning how to record music. In 1957 he recorded a local country band and then released a single on his homemade label, Satellite Records. The record sold few copies, but Jim had caught the fever and decided to get serious about running a recording studio. His first step was buying professional-quality equipment, and Jim went to his sister for a loan. Estelle became his partner, taking out a $2,500 second mortgage on her house to finance the venture, and they built a studio in an empty storefront in a little town called Brunswick about thirty miles east of Memphis. It quickly became a home base for a local rock group called the Royal Spades that featured Estelle's son, Packy, on tenor saxophone. The band was made up of high-school kids from Memphis—including Steve Cropper on guitar and Donald "Duck" Dunn on bass—and the group traveled out to the studio every weekend to rehearse and mess around.

The Brunswick location proved too isolated, too far from the city, to attract much business. About a year later, Jim and Estelle moved their base of operations to Memphis, into the old Capital movie house on East McLemore. The rent was cheap, $100 a month, and they went about transforming the building into a real studio. They ripped out the theater seats, laid down carpeting, built a control room, and padded the walls. To help the acoustics, Estelle sewed large drapes that hung from the ceiling. And to help generate cash flow, the lobby was converted into a record shop—a decision that would quickly become a crucial ingredient in Stax's later success.

Almost as soon as they had finished setting up the studio, a local DJ and R&B singer named Rufus Thomas stopped by to check things out. Thomas worked at a local station called WDIA and had recorded one of Sun Records' first hits—a song called "Bear Cat" that was his musical response to Big Mama Thornton's 1953 hit "Hound Dog." Rufus told Jim that he had written a song called "Cause I Love You" that would make a perfect duet with his teenage daughter, Carla Thomas. Jim agreed to bring them into the studio. The song was released in August of 1960 and Jim Stewart assigned part of the publishing rights to John R., who put the record on the air and gave it a push. With his help, "Cause I Love You" became the first hit for Satellite Records. The song also caught the ear of Jerry Wexler, who paid Jim and Estelle $1,000 for the right to re-release it under the Atlantic label. Carla Thomas followed up that record with a song she had written called "Gee Whiz," which, aided by a big push from Atlantic, became the the studio's first Top Ten hit. "Gee Whiz" climbed to #5 on the R&B charts and #10 on the pop charts. Not long after that, Jim Stewart and Jerry Wexler shook hands and agreed on a deal that gave Atlantic exclusive distribution of his records.

The studio quickly became a hangout for local musicians: Steve Cropper and Duck Dunn and Booker T. Jones, all young kids; Chips Moman (who set up Stax's studio, then had a falling-out with Jim and Estelle and founded his own recording facility); and two songwriters named David Porter and Isaac Hayes. They all seemed to congregate every afternoon at Estelle's record shop, which often was generating the only actual cash coming into the business. "The idea for the store came when I was working as a teller at Union Planter's Bank and my friends wanted records," she said. "So I'd get them and pay 65 cents each and then sell them for a dollar. And what money I had left, I'd buy some more records. I ran the record shop after I got off work, and that's where writers and artists would hang out. It was wonderful. They would listen to the hit records and try to analyze why they were hits."

In the meantime, the Royal Spades had transformed into a tight, well-rehearsed group, finding their first steady gig at a little joint called Neal's Hideaway out by the Millington Naval Base. The band members continued to frequent the studio, and one afternoon someone began playing a goofy riff and the others kicked in behind them. They put it on tape and called it "Last Night." Estelle loved it, but the track languished for weeks on a forgotten reel; Jim was focused on recording Carla Thomas's debut album and he had no interest in putting out an instrumental single. That's when Estelle stepped forward—not only did her son play on the song, but she thought it was a hit. She put a copy in the hands of a couple of local disc jockeys, who began playing it. Even after that, Jim remained noncommittal until Estelle finally confronted him one night. When tears and pleading didn't work, she started cussing up a storm. That did it; Jim finally gave in. "I had to force them to put it out," she said. "My son was one of the writers and he was a musician on it. So I had them put it on the radio and people were coming into the shop wanting to buy the record. And I didn't have it! I finally got it out and it became a million-seller."

Estelle also convinced the band to find a new name, and came up with the Mar-Keys, a play on the old theater marquee hanging above the front studio facade. "Last Night" was released on Satellite Records and shot up the charts—topping out at #3 on the white pop charts and #2 on the R&B charts. Days after the song became a hit, a small California label also called Satellite Records contacted them and threatened to sue. Jim and Estelle had never liked "Satellite" anyway, so they quickly changed the name of the label to Stax Records—the "St" for Jim Stewart and the "Ax" for Estelle Axton.

The second Stax vocalist to hit the charts was William Bell, a local kid who had performed with the Memphis-based Phineas Newborn Band and sang backup on "Gee Whiz." Chips Moman championed William around Stax and encouraged him to come up with an original song to record. When he showed up with a ballad called "You Don't Miss Your Water ('Til Your Well Runs Dry)," Chips put him behind the mike. The song was very much Sam Cooke–influenced, especially

William's lilting and elegant vocals. But the recording veered away from the smooth sophistication of Cooke's records; instead it had a raw emotional feel that was powerful and unforgettable. "You Don't Miss Your Water" became the prototype for what would become the classic Stax sound. Nothing was sugar-coated or sweetened up to appeal to white audiences—Stax's music was unabashedly black and rural. They would later call it "soul music," a genre that was born at Stax Records.

Like the other kids at Stax, William hung out at Estelle's record shop. "It was a fun time, a creative time," he said. "You could go in the studio and cut something, and then bring it up to Miz Axton and play the tape in the record shop. She always had a bunch of kids hanging around listening to records, so you could get a pulse on whether or not you had anything from just that. And it was also a time where the formats at radio stations weren't so tight. You could take something down to the radio station. They had what they called the *Make It or Break It Hour.* And a lot of good songs were probably lost because people would say 'Break it' and it'd never be played again!"

William also was around the studio one day during a recording session when someone suggested an organ would sound nice on a certain song. He suggested a kid named Booker T. Jones, the organist at his church and a musical prodigy who could play with skill nearly a dozen instruments—piano, organ, ukulele, clarinet, bass, oboe, saxophone, baritone saxophone, trombone. Though he was still in high school, Booker already was a veteran of several of Memphis's most prominent bands. He also had a history at Stax; he played baritone sax on Rufus and Carla Thomas's "Cause I Love You" and was a regular at Estelle's record shop.

Booker quickly became a fixture around the studio. He impressed Jim Stewart: He was mature for a teenager, businesslike and dependable and laid-back. He'd go to school during the day, work a paper route, then head down to Stax to play sessions or hang out at the record shop until his nine o'clock curfew. Booker brought in two people who would form the backbone of the early Stax Studio rhythm section—drummer Al Jackson, Jr., and bassist Lewis Steinberg. Both had played with Booker in the band of local icon Willie Mitchell, and Al Jackson was well known as the best drummer in Memphis. He also was a perfectionist. Booker liked to tell the story about playing bass in local bands that also featured Al on drums. Al would usually spend a good portion of every gig yelling at him: "You little shit! Get on the beat! Get on the beat!"

Duck Dunn, who shared bass duties with Lewis Steinberg at Stax, was a fan long before he actually met Al Jackson. "When I was working with the Mar-Keys, Al was playing with Willie Mitchell in a club. And I was playing in a hillbilly/rockabilly club. I'd start at nine, get through at one, and on my way home, I would pass where Al was playing at the Manhattan Club and I'd stop in. I'd never say too much; I'd just sit back there and dream that one day I was gonna play with him. I'd get home around four or five in the morning. I was distributing King Records in those days, married and had two kids and getting about three hours of sleep at night. But I just had to hear him. He was just impeccable, man. There was nothing like it."

In June of 1962, Stax brought in Steve, Lewis, Al, and Booker T. to play a session backing up rockabilly singer Bill Lee Riley. When Riley didn't show, the guys began jamming on a funky blues riff that Booker and Al had sometimes played with Willie Mitchell's band. Jim Stewart heard them, cued up a tape, and asked them to take it from the top. They didn't even know they were being recorded but when Steve Cropper heard the playback he told himself it was the best damn instrumental he'd heard in years. They called it "Green Onions" because they wanted something funky-sounding for the title, and the next morning Steve took an acetate to a local radio station. By the afternoon, the phone lines were lighting up with people looking for the record. The single was released a couple of weeks later on Volt, a newly created sister label to Stax. Then Jerry Wexler told them to withdraw that version and put out the song on the Stax label because it had a track record with DJs and fans. "Green Onions" quickly climbed to #1 on the R&B charts and #3 on the pop charts, becoming the biggest hit in Stax's young history and one of the most instantly recognizable instrumentals in history.

That song sealed the deal. From then on, Booker T. and Steve and Al and Lewis were the Stax studio band. They called themselves Booker T. and the MG's. About a month after "Green Onions," Otis Redding showed up at the studio with Johnny Jenkins.

In retrospect, the chemistry between Otis Redding and the MG's was obvious from almost the first moment they played together in the studio. The first song Otis cut that Tuesday afternoon was "Hey Hey Baby," an up-tempo rave-up that was little more than a Little Richard knockoff and a huge step backwards from the originality of "Shout Bamalama." The most interesting thing about the song was the ascending guitar lines that Johnny played behind the vocals and his intricate, knife-edged solo. The track was good, but no cause for excitement.

Then came "These Arms of Mine." No one anticipated the depth of Otis's voice, the husky soulfulness that gave texture and vitality to what was otherwise a rather pedestrian ballad. The song began with Otis singing the title line alone until the band joined in on the final word. He started out very tentatively, struggling to find the beat. Yet the aching hesitation in his voice gave the song a haunting quality, like someone who shyly stutters as he begins a confession that comes from the deepest, most vulnerable corners of his soul. As he reached the bridge of the song, his voice began gaining strength and confidence. By the second verse Otis was singing with supreme assurance, his voice passionately pleading for the woman he loves as if he believes he will never have her unless he can win her over right here, right now, with this one song. And in that one brief performance, Otis was able to do what few singers could—convey that haunting despair with absolute sincerity.

"These Arms of Mine" was liberating for Otis. It enabled him to finally seek out his own personal vision as a singer. "The thing that brought out a different style in him was when he came up with that song," said Johnny Jenkins. "That took him away from Little Richard. He had that Georgia gospel sound. He didn't just say, 'I love ya; I care about you,' like the average person would say and then be through with it. He'd keep repeating the same thing over and over and over until it *got* you."

"Otis had the talent," Bobby Smith said. "But all the time I had him, I never saw him do nothing but Little Richard–type stuff. And that was the break, when he went up there and did 'These Arms of Mine.' That really opened up his style."

Two days after the recording session—on August 16, 1962—Galkin and Jim Stewart signed a short, three-paragraph contract confirming their agreement and just like that, it was official: Otis Redding was a Stax recording artist. A week later, Phil formalized his professional relationship with Otis—he and Poor Sam signed a contract to become Otis's co-managers. It was a three-year deal, with Phil and Poor Sam holding an additional option for three additional years. The contract gave Phil and Poor Sam a healthy 30 percent of Otis's gross income. The three-page document outlined in great detail the expectations of Phil and Poor Sam. They would get the gigs and champion Otis's career. In turn, Otis agreed that he would "reherse [*sic*] and attend all performances, engagements, and recording sessions which managers shall require, and follow managers' directions and instructions during all rehersals [*sic*], performances, and recording sessions, and further, will travel by all boats, trains, airplanes, and other means of conveyance as and when required by managers." Otis signed the contract on August 23, 1962, three weeks shy of his twenty-first birthday.

There was just one problem: Otis already had a manager. His name was Bobby Smith.

A few weeks after Otis and Johnny had borrowed his station wagon to drive up to Memphis, Bobby got a call from John R. at WLAC. "You seem like a young man who's trying to make it in the music business and you seem pretty straight, so I want to fill you in on some information," the disc jockey told him. "I just came from an R&B convention in St. Louis. Joe Galkin has a tape on your singer, Otis Redding. It's called 'These Arms of Mine.' I heard it."

Bobby was stunned. "You got to be kidding," was all he could manage to say.

"No," replied John R. "You better check your contract."

Indeed. Otis already was under an exclusive recording contract with Confederate/Orbit Records, which meant he wasn't supposed to be making records for anybody else. Bobby confronted Phil, who said he didn't know anything about it. Then he went over to Otis's duplex in East Macon, the one Bobby had gotten for Otis and Zelma. They sat down at the same kitchen table where Otis had signed his recording contract with Bobby. He asked Otis flat out: Did you record "These Arms of Mine" when you went to Memphis?

Otis hemmed and hawed, then finally confessed. "Yeah, Bobby, they just wanted to lay it down on tape," he said. "They just wanted to see how I sounded on it." Finally, Otis suggested that Bobby take a manager's cut, and let them go ahead and release the record.

Bobby couldn't believe it. He wasn't mad at Otis; he figured Otis probably *did* think he was just doing a demo record that was never intended for release. But he was furious with Joe Galkin. He had a signed contract with Otis, and Galkin knew that. He'd worked day and night to make Otis a star. It was about to finally pay off and here was Joe Galkin, trying outright to steal Otis away. Bobby went back to Phil, who still denied everything. "I don't know anything about it," he said.

Then Bobby called Joe Galkin, who confessed with a cool arrogance. "Yeah, I went ahead and recorded him," Galkin said. "He wasn't twenty-one years old when he signed your contract."

Neither was Otis twenty-one years old when Galkin and Jim Stewart signed him. Bobby turned the whole thing over to his lawyer, who negotiated a buyout; Bobby didn't want to fight Otis and he didn't want to fight Phil. "I had a choice," he said. "I could have received 2 cents a record on everything in his career. And not being sensible, I sold his contract right out. I don't want to tell you for how much, but let's put it that way: It wasn't a lot. You come out of a bad wreck with a wife and four children, you do the things you have to do. And I didn't see what the future was going to be. I didn't know the music business; I was learning. And I was mad. They knew what they were doing. They knew what was going down from the very get-go. They figured, That boy down there in Macon, he don't know nothing."

Stax released "These Arms of Mine" and "Hey Hey Baby" in October of 1962 on its new Volt label. And the record did exactly nothing. No chart action, no radio play, nothing. Otis was still in Macon, singing with the Pinetoppers at Club 15 and the Grand Dukes. At first they mentioned the song in newspaper ads promoting their appearances; after a couple of weeks, they no longer bothered. No one had heard of "These Arms of Mine"—why waste the newsprint?

Phil set up a small tour for Otis just after the record was released, hoping to drum up interest in "These Arms of Mine." They turned to

Percy Welch, who had been there the night Otis bombed in that first talent-show appearance with Gladys Williams at Hillview Springs. Since then, Percy had hooked up with Universal Attractions out of New York City, who had put him to work playing behind their touring acts: Roy Brown, Etta James, the Moonglows (featuring Marvin Gaye), the Drifters.

"We got a group together to go out with Otis after he made 'These Arms of Mine,' " said Percy. "He wanted to go on a little tour because his record wasn't doing nothing. It'd done all it was going to do and it wasn't no hit. So he wanted to hit some spots where he hadn't been and make a little money, too. But we didn't. We did about thirty days with Otis. Joe Tex was on that package, along with a vocal group. We didn't get but eight hundred dollars a night. I'd pay Otis his hundred and a quarter. I'd pay a hundred seventy-five to the vocal group because there was five of them. I'd pay Joe Tex a hundred and a half 'cause Joe Tex had that hit record, 'Skinny Legs.' Man, when it got around to paying the band to back them all up, which was my band, there wasn't no money left for me after I paid them!"

Even with the modest tour "These Arms of Mine" continued to flounder. Most stations seemed have listened to "Hey Hey Baby" and never flipped the record over. Then John R. came riding to the rescue. He had fallen in love with "These Arms of Mine," and about two months after the single came out, he called up Jim Stewart to inform him that he thought the ballad was a smash hit. When Jim scoffed, John R. cut him short: "I believe in this record and I intend to play it until it's a hit." Jim was a Southern boy who wasn't about to look a gift horse in the mouth; he thanked the disc jockey and offered to John R. his share of the publishing rights. "He played that song every night over and over, and finally broke it," Jim said. "It still wasn't that big-selling of a record—completely in the R&B market. We couldn't even get all of that because it was just a black, country-sounding record; in Chicago, for example, they were getting away from that sound."

But almost purely on the strength of John R.'s effort, the song eventually crept up to #20 on the R&B charts. Otis Redding had his hit record. Now the trick was to prove it was no fluke.

Pain in My Heart

Not long after "These Arms of Mine" hit the charts, Otis and Bubba Sailor hopped in Bubba's black 1952 Ford one afternoon and rode over to Ballard-Hudson High School. There was a place around back near a big open ditch where the kids hung out, and Bubba parked the car while Otis chatted with his little brother, Luther Rodgers, and one of his brother's friends, David Tharpe. Otis and Bubba both now sported processed hairdos courtesy of Otis's barber, Walter Johnson, who owned the House of Johnson barbershop on Broadway just down the street from the Douglass Theatre. While they were talking, a group of girls spotted Otis and within minutes Bubba's car was surrounded. Otis laughed with embarrassment when they all began demanding his autograph. He didn't know what to do or even what to write; nobody had ever asked him to sign anything before. At the suggestion of David Tharpe, he simply wrote, "Love Always, Otis Redding," and wound up hanging out behind the school for nearly an hour before making an escape.

Otis was a country boy who comfortably grew into the role of "star" as he matured into manhood. Celebrity wore easily on Otis because he wanted it so badly. He never ran from fame; he always embraced it and encouraged it. He'd tell people all the time that he was going to be famous. Even when he was doing fraternity gigs in the backwoods of Alabama with the Pinetoppers, Otis always seemed assured of his fate. "I'm gonna to be a star, man, and when I do, I'm going to be a real motherfucker," he'd tell anyone willing to listen.

"It didn't matter to him; he just wanted to be big and famous," Johnny Jenkins said. "It's exactly why he was easy to go into anything without thinking. He was like that his whole life. Otis, if you drew a gun on him, he'd tell you to shoot him, then walk up and take it if you don't shoot. There's people like that in the world and Otis was one of them."

Some thought it was an arrogance that ballooned after he had his first hit record. "He changed like the weather," said Percy Welch. "He was always humble and always ready to do something for you, ready to help you do something. As soon as the son of a bitch had that hit record, you could feel the change in him by the day."

Others took it more benignly, as Otis expressing his confidence in himself. Like as not, everyone seemed to notice it. "I thought he would make it locally, but I didn't think he'd ever get *that* big," said Charles Davis. "But I don't think Otis ever doubted it."

The success of "These Arms of Mine" marked the beginning of a parting of the ways between Otis and Johnny. The original plan was for the two of them to continue performing together as they always had, simply taking their act out on the road. It made perfect sense. They worked well together and Johnny had a true feel for playing behind Otis. Johnny also had his own hit record and possessed the kind of flamboyant stage moves that Otis would never have. There was just one catch: Johnny refused to go on the road.

There are those who attribute it to jealousy, Johnny's bitterness that Otis had shot to stardom at a recording session that was supposed to be his own ticket to fame. Johnny insists the reason was more elemental—his fear of flying. As the Pinetoppers broke apart, Johnny's drinking took a turn for the worse. People say his life and career soon slipped into an alcohol haze, and he would never have another hit on the scale of "Love Twist" even though there are many who think stardom was within Johnny's grasp. "Johnny, right now, could have been a millionaire if he'd wanted to," Ish Mosley said. "Otis really wanted to take Johnny with him."

Otis wanted to take them *all* with him. When he began searching for musicians for his new band, he concentrated on old friends from Macon. Most were content to stay right where they were. Like Johnny, they were comfortable in their simple and safe surroundings, fearful of how the road and fame might indelibly alter their lives. None of the Pinetoppers went with Otis. Charles and Benny Davis moved to Chicago with their family. Poor Sam decided to concentrate on his managerial skills, which were far greater than his ability on the bass. Ish also dropped out, even though Poor Sam pleaded with him to leave his day job at Robins Air Force Base to go on the road with Otis. "Listen, this thing is about to get big," Poor Sam told him. "I want you to quit Robins."

For Ish, there wasn't much of a debate. He was married. He had five children to support. His job at the Air Force base was good. The checks were steady. They came every week. "No, man," he told Poor Sam. "I can't do that."

"We'll guarantee you $500 a week," Sam countered. When Ish still resisted, Poor Sam didn't beat around the bush. "Well, Ish," he said. "We're gonna have to get somebody else to play saxophone. We're gonna hate to lose you."

Poor Sam himself wasn't to remain in the picture very long. By May of 1963, he was no longer helping manage Otis. Phil would say later that he met with Otis and Sam and they all agreed that Sam would part amiably. Sam disagreed with that assessment, and filed a lawsuit a couple of years later that claimed he still had a valid managerial contract that entitled him to a share of Otis's income.

While Phil took over as Otis's sole manager, the behind-the-scenes power broker was Joe Galkin. He got Otis's career off the ground and gave it direction. Because Galkin represented Atlantic Records, he held much sway over radio stations across the South and didn't hesitate to use his muscle. If a station didn't want to play an Otis Redding song, he was known to dramatically demand the immediate return of every Atlantic record on the station's premises. "Joe promoted Otis day and night," Jim Stewart said. "Joe was the one that kept pushing and pushing. He was the motivating factor behind myself and Jerry Wexler and Phil Walden, kicking us in the butt, saying 'Let's do this; let's do that.' And he never really got the publicity or credit for that because he was behind the scenes so much."

The one person who would reap the publicity was Phil Walden. "Our relationship was very unusual for that place and that time," he told one reporter. "Our lives were very entwined. Otis had such a big heart. He could overwhelm you with his personality. You couldn't hate this guy. He made friends with all people—bankers, police officers. I watched him with this redneck sheriff one night, and he just charmed him. They were trading hats by the end. I'd catch hell from redneck whites, and he'd catch hell from militant blacks. We were right there on the cusp of social change. I used to talk to Martin Luther King all the time, and Rap Brown. It was a historical time."

While Phil certainly had the gift for self-promotion, he and Otis did have a very close relationship in the early days and he earned the respect of Otis's circle of friends. One thing that impressed them was that Phil didn't treat his friendships with blacks as "man/boy" the way most whites treated people of color. His relationship with Otis was symbolized by an incident that happened while Phil was still a student at Mercer University. Phil paid his own way through college, but he was never shy about spending money on fancy clothes and the finer things in life, and occasionally he tapped himself out. After one spending spree, Phil didn't have enough money left over for tuition. His father wouldn't loan him money, saying Phil needed to learn fiscal responsibility. Phil was back at the office when Otis paid his regular lunchtime call. He saw that Phil was depressed and asked what was wrong. After Phil explained his dilemma, Otis asked him how much money he needed and then told him to sit tight. "I'll be back in a little while," Otis said. He came back a few hours later toting a crinkled brown paper sack filled with change and dollar bills, just enough money to pay Phil's tuition. "You do the learning," Otis told him. "I got to do the singing."

"Back then, Phil was like a brother," said Johnny Jenkins. "He was somebody that cared and he was somebody that would stand by you. We all drank together. We played and sung, and if we needed anything, we'd go to Phil to get it. It wasn't no 'black boy' and no 'white boy,' one's got, the other ain't got. If one had, the other had."

"Phil had no racial bias; he wouldn't let that stand in the way of what he wanted to do," said Charles Davis. "He was always talking about one way a black man can make it out of poverty is through music. He was always pushing Otis to achieve those things. He was strictly a businessman, although he had a good sense of humor sometimes. He bought us some of the clothes we had, and our instruments."

Phil retained much of the same basic philosophy that he had adopted as he was first getting into the business. He booked the gigs and ensured that the act showed up. When someone in the band needed a new instrument, Phil made sure he got it. When there was a gig that called for nice clothing, Phil went down to his dad's clothing store on Cherry Street and rented suits for everyone. If there was trouble on the road, he got them out of it. If someone in the band was unhappy, Phil tried to smooth the waters.

"Phil was good to me," said Ploonie. "Treated me real good. When I quit the Pinetoppers, I was tired of playing that rock 'n' roll; I wanted to play jazz. We were supposed to go to Tuscaloosa and play a fraternity house. I called Poor Sam and told him I was quitting, I wasn't going. Phil got on the phone and said, 'Don't go anywhere; I'll be right there.' He asked me what was wrong. I said, 'I don't know.' He asked if I wanted something. I said, 'Yeah, I want a big cymbal.' He said, 'That's all you want? That's all? I'll buy it.' It didn't matter; I still didn't go to Tuscaloosa. But I liked Phil. Phil was fine."

It didn't take long for Otis and Bobby Smith to renew their friendship. For a while, Bobby was red-hot mad. Then Otis went to see him. He didn't want any hard feelings, and Bobby couldn't find it in himself to remain angry. Within weeks of breaking his contract, Otis was helping Bobby build his first studio down on Mulberry Street next door to the Grand Opera House. Bobby hadn't stayed down very long. In fact, had he managed to hang on to Otis for just a little while longer, the future course of soul music might have veered very dramatically—instead of hooking up with Stax under the guardianship of Atlantic Records, it is very possible that Otis would have signed with Atlantic's chief rival at that time, King Records out of Cincinnati.

For months Bobby had sent Wayne Cochran tapes to every record label and radio station he could find, to virtually no response. Then, in the course of a single day, Wayne Cochran suddenly became a hot property. First, a representative from Mercury Records called Bobby to offer Wayne a recording contract. Bobby asked him about the money. The rep said he had to ask the president of the label, but would get back to him later in the day with a firm financial offer.

Just an hour or so later, the phone rang again. Bobby picked it up and a woman told him, "Please hold for Mr. Nathan." His heart skipped a beat. "Mr. Nathan" was Syd Nathan, the founder of King Records, and nobody interested in music around Macon had to ask about King Records—that was James Brown's label. A few seconds later, Nathan came on the line. His voice was unforgettable: rough, husky, full of verve. Nathan began talking about how much he liked the Wayne Cochran tapes, and asked Bobby how he and Wayne had hooked up. So Bobby told him about the car accident and how he was just getting started in the music business. He also happened to mention that a Mercury rep had made an offer and was asking his boss about a firm dollar figure. Nathan didn't skip a beat. "I don't have to ask nobody," he said. "Here's what I'll do." Nathan made an offer and Bobby quickly agreed to a deal.

About a week later, he called Bobby and told him to come down to Miami for a meeting. Bobby turned down the invitation, explaining that he couldn't afford to make the trip. "Don't worry about it," replied Nathan. "I'll send you the money." Bobby arrived in Miami and caught a ride to Nathan's address, which turned out to be an ocean-front condo. He walked in the lobby, saw a circle of people gathered around someone. Bobby heard Nathan's unmistakable voice ringing out from the center of the crowd and went over to introduce himself: "Mr. Nathan, I'm Bobby Smith from Macon, Georgia."

There was no shame in being awestruck by Syd Nathan—he was one of the founding fathers of R&B music, starting King Records in Cincinnati in 1945. He quickly made it the premier label for black performers during the 1950s. He gathered an incredible roster of future R&B legends: James Brown, Hank Ballard and the Midnighters, Bill Doggett, Big Jay McNeely, Earl Bostic, Little Willie John, Wynonie Harris, Eddie "Cleanhead" Vinson. And as if to show his nose for talent was no fluke, Nathan also made a big impact on country music, signing up stars such as Moon Mullican, Grandpa Jones, Webb Pierce, the Delmore Brothers, Hawkshaw Hawkins, and Ferlin Husky.

Nathan could have easily looked at Bobby Smith as a rube, a country bumpkin to be taken advantage of. Instead, Bobby's earnest sincerity seemed to impress him. They spent two days together in Miami, talking music and getting acquainted. "I'm gonna put you in the business," Nathan told Bobby before he left for home. "I like you. You have a good ear. Go back to Macon. Find a place to put a studio, put one in, and go to work for King Records."

Bobby wasn't sure if he believed him. He already had been burned once and his innocence was gone. Bobby could imagine himself incurring all sorts of debt building a studio only to see Syd Nathan give him the bum's rush. So Bobby went home to Macon and basically forgot all about it. Then a few weeks later, Nathan called. "Have you found a place yet? No? Well, get out there and find it!" That stirred Bobby into action. He looked around town and found a space in the old Georgian Hotel just down the street from his office and right next door to the Grand Opera House. The hotel was falling into disrepair, so they had closed the restaurant and dining room area, boarding it off from the rest of the hotel. Bobby leased the two rooms and then Syd Nathan quickly sent him a check to pay for everything.

"Otis and I, we built the studio, literally," Wayne Cochran said. "We took two or three rooms that were like closets and we were going to make an echo chamber. So we went in there with chicken wire and put it on the walls and covered it with plaster. Then took varnish and shellac and painted it. And this was a closed-off space. We put about ten coats on it. And just breathing that stuff, man, it was horrible. It's a wonder we didn't die from the fumes."

"It was a funky place," said Bobby Smith. "You had the studio and then four steps up to the control room. And you had a door up under the control panel where you'd go work on equipment. Wayne had bought this ocelot cat; it looked like a tiger but it was trained, tame. One day it got loose and went up under the control panel. And Oscar Mack came in. Wayne told him to go in there and get out that 'little kitten' for him. Oscar went in and that cat growled at him. And Oscar came up out of there, and he just shot out the back door!"

The Macon Recording Studio would prove to be an important learning ground for Otis. Although he was signed to Stax Records and all his recordings in Bobby's studio were done surreptitiously (and in obvious violation of his Stax contract), Otis was down there just about every day he wasn't out on the road somewhere. Just as Stax became a gathering spot in Memphis, Bobby's studio attracted aspiring musicians in Macon—Otis and Johnny Jenkins and Little Willie Jones and Wayne Cochran and Percy Welch and Oscar Mack were all fixtures, as was Phil Walden.

Some of the first recordings they made in the studio featured Otis and Oscar singing duets. The material has never been released, but represents an important moment in Otis's career. He and Oscar sang in much the same style that Sam and Dave would later develop at Stax, trading verses and lines. Oscar Mack's fluid, soaring voice was the polar opposite of Otis's, and made for an interesting contrast when they sang together on songs such as "Dream Girl" and "A Little Bit of Soul." Yet the recordings also show a startling similarity in the way Oscar and Otis approached a song, from the phrasing of the lyrics to the gospel feel in their voices. On one of the songs, someone begins scatting on the coda "Got-ta, got-ta, got-ta, got-ta!" It's an exciting moment to hear, the first evidence of the stuttering "got-ta" that would soon become an Otis Redding trademark. Then you realize it's not Otis singing; it's *Oscar Mack*. "Otis's style really comes from Oscar Mack," said Newt Collier, who was hanging around the studio as he learned to play trumpet, and possesses copies of the tapes. "You can hear that Otis sound on these tapes and it's all Oscar Mack."

Recording in Macon gave Otis important experience working in a studio, something he certainly wasn't getting up in Memphis. Despite the success of "These Arms of Mine," Stax seemed reluctant to bring him back. It was a full eight months before Otis returned to Memphis to record two of his own songs: "That's What My Heart Needs" and "Mary's Little Lamb." The session followed a standard formula of the time—record a ballad for one side of the 45 and an up-tempo song for the other. It allowed a record company, especially a struggling one like Stax, to hedge its bets; if stations didn't like the slow song, then maybe they would flip the record over and play the fast one.

Otis's second session contained little of the magic of the first. "Mary's Little Lamb" was little more than a throwaway, and the ballad "That's What My Heart Needs" was a weaker cousin to "These Arms of Mine." Yet Otis transformed the song in the last sixty seconds when his voice cried out in a mournful series of wails that seemed to resonate from his very soul. As with "These Arms of Mine," Otis's performance rose above the level of the material; without his ability to sell the song, to make the emotions seem personal and real, "That's What My Heart Needs" hardly would have been memorable at all. The record was released in June of 1963. It rose to #27 on the

R&B charts, a step backwards from "These Arms of Mine," and then faded away.

While the material on his second session didn't leave Otis a lot to work with, his confidence in the recording studio was growing. He had a better sense of what he could do, what he *wanted* to do. And if he wasn't quite reaching it yet, he was beginning to reach toward it. "That's What My Heart Needs" marked the first time that Otis would make effective use of the Stax horn section, using crisp and darting lines to accent the vocals. Otis had spent time at the studio in Macon playing around with horn arrangements, learning from Oscar Mack and Little Willie Jones how to compose musical riffs for the horn section. Since Otis couldn't write music, he was taught to hum the parts to the musicians. "He got that down at Bobby Smith's studio," Newt Collier said. "We'd all work on the horn arrangements, together at one time. Otis also took a lot of Oscar Mack's style with the horns. Willie Jones had the communication skills to translate raw musical ideas to the band and make them see what was happening. Otis used to watch him do it."

Just as Otis continued to seek out opportunities for Johnny and the rest of the guys from the Pinetoppers, he also looked out for the friends he knew from the recording studio in Macon—when he traveled to Memphis for the "That's What My Heart Needs" session, he brought along Oscar Mack and a blues guitarist from South Macon named Eddie Kirkland, and convinced Jim Stewart to record them. One of the songs, Kirkland's "The Hawg," even turned into a minor hit.

Oscar and Eddie were each on the bill when Otis headlined the most important show of his young career, a Homecoming Show at the City Auditorium in Macon on July 30, 1963. To ensure its success, Stax rolled out its A-list of recording stars. Carla Thomas was there; so was her father, Rufus, who'd just had a hit with "Walkin' the Dog." Deanie Parker, a budding singer who would soon become the Stax public-relations director, did a short set. Booker T. and the MG's made a rare appearance outside the studio to back up everyone. It worked. People were lined up outside waiting to get in—black kids who had seen Otis at Hillview Springs or the Douglass or Club 15 crowding onto the floor of the Auditorium, white kids who had seen him at Lakeside Park and fraternity houses over at Mercer packing the balcony. They cheered every move Otis made. He had come home. And his home had embraced him as the returning prodigal son.

Otis was back in Memphis in September for his third session at Stax, recording what would be his first great record, a ballad called "Pain in My Heart" and an up-tempo B-side called "Something Is Worrying Me" that credited Otis and Phil Walden as the songwriters. The fast tune was another throwaway, a Little Richard–flavored song that sounded as if it was recorded under duress with the studio clock winding down. All the time and care obviously went into recording "Pain in My Heart." It was the first Otis Redding recording to have a fully realized arrangement with intricate and well-thought-out horn lines. From the very first moments of the song, it was obvious this was a different Otis. He exuded confidence and it seemed to rub off on the musicians playing behind him. It was as if, suddenly, they were beginning to get it, to understand what Otis was about and how to capture his sound.

The lyrical premise of "Pain in My Heart" differed little from his first two ballads at Stax—the singer aches for the woman he loves, begging her to come back to him. The revelation was Otis's voice. He took it places only hinted at in "These Arms of Mine," singing with a deep richness and husky warmth that transformed his voice into an expressive instrument; it was mature and bristling with emotion. Like a gruff and sweet tenor saxophone, his voice would reach for a musical destination and then subtly hover around it in a fading whisper. He also was learning to use it to tease. When Otis slowed down the tempo of "Pain in My Heart" to croon, "I want you to love me, baby, 'til I get enough," the implications were obvious. Yet he sang it as if he were winking at the audience, causing the women to swoon and squeal with laughter at the same time.

There was no better illustration of this than a show featuring Atlantic Records artists at the fabled Apollo Theatre in Harlem on November 16, 1963, that was recorded for a live album. The Apollo gig was Otis's first taste of being treated like a star outside his own hometown and it carried great meaning for him—the Apollo was the most famous stage in America for blacks, the place Otis had dreamed of singing at at the Douglass. He rode up in a 1963 Ford convertible with Huck behind the wheel even though Huck didn't have a driver's license. They stayed at the Hotel Theresa and ran into Cassius Clay, the brash young Louisville fighter who predicted his knockouts by the round and had just signed to fight heavyweight champ Sonny Liston. Clay was in town to promote the Liston fight and had the entire seventh floor, so Otis went up to his room to meet him before the show. "They paid us $400 and had a house band, so we thought it was lots of money," Huck told writer Peter Guralnick. "But then we had to get the music arranged—Otis used to just go up and tell people [what to play], but this was the King Curtis band and they wanted sheet music. So that cost us $450 and we had to wire back home to Phil to send us some more money."

It was a breakthrough show for Otis. He sang "Pain in My Heart" and "These Arms of Mine" in a revue that featured King Curtis, Ben E. King, Rufus Thomas, the Coasters, and the Falcons (featuring Wilson Pickett). The nervousness in his voice is obvious; you can hear it trembling in the first few bars of "These Arms of Mine." Yet he clearly connected with the crowd, especially the women. Throughout his performance of "Pain in My Heart," there were orgasmic female squeals from the audience. At one point, Otis sang, "Where can my baby be?" And a woman screamed back, "Right here! I'm here, baby!"

Otis did it all on the sheer strength of his voice. He had no real stage act. He didn't swivel his hips like Elvis, or fall to the floor and moan like James Brown. He simply stood at the microphone and sang, arms outstretched or emphasizing lyrics by bending at the waist. "You could feel this plea coming from him," Atlantic's Jerry Wexler said. "He didn't know how to move in those days. He was inept onstage. Yet in spite of his inertia, the women at the Apollo loved him, not only for his looks—he was tall, strapping, and handsome—but for his voice and vulnerability as well. Otis had chops like a wolf; his voice was big and gorgeous and filled with feeling."

Meanwhile "Pain in My Heart" was scooting up the charts and surpassing "These Arms of Mine." In an early nod to political correctness, *Billboard* magazine had discontinued the R&B charts and folded everything under a single "pop" chart that included music by both black and white musicians. "Pain in My Heart" rose to #61 on the *Billboard* pop charts, Otis's highest position yet. Had *Billboard* not abandoned the R&B charts, Otis certainly would have had his first Top Fifteen R&B hit.

Even as "Pain in My Heart" became his biggest record to date, Otis was hit with an accusation of plagiarism—a charge that had popped up before and would continue to follow him throughout his career. Stealing and remaking other people's songs was a long-standing tradition in blues and R&B music. Elmore James, for example, rode to fame on "Dust My Broom," a Robert Johnson standard that he took full credit for writing; he also took credit for writing the classic "It Hurts Me Too," which was actually written and recorded by Tampa Red a dozen years before James ever touched it. Copyrights in that era meant little—ownership of songs was often sold for $20 and the original author might never receive credit.

"Pain in My Heart" was a little too obvious. It sounded as if it was directly lifted from the Irma Thomas hit "Ruler of My Heart," a song written by New Orleans legend Allen Toussaint using the pseudonym of Naomi Neville, his mother's maiden name. Otis was sued and a settlement quickly reached; the song was thereafter credited to "N. Neville." That wasn't the first time the question of authorship had risen over a song credited to Otis. Bobby Smith heard rumblings that "Shout Bamalama" wasn't actually written by Otis. "I've heard stories that somebody else wrote it, but I have never confirmed that," said Bobby. "I've got to take Otis's word for it. He said he wrote it. He got the copyright on it."

Huck told people that he actually wrote "Mary's Little Lamb" even though it was credited as an Otis Redding song. And more than one person claims authorship of "These Arms of Mine." Percy Welch maintains the song was written by a guy named "Hot Sam" from Alabama. "Otis never wrote nothing," Percy said. "But he stuck his name on it."

The actual source may be Benny Davis, Otis's childhood friend who played guitar with the Pinetoppers for a time. He said that he wrote "These Arms of Mine" and his brother, Charles Davis, backs him up. "Benny just sang and wrote songs," Charles said. "And he wrote

'These Arms of Mine.' When Otis took it, my brother didn't like it at all. He felt like he should have got money for it. But different ones stole songs from Benny, even James Brown. Benny wrote a lot of different songs he didn't get no credit for."

Benny said it was a song that he wrote for Otis when they were together in the Pinetoppers. "It was just something I came up with," he said. "We used to do it with the Pinetoppers and the next thing I knew, I was living in Chicago and hearing it on the radio. I thought it was a rotten thing to do. I don't think he should have did me like that because we was real good friends. And that was one of the real big hits. I always thought he'd do the right thing about it, you know? But he never did."

In late 1963, Jim Stewart decided that Otis had compiled enough songs to warrant a full LP of material. At that point, albums mattered very little in popular music. The money was in 45s, aimed at teenagers enthralled by the jukebox and AM radio. No one viewed albums as artistic statements; they were afterthoughts, usually made up of two or three hit singles surrounded by filler material and used as a way to milk a little more money out of old hits.

Pain in My Heart fit right in that mold. The album was anchored by the songs "Pain in My Heart," "These Arms of Mine," and "That's What My Heart Needs." There were songs Otis had performed with the Pinetoppers—homages to his heroes: a cover of Sam Cooke's "You Send Me," a version of Ben E. King's "Stand By Me," and Otis's take on the Little Richard classic "Lucille." The album also included Otis's upcoming single, "Security," a song that represented both a change in direction and a maturation of his style. Otis was credited as the writer of "Security," although Huck said it was another song he had written for Otis. According to Huck, a girl who lived in Tindell Heights gave Otis the rough idea. He liked the title and concept, but the words didn't rhyme. So he gave it to Huck and told him fix it.

No matter the source, "Security" was a startling departure. Until that point, Otis had made his mark with slow and pleading ballads, one after another to the point he was in genuine danger of digging himself into a rut. "Security" broke that mold and forged a newer and better one. From the moment the song kicked off with a fast and sassy horn riff, "Security" *rocked.* This was the first Otis Redding song where the backbeat mattered more than the words. It was a song built on riffs and hooks, from the recurring horn lines, to Steve Cropper's succinct guitar licks, to Otis's repetition of the word "security." Most of all, "Security" marked the first up-tempo song where Otis rose above his Little Richard influence and began molding his own, unique sound.

As Otis grew as an artist, so did the MG's as a band. They were truly a *unit.* None of the band members possessed true virtuoso skills. Yet, put them together and they formed what many believe is the greatest band in the history of rock 'n' roll. One of their secrets was their ability to play with complex simplicity. Every note, every drum lick, had its place and fit into the whole. Nothing ever seemed to clash. Sometimes the band was so in sync that it was difficult to separate and hear each instrument: They didn't sound like four musicians playing in a band; they sounded like a band that happened to have four musicians.

The creative force behind the MG's was guitarist Steve Cropper. "Steve is the greatest rhythm guitar player I ever worked with," Duck Dunn said. "His timing is just incredible. Steve got notoriety for finding holes to play in, little licks. He's not known as a great soloist, but he's played some great solos. To me, when he plays rhythm, that's when he excels."

Steve and Duck's friendship went back to childhood. They met in the sixth grade and grew up on the same block. They went to school together, played football in the fall and baseball in the summer. But it was music that provided the bond for a friendship that would last a lifetime. They both began playing the guitar as teenagers, spending much of their spare time practicing together and jamming on rock-and-roll songs. They listened to the same records and studied the same guitar players: Scotty Moore, Chuck Berry, Billy Butler, Chet Atkins, Tal Farlow, Hank Garland.

Of the two of them, Steve was clearly the more talented player. Duck struggled to grasp the guitar; his fingers felt too clunky to play the tiny strings. Then he spotted a picture of an electric bass—then newly invented by Leo Fender and still trying to catch on in the music business. The bass looked like an oversized guitar with four big strings, and a single thought flashed through Duck's mind as soon as he saw it: Hey, four strings; I bet I could play *that*. "I bought a 1958 Precision and started working," he said. "The electric bass was starting to show up on a lot of R&B records, but when I signed with the union in Memphis, I think I was only one of three players listed."

With the electric bass, Duck had found his voice. He and Steve helped form the Royal Spades in high school. In the fall of 1960, Steve enrolled at Memphis State to study engineering, and because of the band his schedule was absolutely brutal. During the week he attended classes in the morning, worked in a grocery store in the afternoon, then drove forty miles to a club called Neil's Hideaway and played until two A.M. He spent much of his spare time—what little there was of it—at Stax, working in the record shop and playing sessions, learning the tricks of the recording studio, and teaching himself the craft of writing songs.

The Royal Spades became the Mar-Keys, and as "Last Night" hit the top of the charts, the band went on a breakneck tour to push the single. Steve quickly tired of living out of his suitcase, quit the band, and went back to Memphis to concentrate on the studio. When Chips Moman left Stax in a dispute with Jim Stewart in 1962, Steve stepped into his role—maintaining the equipment, running the control board during sessions, and scouting out talent. He spent nearly every waking hour at the studio, in an unpaid role at first until Estelle insisted that Jim pay him $50 a week.

Steve was with the MG's from the beginning, and the band really began to jell when Duck Dunn became the full-time bassist. The interplay between Duck and drummer Al Jackson, Jr., was crucial to the sound. "It was like a perfect marriage with Al, Booker, myself, and Steve," Duck said. "It's no doubt the best band I've ever had anything to do with. There's no doubt. And mainly because of Al. He had the secret to that groove, that big pocket with the delayed feel. Al just had this amazing sense of time. Believe me, he was simple but he could *play*. And he could control me. I have a tendency to rush every now and then. And Al would go, 'Dundy-Dunn-Dunn'—that's what he called me—'now back it off; wait on the two; don't beat me there.' He knew how to shape a song. Every band has arguments about how a song should go, but it became clear pretty quickly that when Al came up with something, it was going to end up being perfect for the song. I just stuck with him; we locked down. Like I say, if the drums and bass ain't happening, *nothing's* happening."

In retrospect, it was a fortuitous twist of fate that led Otis Redding to Stax Records. Stax was small, an independent label without expectations. Otis faced no pressure. No one was making hit records so no one was demanding hit records. The label offered a nurturing ground for someone like Otis who had obvious talent but needed time to develop. Stax was willing to be patient and build for the long term. Jim Stewart and the others weren't sure of what they had with Otis, but they were sure they had *something*. "After about probably the third single, I really began to understand what Otis was about and how special he was," Jim said. "His music was so raw and so earthy; without being trite, it was right from the soul. I'd never really worked with a singer who could reach down so deep and bring out that warmth and that feeling."

Mr. Pitiful

While Otis had recorded several good records—"These Arms of Mine," "Shout Bamalama," "Pain in My Heart"—he had yet to write a true hit, much less a song for the ages. In fact, "Security" stalled on the charts and barely cracked the Top 100. Otis stayed on the road, playing the "chitlin' circuit" up and down the East Coast, trying to build career momentum. Most often, Huck was with him everywhere he went. Huck remained the muscle man, making sure things were taken care of and that Otis was always paid. "Sometimes nobody got paid but us," Huck said. "You had to show strength."

Otis was never afraid of a fight. He'd grown up in Bellevue. He was big and strong. And he knew how to protect himself. The fighting skills he learned as a kid sometimes served him well on the road. One night he was driving the women crazy at a gig in North Carolina and a man out in the crowd became jealous of the effect Otis was having on his wife. The jealous man decided he could take it no more and stormed up to the bandstand. Otis was down on his knees, his eyes closed, singing "These Arms of Mine." The man stepped onstage, reached Otis, and sucker punched him in the face. It was a hard shot. Otis didn't even fall. He continued with the song. But when he finished, he stood up and calmly put down his microphone. Then he walked offstage, rushed his assailant, and proceeded to whip the hell out of him. A cop working security at the show watched the whole thing and didn't move a muscle, except to yell out encouragement: "Hit him, Otis! Hit him! I don't see a thing! Hit him, Otis!"

Another time, Otis was performing at the Howard Theatre in Washington, D.C., and a woman in one of the front rows began violently heckling him. One of Otis's bodyguards, a guy nicknamed "Bear," went up to the woman and tried to calm her down. A couple of minutes later she snuck up behind Bear and whacked him on the head with a claw hammer. Everyone's eyes were glued to the stage—where Otis was in the middle of a song, down on his knees—and few people noticed the assault. Seconds later, Otis glanced up and saw the woman standing directly in front of him, raising the hammer and aiming it at his head. As she swung, he leapt to his feet and jumped back, ending up against the drum kit, within the safe perimeter of the band. Nobody in the band ever accused Otis of being slow after that.

In 1964 Otis landed a spot on a show called *Hot Summer Revue*, sharing the bill with Solomon Burke and Garnet Mims. It was around that time he picked up a new backup band, a group called the Rockin' Cabanas, out of Washington, D.C. And inspired by the Mar-Key horn section at Stax, Otis brought horns with him on the road. One was Newt Collier—Otis's buddy from the Macon Recording Studio—who went out with Otis to play the trumpet.

"It was interesting because you didn't actually know the magnetism of Otis until you sat down and played with him," Newt said. "You could hear about it but until you got out there, you didn't understand. All of a sudden, you'd hear the emcee say, 'Otis Redding!' Then you heard the crowd. That's how big Otis was. He'd come tumbling out onstage. There was nothing easy about it, nothing graceful. He'd just come motoring out. But his presence, the way he handled the audience, let you know he was in control, he was *the man*."

Whenever he was home, Otis hung out with the fellows. When he wasn't over in Bellevue or holding court down on Broadway at Walter Johnson's barbershop, he'd be at Phil's office or else over at Bobby Smith's studio hanging out with Bobby and Wayne Cochran. "We'd ride around together," Wayne said. "We'd talk to one another. We'd try to write songs together. Between the band and my job at a dry cleaners', I'd made a little money and I'd bought me a used 1955 Buick Century convertible. It was yellow, with a black interior. Otis really liked that convertible—so every so often I'd leave it in Macon and let him drive it for a week. Then he had 'Security' come out. He was the talk of the town. And all of a sudden he had a new 1963 Ford convertible, purple with black leather interior. Otis looked so proud in that car; he'd ride all around Macon."

Wayne actually owned the publishing rights to "These Arms of

Mine" through a company he set up called Cochran Music. In 1964, Wayne left Macon after a falling-out with Bobby Smith. He needed money to buy a reverb unit for his PA system and had no money; he sold the publishing to Phil Walden for a grand total of $69.

The division between Wayne and Bobby was so bitter that even today Wayne refuses to refer to Bobby by name, often referring to him as "that used-car salesman." It began when Wayne wrote a ballad called "Last Kiss" that was released on King Records. Wayne thought it was a sure hit, but it languished without any push by the record company. It was, however, the #1 song in Odessa, Texas, where a guy named Joe Frank Wilson heard it and recorded his own version. Wilson's recording was released and immediately began to climb the charts and became a major hit. Wayne was livid, confronting King Records president Syd Nathan and demanding to know why somebody else had had a hit with *his* song. He also says he never saw a dime of money as a songwriter, just a brand-new Ford that Bobby bought him. For Wayne, that was the end.

By then, his musical direction had been drastically altered by the release of James Brown's "Out of Sight." When Wayne heard the record, he was stunned. It was *exactly* the sound he wanted to have, so he put together a full-blown soul revue that was based on James Brown's *Live at the Apollo* album. James had just debuted a new bouffant hairstyle, which Wayne also decided to mimic. Only he decided he wanted his bleached white. "I'd played with four young guys from Beaumont, Texas, called It and Them. They played R&B. Two brothers and two other players. The two brothers were albinos and every time they'd stand under the lights, their hair would change colors. I said, 'That's it; that is just *so* cool.'" The two albino brothers were teenage musical prodigies—Johnny and Edgar Winter.

Wayne could find no one who would bleach his hair albino white; everyone told him it would make his hair fall out. A few weeks later he traveled to Muncie, Indiana, for a four-week gig at a place called Woodberry's Supper Club. Opening night was horrible; nobody was there. It was just as bleak the next night and the night after. Wayne was called into the manager's office and told that he had to turn things around by the end of the week or else he'd be fired. Wayne decided he *had* to get his hair fixed and found a Muncie hairdresser

named Joe Gibbons who agreed to bleach it. They did it three different times and the result was always the same: Wayne's hair came out
with a pinkish strawberry hue. When he showed up at the club that
night, the manager took one look and said, "That's it. Get rid of the
hair or you're gone."

That's when Wayne came up with an idea that would jump-start
his entire career. "I'd just had new suits made up for the guys in the
band, the bolero-style short jacket with the cummerbund," he said. "I
had a long black satin cape with a red velvet lining. So I got this idea.
We pooled all of our money together. I'd heard of this place in town
called the Fox's Den where all the businessmen went for lunch. I
called and made a reservation for Wayne Cochran and the C.C. Riders. The guys in the band put on their dinner jackets and I put on my
stage outfit with the black cape and my hair done up in the strawberry
bouffant.

"We had enough money for the band members to get a salad and
for me to get a full meal. I worked up a thing with Joe Gibbons and
the band: We got to the door and they lined up four on each side.
Joe went in and he had on evening tails. He clapped his hands (*clap*,
clap) and they walked in and lined up on each side. Then I came in,
walked over to the table, and they all stood around me. Joe took my
cape off and I sat down. He went (*clap*, *clap*) and they all sat. He
couldn't eat because we didn't have enough money. We told the wait-
ress that he was my food-taster. In case of poison. And you could
just *hear* the forks dropping in that restaurant. We finished our meal.
Joe went (*clap*, *clap*) and the band stood up. And then I stood up.
Then they formed two lines at the door and I walked out. Then Joe
went back in and said, 'Ladies and gentlemen, you just had dinner
with Wayne Cochran and the C.C. Riders; he'll be appearing tonight
at the Woodberry Supper Club.' So we get to the club about six
o'clock. There's a line waiting outside.

"We went in and the room was *packed*. This was going to be our
last night, so I was going to do something different. We went into
'Shout' and I got down on the floor and I was laying on my cape.
Then I went into the audience hollering and screaming, and getting
them to holler and scream. Out in front there was a big plate-glass
window. And I took a chair and threw it through that window. Now,

this is the wintertime. It's cold outside. The chair went through the window, rolled downhill, and hit a Corvette. It was so loud inside, you couldn't hear the glass break. And all these thousands of fragments of glass went everywhere. And people went nuts! *Nuts!* So we finished and the guy calls me in his office and says, 'I'd like to keep you over for three more weeks.' And we packed the place every single night."

From there, Wayne Cochran and the C.C. Riders eventually wound up in Las Vegas, making upwards of $5,000 a night without ever having the benefit of a hit record, or *any* record for that matter. "That was big money," he said. "In the end, it wasn't music to me; it was a cause. To me, R&B and soul music was the finest music ever produced in America. It's so much better than rock 'n' roll. It had intensity. It had emotion. It was more musical. It was a bigger sound. And yet it had never been accepted in the masses of American culture. It was a minority music. That was my cause. I was going to make R&B be accepted by the masses. And I was the first R&B band ever to get accepted in Vegas. And I talked to them constantly. Ike and Tina Turner were there. Finally, Joe Tex was brought in. And they finally brought more soul acts in. What we did, we took soul and R&B music and dressed it up like Las Vegas. And while they weren't lookin', we snuck up behind them."

Wayne Cochran wasn't the only one getting a taste of success. Otis's lifestyle had improved significantly. He'd made enough money to buy his own house, at 3226 Commodore Drive in the Shurlington area of East Macon. He bought Zelma a champagne-colored Ford Fairlane that he squired around town. "There was a ball field near Mercer," said David Tharpe. "I used to go up there as a kid and when the guys knocked the ball out of the park, they'd give you so much money to bring the ball back. I remember seeing Otis up there in that Fairlane. He was in a suit. He'd got his process cut off and he had a hat on— wearing a hat was a rare thing for him. And the next year he bought his daddy a new Ford."

Even though he was enjoying his newfound celebrity, if he was home you could inevitably find Otis hanging out in Bellevue and being given the celebrity treatment—everybody knew Otis and everybody liked him. One afternoon a group of kids were hanging out playing pinball at the Perry Hills barbecue joint when Otis came in wearing a sleek corduroy suit with a leather shirt. Everybody's favorite meal at Perry Hills was the basic red-link sandwich with ketchup and mustard; nobody went for frills like slaw or chili. Otis ordered himself a red-link and surprised everyone when he asked the lady to put slaw on the top. She smiled and teased him. "Otis, you want *slaw* on your sandwich? Oh my! You done got rich now." Everybody in the joint burst out laughing. But after that, all those kids began getting slaw on their red-links, just like Otis.

He still hung out with the same basic crew—Huck, Bubba Howard, and Bubba Sailor. Bubba Sailor was married by then, with two kids, but little else had changed. Bubba Howard still had his fiery temper, and Huck was in and out of trouble with the law. Otis himself was arrested in 1963 for disposing of mortgaged property. He had bought a 1955 Buick Roadmaster for $65 from a garage on Napier Avenue, and they let him pay on time. Then he sold the car before he had paid off the loan, and they swore out a warrant. He pleaded guilty in Bibb County State Court and paid a $35 fine.

But, comparatively speaking, that was small potatoes. Huck was still the enforcer of the group and in the spring of 1961 Otis and Bubba Howard were at Jack's Snack Bar on Earl Street when Bubba got into a fight. The brother of Bubba's opponent tried to intervene— a friend of Huck's named William Shelley—and Huck smacked him in the mouth with the butt of a gun and threatened to kill him. Shelley escaped further punishment by lying on the floor and pretending he was unconscious.

Huck was arrested for assault and battery, and as his trial approached, he put out word that he was going to jump anyone who dared testify against him. A man named Terry Jackson failed to take heed and took the stand against Huck at the trial. Huck was livid. He vowed payback. A few days later, he spotted Jackson walking up Mumford Road. Huck pulled his car off the road, parked it, sat inside, and waited. When Jackson got close, Huck jumped out, slugged him, and pulled a pistol before he let him get up and run away. Once again Huck was arrested for assault. Then, in March of 1962, he was arrested for operating a dive, a non-licensed private club, and for selling beer without an alcohol permit. He was fined $100 and given twenty-five days in jail. Two months later, Huck was arrested again for almost the exact same crime.

And it was Huck who would take the fall for the gunfight that broke out on July 4, 1964, just before Otis was to play another Homecoming Show at the City Auditorium.

It began over almost nothing at all. In their circle of friends were the two Ellis brothers, Herbert and Arthur. Herbert Ellis caught his girlfriend talking to another guy, a seventeen-year-old kid named David McGee. When Herbert took offense, he was jumped by a group of McGee's friends. So Herbert went to Otis and Huck to get retribution. "See, we was family," said Bubba Sailor. "So when they whupped him up, he came to the family to get them back."

There was never a debate. It was a given—there was going to be payback. Otis gathered the gang together: Huck, Bubba Howard, the Ellis brothers, a friend named George Watson. Bubba Sailor missed the actual showdown because he was off with his wife visiting her family when Otis tried to reach him. They armed themselves with pistols and shotguns, hopped into Otis's Cadillac, and drove over to David McGee's house at 2755 Roy Street. They surrounded the house and the shoot-out began. Otis opened fire. McGee and his brother grabbed their own guns and shot back. Otis was crouched in front of the house, armed with a .38-caliber pistol, and spied McGee inside the house. It was apparently Otis who fired a shot that hit McGee in the right thigh just above the knee. McGee's brother, Willie, was hit in the abdomen and someone shot out the tires of his truck so he couldn't give chase when they left.

After a brief but intense firefight, Otis and the others finally retreated. Otis was hit with birdshot and Bubba Howard was hit bad enough to warrant a trip to the hospital. The Cadillac was hit, too. "They had the shoot-out over there and when I came home, my phone rang," Bubba Sailor said. "It was Bubba Howard and he wanted me to come to the hospital. I said, 'For what?' He said, 'We just got shot, man. Get your gun; meet us at the hospital. We're going back.' I was going because we'd always done everything for one another. I told my wife what I was going to do and she said, 'No, Willie, don't do that; you have me and these two kids here and you might be the one they kill.' So I did something I shouldn't have done—I didn't go. They felt like I betrayed them. Otis changed toward me. We never did get together no more too much. It really bothered me."

They never actually went back to the McGee house that night, but Otis still had to perform the Homecoming Show a few days later and there were wild rumors going around Bellevue that friends of the McGees were going to gun him down when he took the stage. Otis almost didn't go on. He performed without incident although his eyes were glued to the crowd all night, on the lookout for anyone who might be carrying a gun, and he also had his friends scouting the audience for signs of trouble.

After the gunfight, Huck was arrested for assault with intent to murder and discharging a firearm. He pleaded guilty and got off with two years of probation. And Otis was sued by both McGee brothers. David McGee was represented by two prominent white Macon attorneys, Denmark Groover and Wilbur D. Owens. Groover would go on to become a politically powerful state representative; Owens would go on to become a federal judge and preside over the trial of former Allman Brothers Band road manager Scooter Herring, sentencing him to seventy-five years in prison for supplying Gregg Allman with drugs.

The suit against Otis went to court later that year. He lost a non-jury trial, but got off lightly—he was ordered to pay David McGee $500 in damages. Otis then settled with Willie McGee for an undisclosed sum.

Had Phil Walden been around, it might never have happened. Phil fixed messes like that. But Phil was in Germany, in the Army. He'd left things in the hands of his twenty-year-old brother, Alan Walden.

Alan was young and innocent, rail-thin and hawk-nosed. They called him "Red" because of his sandy reddish-blond hair. And nothing he'd ever experienced prepared him for going on the road with Otis Redding. "In those days, we would go out thirty-five to seventy days straight," he said. "Sometimes it was like going to war. I carried a gun. All of us carried guns. You had to in those days. If some fucker was gonna mess with you, you had to be prepared to blow him away. I wasn't going to get written off like some of them civil-rights workers by the side of the road. I'll tell you, with Otis, it was never dull. There was always something going on. He had tremendous sex appeal to the ladies. There were always flocks of ladies backstage waiting just to touch his hand. Being single, I thoroughly enjoyed traveling with a guy who had such an appeal. I stayed in his room one time and had more sexual conquests in one week than I'd had maybe in a year before—and all I was doing was answering the phone." Word around Bellevue was that Alan was particularly shocked to discover that a good portion of the women calling Otis were white.

As a manager, Alan was hopelessly lost. He'd had about a day's worth of training in the music business, then found himself in charge of his brother's entire company. He almost immediately began losing money and it wasn't long before Alan dropped every one of Phil's acts except Otis. While it may have cut down on overhead, it also cut down on revenue. Nothing seemed to abate the worsening financial straits and when Alan tried to get a bank loan to keep them going he was too young to qualify. Growing desperate, he began seriously contemplating closing the business. He called Otis one night in Washington, D.C., where Otis was performing at the Howard Theatre, to tell him he didn't think he was going to be able to continue doing the booking any longer. "Up until that point, I had never seen an angry side of him," Alan said. "He'd always been a likable, affable person. But he flew home to Macon and commenced to get all over my butt."

Otis went over to the office and laid down the law. "Man, we gotta do anything we have to do to keep this company going 'til your brother gets back," he told Alan. "If it takes me putting all my money into the company, that's what we do." And then they went to Alan's father, who was sick and confined to his house.

"Pop, we need you," Otis told Mr. Walden. Otis knew how to charm him, and summoned all he had that night. Mr. Walden was old-school, a Southern gentleman; Otis had always used psychology on him, acting like "the help." It worked again. Alan was still living at home and when he got up the next morning to go to work he found his father waiting for him at the back door. Mr. Walden announced that he was going to the office with Alan. For the next few crucial months, there were three of them—Otis, Alan, and Mr. Walden—who combined to keep the company up and running until Phil came home from Europe.

What they needed more than anything else was a breakthrough

record from Otis. By most definitions, his career had stagnated. After "Security," Otis had recorded a series of songs that were well-crafted and professional-sounding. But none of them was strong enough to climb to the top of the charts. "Come to Me," his follow-up to "Security," was yet another weepy, slow ballad, a plodding song that ended by quoting lines from both "These Arms of Mine" and "That's What My Heart Needs." It climbed to #69 on the charts, far exceeding "Security" but not making the kind of mark Otis needed. The next single was "Chained and Bound," released on September 9, 1964, Otis's twenty-third birthday. It was yet another ballad. And even though it was an artistic step up from its predecessor, it only hit #70.

Otis found himself pigeonholed as the guy who sang those pleading, heartbreaking ballads. In fact, a WDIA disc jockey in Memphis called "Moohah" (A. C. Williams) had already nicknamed Otis "Mr. Pitiful" because he sounded so pitiful when he sang all those sad songs. "Security" had failed because he broke that mold and people were hesitant to accept it. Otis badly needed a change of direction. And when he came back to Memphis just after Christmas to record his next single, everyone was aware of it.

One of his heroes, Sam Cooke, was killed on December 11, 1964, in a suspicious shooting outside a seedy hookers' motel in Los Angeles. Otis was at a gig with soul star Jerry Butler in Jackson, Tennessee, when the news came over the radio, and he was still grieving when he arrived at Stax. Cooke was the crown prince of R&B and his death left the industry stunned. It hit Otis harder than most. "When Sam Cooke died, Otis was just like somebody died in his family," Zelma said. "He loved that man. That was his idol, Sam Cooke, and Little Richard." Otis always thought Sam Cooke was the prettiest singer he'd ever heard. He had what Otis longed for, one of those soaring and beautiful tenors that seemed to float above the melody like a voice from the heavens. Otis had met his hero once at a layover in a Washington, D.C., airport, and he was thrilled because Sam Cooke knew of him and was nice to him. "Be natural; be *you*," Cooke told him. "You're a great entertainer." That's when Otis had Walter Johnson cut off his processed hairdo; from then on he wore his hair in an "I'm black and I'm proud" natural Afro, just like Sam Cooke.

Otis rehearsed with the MG's on December 27, working up two new songs for his next single, including a ballad called "That's How Strong My Love Is." The next morning Steve Cropper was in the shower and began chuckling because it was another slow and pleading song that would only add fuel to the fire for Moohah and the other DJs who called Otis "Mr. Pitiful." Then it came to him, a single musical line that he sang aloud: "They call me Mr. Pitiful." The lyric had an immediate irony because the melody Steve imagined was fast and upbeat, a goof on Otis's reputation for singing sad songs.

Steve immediately realized he was on to something. He had to go pick up Otis at the Lorraine Motel to take him to the studio, and he hummed the song the whole way over so he wouldn't forget it. As soon as Otis climbed in the car, Steve said, "Hey, what do you think of this?" As he sang the opening line, Otis grew excited. He immediately grasped the whole premise and loved it. It was a ten-minute drive to Stax and by the time they arrived they had written the song. They hustled into the studio, quickly taught it to the MG's, and had it worked up by the time Jim Stewart showed up.

"Mr. Pitiful" proved a landmark for Otis. Like "Security," the song kicked off with a screaming horn riff. Then Al Jackson and Duck Dunn locked in on the pulsating beat. Otis's voice sounded as if he were winking as he sang the first lines: "They call me Mr. Pitiful / Baby, that's my name." The song moved at a brisk pace, stopping just before the bridge for a series of three superquick horn bursts. Otis came up with the riff on the spot, humming the lines to the horn section just as he'd watched Little Willie Jones do it at the Macon Recording Studio. The horn lines Otis composed were so unusual, so unique, that the musicians couldn't grasp them at first; the song kept falling apart every time they reached the horn break. But once they nailed the lines, they decided it was the coolest thing they'd ever played, a riff that seemed closer to Woody Herman than James Brown. They were all astounded that this musically untrained backwoods kid from Macon could come up with horn lines that sophisticated, that strikingly original.

The song was recorded with just two or three takes. During the "keeper," Otis forgot some of the lines and made up new ones as he went along. He wound up singing, "I lost everything I had / I lost someone just like you," rather than the lyrics he'd written with Steve. "What he sang doesn't make any sense," Steve said. "It wasn't 'I lost you, baby' or however it originally was, but 'I lost someone *just like you*.' It doesn't even rhyme, but it works in the song. It feels great." The line gave "Mr. Pitiful" an added and intriguing dimension—the singer was now using his sad story as a come-on line to a woman.

When Otis and Steve began writing songs together, that was the final element in the equation. That's when the label's patience with Otis finally began to pay off. The great equalizer in music has always been the songs. Give a great song to a mediocre singer and you can still have a hit record; give a great song to a great singer and you can have a record for the ages. Without his ability to write rock 'n' roll poetry within a three-minute song, Chuck Berry would have spent his life playing in East St. Louis bars. Without their original songs, the Beatles might have been nothing more than another bar band playing the mean streets of Hamburg on a diet of Chuck Berry covers; the Rolling Stones might be footnote in rock history. And even though Elvis Presley never wrote an original song in his life, he had the talent to find great material and then make it his own.

"Mr. Pitiful" worked on every level. And it did something that no Otis Redding record had done before: it shot up the charts. By then *Billboard* had reinstituted its R&B charts, and "Mr. Pitiful" hit #10 and peaked at #41 on the pop charts; it was by far Otis's strongest showing. Not only that; it became a two-sided hit. The B-side, "That's How Strong My Love Is," did almost as well, hitting #18 on the R&B charts and #74 on the pop charts.

Otis Redding had at last come of age.

The Big O

Otis was back at Stax in January of 1965 for a quick recording session to flesh out his upcoming second album, *The Great Otis Redding Sings Soul Ballads*. The album would be anchored by "Mr. Pitiful" and represent a collection of his most recent singles—"That's How Strong My Love Is," "Come to Me," "Chained and Bound," "Your One and Only Man"—augmented with several throwaway cuts. The cream of the new material was a sparse and atmospheric cover of the 1958 Jerry Butler classic "For Your Precious Love." Ironically enough, just a few weeks after the session Otis ran into Jerry at the airport in Atlanta in the Delta first-class lounge. They had met a year or so earlier, performing together on a package show, and Otis's face broke out into a broad grin when he looked up and saw the "Ice Man" walking towards him.

"Hey, man," Otis greeted him. "How are things going?"

"Great," replied Jerry. "Where you going?"

"I'm going to Buffalo," said Otis.

"Me, too. What are you doing in Buffalo?"

"I'm playing a show there in the auditorium."

Jerry broke out into a grin. "Hey, me too!"

They stayed at the same hotel and after the concert Otis invited Jerry to come hang out in his room. They sat around catching up on news and swapping gossip for a while, but it wasn't long before Otis picked up his guitar—a battered acoustic that looked as if it had cost him about five dollars at a Sears and Roebuck store. He carried it everywhere he went, using it to write songs and work up arrangements to show to the guys at Stax. "Hey, man, listen to this song," Otis said. He started strumming a chord, then sang a few lines. He stopped and shrugged. "It's one I've never been able to finish."

Jerry wasn't overly impressed. But he had his own unfinished song, and decided to run it past Otis. He took a deep breath and then began singing a slow, mournful melody: "I've been loving you too long / To stop now / You are tired / And you want to be free." Jerry stopped singing and shrugged. "Man, I've been messing with this song for almost three years and can't get past that 'You've grown tired and you want to be free' line."

Otis's eyes were wide. "Hey, man, that's a smash," he said.

"You really like it?"

"Oh, man," exclaimed Otis. "I *love* that song." He began picking out chords on his guitar, messing around with the melody and trying to figure out how to play the song. "I'll tell you what," he announced after a few minutes. "Let me go and mess around with it. Maybe I'll come up with something."

Two weeks later, Jerry was in Detroit for a show and Otis tracked him down on the telephone. Jerry had no sooner said hello than Otis blurted out: "Hey, man, it's a hit! I told you that song was a hit! I told you!"

For a moment, Jerry was completely confused. He finally realized Otis was talking about the song he'd shown him in Buffalo. "How do you know it's a hit?" Jerry asked.

" 'Cause it's on the street."

"What? You're jivin' me."

"No, man," said Otis. "It's all over the place. People are running to the stores like it's something good to eat."

"No fooling," Jerry said. He was taken aback, unsure of how he felt. For one thing, he needed a hit record every bit as much as Otis did. It was *his* song—and it was a hit record for *Otis*?

A couple of days later, Jerry got a call from a friend in Atlanta. "Have you heard that new Otis Redding record?" she asked.

"No," he responded. Then he added a rueful laugh. "But I wrote it."

"Well," she said, "it's the most beautiful thing I've ever heard in my life."

With that, Jerry decided he'd better hear this record. He called Otis and asked him to play it over the phone. As he listened, his jealousy vanished. Otis had taken the song to places Jerry had never envisioned. The arrangement was so simple, yet so ingenious. And there was a magical quality in the *feel* that Otis had captured. The song was carefully crafted so that every single note, every nuance of the music, conveyed drama and emotion. There was an exquisite hesitation in Otis's voice as he sang the opening lines over the muted accompaniment. He might have been singing to a girlfriend. A wife in a troubled marriage. A woman in an illicit affair. Or a lost true love. That was the beauty of the lyrics: they were so universal that they struck an instant chord with almost anyone who heard them.

After the first line, a sharp drum shot came out of nowhere and the horns played an ascending progression that sounded like a voice rising in anguish. Otis's voice soared behind them, and then, as the horns faded, his voice was left alone and calling out in a hoarse whisper. This verse ended differently than the first, with a series of dramatic, three one-note stops. For just a moment, there was complete silence. Otis's voice came back in, alone and vulnerable. Finally, just before the coda, the song made a dramatic shift when the MG's suddenly changed the key from A to B-flat. As "I've Been Loving You Too Long" reached its coda, the intensity began building. The horns played rumbling riffs that echoed a New Orleans funeral dirge. The drums rang out just a little harder. The guitar was a little louder, the piano a bit more pronounced. And, above it all, Otis's voice was calling out in an aching wail of undying love.

"Nobody else on the face of this earth would have gotten that song because it was intended for him," Jerry Butler said. "I've since heard it recorded by Tina Turner, Aretha Franklin, Joe Cocker. *I* recorded it. And I *still* say it was Otis's song. I was just the conduit. I never would have approached it the way he approached it. He sang 'I've been' and then he just paused and let you think about it: *I've been what?* Okay, 'lovin' you.' And then he stopped again. Then 'too long.' And he made 'long' a ten-syllable word! When he sang 'You've grown tired,' that was every wail and cry and moan that any man has ever sang. Like when Ray Charles says 'Georgia.' It was a statement. It was a paragraph. It was just beautiful."

It also was one of the great ballads of the soul era.

"I've Been Loving You Too Long" was pressed up and released almost as soon as it was recorded on April 19, 1965. Backed with a sharp-sounding up-tempo song called "I'm Depending on You," the record zoomed up the R&B charts and rose all the way to #2. Even more, the record hit #21 on the pop charts and represented Otis's first true crossover hit.

One of the first things he did after the record hit was to surprise his father on his birthday. By then, Mr. Redding had taken over as pastor in a little church called Lundy Chapel in North Macon, a job that the Reverend Moses Dumas helped him find. "It was a small church, but a strong church," Reverend Dumas said. "He was acquainted with the previous pastor and he had attended that church on different occasions. And he had preached for me; many times I'd use him when I couldn't be at my church myself. He was a good preacher. He was a deep preacher. He was sincere; there was no doubt about it."

Even with his son's success, Mr. Redding remained skeptical and mocked Otis's singing career. It must have been a sweet feeling for Otis when he called together several of his father's friends for a birthday-party dinner at his new house on Commodore Drive, and then surprised him with a brand-new blue Ford Fairlane 500. "There he was, saying, 'You the *worst* child I had and you just worry me to death and you won't ever amount to nothing'—well, sometimes we have to eat words!" Reverend Dumas said with a laugh. "Sometimes, the worst turns out to be the best! Man, you should've been there. Because when that boy and that car drove up there, I'll tell you, it was something else. His parents were still living in the projects and barely making it. Not long after that, Otis moved them out of there."

As "I've Been Loving You Too Long" lingered at the top of the charts, Phil returned from the Army to take back his role as Otis's manager. "Everything was so up," Phil said. "Otis was finally feeling like he was a star. You could sense it. Everything happened right, just knocking out songs like this (*snaps fingers*)." Phil jumped back into the equation with gusto. He set up Jotis Records, which was named for Otis and Joe Galkin. He signed the label's first artists: a singer named Billy

The Teenage Party drew lines of crowds at the Roxy Theatre before it moved downtown to the Douglass Theatre. (Courtesy of the Middle Georgia Regional Library Archives)

The Pinetoppers: (*left to right*) Samuel "Poor Sam" Davis on bass, Willie "Ploonie" Bowden on drums, Johnny Jenkins on lead guitar, Otis Redding on vocals, and Ish Mosley on saxophone. (Courtesy of Mark Pucci)

One of his earliest
publicity photos.
(Michael Ochs Archives)

Otis (*left to right*)
with Stax founder
Jim Stewart, Rufus
Thomas, Booker T.
Jones, and (*seated*)
Carla Thomas.
(Michael Ochs
Archives)

Otis and his processed hair style just as "These Arms of Mine" became his first hit record. (Michael Ochs Archives)

Below: Otis didn't know how to dance, but he still *moved* on stage and knew how to convey the emotion of the song. (Michael Ochs Archives)

Phil Walden helped Otis fashion his
sense of style.
(Michael Ochs Archives)

Otis (*left*) presents his father with a Christmas gift in 1964: a new Ford Fairlane.
(Courtesy of the Middle Georgia Regional Library Archives)

Left: By 1966, Otis had a fully developed stage persona. (Michael Ochs Archives)

Below: Otis with Jerry Wexler, vice-president of Atlantic Records. (Michael Ochs Archives)

Otis in Europe, with the Stax/ Volt tour. (Michael Ochs Archives)

The great
Otis Redding.
(Michael Ochs
Archives)

Singing "Shake" at his
legendary performance
at the Monterey Pop
Festival.
(Michael Ochs Archives)

Left: Always a country boy at heart, Otis loved to hunt. (Michael Ochs Archives)

Below: A moment of contemplation at the farm in Round Oak. (Michael Ochs Archives)

After throat surgery, Otis was eager to return to the studio to record "Dock of the Bay." (Michael Ochs Archives)

Above: A pensive Otis ready to record at Stax. (Michael Ochs Archives)

Zelma Redding (*left*) with Phil Walden holding two Grammy Awards awarded to Otis Redding posthumously in 1969. (Courtesy of the Middle Georgia Regional Library Archives)

Young, whom he had met in Germany, and another named Arthur Conley. He set up a production company for Otis called Big O Productions in honor of Otis's nickname. He began setting up Redwal Music, a partnership between Otis, Phil, and Alan, who'd had so much fun managing Otis in his brother's absence that he had decided to forgo college and stay in the music business.

Most of all, Otis stayed on the road playing night after night. That's where the real money was made; that's where the records were promoted and a singer's reputation was established. One of Otis's constant companions was a budding singer from Macon, Earl "Speedo" Sims. Speedo had sung with a local group called the Peppermint Twisters back when Otis was with the Pinetoppers; he also knew Otis from the Macon Recording Studio. As Otis's career began to take off and Huck wasn't always around, Speedo became the road manager. He was friendly, with a quick wit. He could think on his feet. And he was absolutely devoted to both Otis and Phil Walden.

Speedo also could sometimes be forgetful. One night Otis had performed at Constitution Hall in Washington, D.C., on a bill that included William Bell. Afterwards, Otis and William were going to fly back to Memphis for a day, then join up with Speedo and the road band at the next gig a couple of days later. As they drove up to Constitution Hall, Otis reminded Speedo to make sure he gassed up the car before they left for the airport—a reminder that Speedo promptly forgot all about. After the show, they loaded up the car and rushed off to Dulles International Airport, racing to catch the flight before it left. As they came within sight of the airport, the car began sputtering and finally died on the side of the road.

Otis turned to Speedo and glared. "Speedo," he finally said. "Did you gas up?"

"Oh God," Speedo replied, his voice dropping. "I forgot."

Otis was hot. What made things worse was the car had died within full view of the airport. In fact, the back of the terminal was only a few hundred yards away. But it was unreachable, behind a fence and past an active runway; the actual public entrance was about two miles down the road. It was raining and they had about fifteen minutes to catch the plane. Otis climbed out and stared through the fence at the terminal. He stood there for a moment, then suddenly announced, "Let's go." William hesitantly got out of the car and watched Otis calmly bolt over the fence—still wearing his stage clothes—as if it were the football stadium back home. William looked at Speedo and shrugged, then scampered over, too. They crossed the runway and ran through the rain to the terminal. They managed to find an open door leading inside and arrived at the check-in counter, breathless and drenched with rain. At first they were told the plane was about to back out of the gate. Then a woman at the counter recognized them and she radioed the pilot: "We have Otis Redding and William Bell out here; could you hold the plane for five minutes, please?"

The two of them finally ran on board and collapsed into their seats, Otis still hopping mad. "Wait till I get Speedo," he kept saying. "I'm gonna *kill* him!" Finally they looked at each other and burst into uncontrollable laughter. What were they thinking? Two young singing stars hopping a fence at a busy airport in the rain and running across a runway to reach the terminal?

The package tours Otis shared with William Bell and Jerry Butler were standard fare during that era. The performers called them "cattle call" shows because the performers would come out, do just a few songs, and then scamper offstage. "You'd have six or seven acts—Otis, Gladys Knight and the Pips, the Impressions, Jerry Butler, Jackie Wilson—and you'd do a forty-five-day tour," William said. "You'd have two buses on tour. All the performers would ride on one bus. The band and the equipment would be on the other. You'd play day after day, all one-nighters. But you had fun and you got to know your craft. That's how I really became friends with Otis. A lot of the time, the acts didn't even speak to each other because there was so much animosity between them. But it was never that way with Otis and I. Onstage, it was competitive to where you'd want to do a good show. But offstage you'd go out and hang out and party and have a good time. He was totally down-to-earth. He was the kind of guy, you meet him and think you've known him your whole life. There was no pretense, no nothing. He was always approachable. Nobody felt weird about just coming up and talking with Otis."

William also sometimes traveled to Macon with Otis. "It was just amazing," he said. "We'd go around to these little joints and sit around and eat pig's feet and all that other stuff. That's the way he was. He was one of them. I think that was one of the things that gave him so much appeal, why he became so popular. Even when he became a gigantic superstar, he was still just one of the guys from the neighborhood."

Being young and black and traveling on the road was still a hazardous way to make a living, especially in the racially charged Deep South. The entire region was in turmoil. Dr. Martin Luther King, Jr., had led the march on Washington in 1963 and delivered his "I Have a Dream" speech. President Johnson had called for a "Great Society" and demanded the end of poverty and racial injustice. People were marching across the country for racial equality. In the spring of 1965, Dr. King led a fifty-four-mile march from Selma, Alabama, to the state capital in Montgomery to demand the right to vote. The marchers were pummeled and beaten by state troopers at the Edmund Pettus Bridge outside Selma, images that stunned the nation when they were captured on film and broadcast on television.

"It was the best of times and the worst of times," said Jerry Butler. "I know you've heard that one before, but that's what it was. We were a bunch of young kids that had become instantly famous. We had a few bucks in our pockets, drove pretty cars, winked at pretty girls, wore some pretty clothing. I mean, come on. For some kids who grew up in the ghettos of Chicago and New York and Macon, Georgia, that was *wonderful* stuff. Trying to find a place to sleep at night, that was the bad part. You had to go into a town and search for someplace to eat. You had to go into a town and ask somebody, 'Where is the black side of town?' And having to do shows when the audience was segregated. You didn't know which side of the room to sing to. You'd say, 'Do I sing to the black folks first or the white folks first?' If you sing to the white folks first, the black folks will think you're an Uncle Tom. If you sing to the black folks first, the white folks will think you don't like them."

Jerry would go on to be elected a Cook County Commissioner in Chicago, and his interest in politics grew out of living in that environment. "When people ask me how I got into politics, I say, 'What you do mean? I grew up on it. I was out there on the road.' People would say, 'Hey, the kids over at AT&T or over at Spellman or over at Clark, they having a rally today and they want you all to come join them.' Because we were stars and they figured if we showed up, the press would show up and if the press showed up, they'd get their message out. Otis did it; all of us did it. How could you avoid it, when the people you were singing to were the people who were actually in the fight? People talk all the time about Martin, and God knows he did a wonderful job. But it was the college kids that really turned the damned country around. Black and white. They were out there putting their lives on the line."

The performers at Stax often caught it both ways, since half the MG's were white. The MG's seldom went on the road, but in the early days of the label they did occasionally go out and play with the Stax artists. William Bell remembers a late-night visit they made at a truck stop in Alabama. He walked inside with Booker and Al, and the manager refused to serve them unless they went around to a back window. After they walked out, Duck Dunn went in and placed an order for forty hamburgers. He watched them prepare the burgers and then bag them up. And that's when Duck simply turned and walked out the door, leaving the grill holding forty hamburgers with no one to eat them or pay for them.

"We'd always really stick together," said William. "The prejudice worked on both sides. We were in an all-black club in Illinois once. I was onstage and the MG's were playing behind me. The stage was kind of high, so I was looking down on the audience. All the girls were down front at first. Then I saw all these guys starting to crowd around the stage and I'm thinking, 'Uh-oh, something is in the works here.' And, sure enough, they didn't like it that Steve and Duck and Wayne [Jackson, of the horn section] were white. So they're standing there making all of these gestures and I just stopped and said, 'Guys, we're all in this together. Let's have a good time. If you can't have a good time, then if you go for them you've got to go through all of us.' And they looked and they thought about it for a while and I guess they decided, 'Oh hell, let's have a good time!' And we went back to playing. It was definitely strange back in those days. You'd go down through Mississippi and if you were black and had a brand-new car, every two miles the highway patrol was pulling you over. Even in Memphis back then, we were harassed quite a bit leaving the studio at night by the police and stuff because everything at Stax was just about fifty-fifty black and white. It was a sign of the times. We got through it. It made us stronger as a team."

As "I've Been Loving You Too Long" faded from the charts, Stax wanted Otis to record another album to capitalize on the momentum. There was just one problem: Otis was booked solid on the road. They finally managed to set aside a three-day window in the summer of 1965—Otis could come in and rehearse for an afternoon, have a marathon recording session the following day and night, then catch a little sleep and fly out to his next gig the following evening. Otis had but two new original songs and time was short, so expectations were humble: Follow the formula of the day and put out another album padded with lots of filler material and a couple of hot singles. It was just something to get on the market and sell, that's all. Yet somehow what emerged was one of the great R&B albums of all time, recorded in one amazing and frantic and inspired twenty-four-hour period. They also captured one of the classic songs of modern music—it was called "Respect."

The recording session began on July 9. The MG's were there—Booker T., Steve, Duck, and Al. So was the studio horn section, the Mar-Keys: Wayne Jackson on trumpet, Andrew Love on tenor sax, and Floyd Newman on baritone sax. Rounding out the group were Isaac Hayes on piano and Gene "Bowlegs" Miller on trumpet. Otis was energized and confident. The crowds coming to see him were getting bigger and more enthusiastic; he could sense that his life was quickly changing. "I think he was more sophisticated and aware of who he was," Phil Walden said. "He was successful and he liked that lifestyle, being a star and having people like him. He was into being Otis Redding, and I think it reflects in his music. He was a real star finally, not something we tried to fabricate."

But he faced the daunting task of cutting an entire album's worth of material in just one day. And no one was exactly sure what they were going to record. Otis knew he wanted to pay homage to Sam Cooke by recording some of his songs. But he had nothing in the way of new original material beyond "Respect" and a song called "Ole Man Trouble." The rest of the album was improvised as they went along.

They started at ten A.M. There was no air-conditioning system and by midafternoon the studio was hot and sticky from the Memphis heat. Otis had his shirt off, his black skin glistening with sweat as they worked to get enough tracks for a full album. Late in the afternoon, they took a break when Otis had to leave to take a physical for an insurance policy. While he was gone, Steve Cropper wandered over to Estelle's record shop to scout for material. "Satisfaction," the Rolling Stones' breakthrough single in America, was playing on the radio and Steve began imagining Otis singing it. He could hear it—it might not be great but it would do in a pinch. He grabbed a copy, took it down to the studio, and taught it to the band while Otis was gone. When he came back, they quickly cut a version.

The session broke up at about eight P.M. because some of the guys had to go play club gigs. Then everyone gathered back at about two A.M. and they recorded the rest of the album. "That was tough," Duck Dunn said. "We did it, but I don't know how. It liked to have killed us all. I mean, your eyes start crossing at about four in the morning." Yet some of the best tracks from the album come from that late-night session—Sam Cooke's "A Change Is Gonna Come" and a fresh version of "I've Been Loving You Too Long." They rounded out the session with a blues song, "Rock Me, Baby," and a sleepy-sounding take on William Bell's first hit, "You Don't Miss Your Water ('Til Your Well Runs Dry)."

They had somehow done it, recorded an entire album in one single day. That was one victory. The greater victory became obvious when they listened to the tracks later on and realized they had captured a special moment in time, that desperation had resulted in inspiration. For the first time in the history of the young label, the Stax musicians felt challenged in the recording studio. They had played on hit records before. But this was different. They instinctively understood the stakes were being raised, that Otis was on the cusp of greatness. "I started realizing that about the time we did 'I've Been Loving You Too Long,'" Jim Stewart said. "That, to me, was the beginning of him being more than just an R&B singer or soul singer. I really felt he was that superstar that you always dream of working with in your lifetime."

Otis Blue—Otis Redding Sings Soul was released in September of

1965. The album kicked off with a midtempo rocker called "Ole Man Trouble." Fueled by Steve Cropper's country-inspired guitar licks, it was obvious that, even on that first track, a newfound sense of confidence was shimmering through the music. The performances were sharp, the arrangements thoughtfully conceived and fully realized.

"Respect" is the song where everything melded together. The song kicked off at a breakneck pace, the backbeat pulsating like a steady jackhammer. Then, over a darting bass line and sassy horn riffs that perfectly set up the song's attitude, Otis came in with the first verse: "What you want / Honey, you've got it / What you need / Baby, you've got it / All I'm asking / Is for a little respect when I come home." His voice sounded like a guy trying to smooth-talk a girl—playful and cocky, with just the hint of a wink. The title gave the song an infectious, instant hook for listeners and then Otis gave it a second one, calling out a joyful "hey, hey, hey!" at the end of each chorus that featured William Bell singing the "hey, hey, hey" lines with Otis.

Duck Dunn's thundering bass propelled "Respect" and became regarded as one of the great bass guitar performances. "You know, that bass in 'Respect' was almost a rock 'n' roll bass line," Duck said. "And when Otis kicked that off: *dawnt, dawnt, dawnt, dawnt* . . . and then when he did those horns . . . you know, he's the one that went up and hummed those horn lines to the guys. They had never heard that kind of thing before. They were used to playing whole notes and stops. And Otis came in with those lines; they kind of looked at each other a little baffled. That style, I thought it changed rhythm-and-blues music. It really did. So with all that going on, I had to come up with *something*. And Al played such a groove that it just fell in my lap. That's all I can tell you; it just fell in my lap. And then in the ending, I really walked it down. I liked that, too." The bass line from "Respect" reportedly acted as an inspiration for Paul McCartney's "Drive My Car," which would be featured on the forthcoming Beatles album, *Rubber Soul*. "I don't know if that's true or not," said Duck. "I try to be meek and humble. But if it is, that's some compliment."

From the high energy of "Respect," the album shifted in mood to Sam Cooke's haunting "A Change Is Gonna Come." Recorded shortly before his death, the song came to be viewed as Cooke's self-penned eulogy. His performance was elegant, sweet and sad, and with a

Sinatraesque arrangement that featured flowing strings. There was a resignation in his voice, a poignance as he sang, "It's been too hard a-livin' / But I'm afraid to die / I don't know what's up there / Beyond the sky." If Sam Cooke sang the song like he already was a homeward-bound angel, Otis approached it as a man slipping past the edge of despair and looking to the heavens for redemption. His arrangement was simple and sparse, punctuated by Steve's subtle guitar fills and a gospel-flavored, understated piano. Otis muffed a couple of lines; at one point he sang, "It's been too hard a-livin' / And I'm afraid to die / I don't know what's up there / Beyond the clouds" and somehow managed to make "die" and "clouds" rhyme. As the song reached the bridge, there was a subtle rise in intensity. The horns came in, playing in unison with Al Jackson on a dramatic triplet beat that was only hinted at in Sam Cooke's original. The music continued building in drama through the final verse until there was one final quiet moment where Otis made one last desperate plea: "It's been a long, long time coming / But I know, well I know, a change has gotta come." It was a breathtaking moment—the way he accented certain words in the phrase, stretching them out and repeating them and conveying the emotion of someone who is reaching out for signs of hope and is no longer sure he's going to find them.

The album then jumped into an up-tempo, playful version of Solomon Burke's "Down in the Valley." The song undoubtedly had caught Otis's ear when he toured with the self-proclaimed "King of Rock 'n' Soul" during the summer of 1964. Solomon Burke's original had been a solid hit, but the recording sounded like a song unfulfilled. The arrangement was wooden, almost amateurish, and featured what sounds like a tuba playing a very rudimentary two-note bass line. Otis gave the song *swing*; he gave it sass and vitality. His voice was teasing and he was scat-singing between verses from almost the first line. He also introduced for the first time on record something that would soon become his trademark device, that stuttering "Got-ta! Got-ta!" sung over and over and over again like a man bubbling with so much giddy happiness that he just can't possibly get out all the words to fully express himself.

It was followed by a new version of "I've Been Loving You Too Long." This recording was slightly faster than the first one, losing some of its weariness but gaining in precision. Otis's voice was appreciably richer, more in command of the song. He'd recorded it the first time only days after he'd finished writing the song, before he'd had time to learn the nuances of the vocals. Now, after performing the song night after night on the road, he had honed his attack to perfection. Everything about the recording sounded more assured—the horns, the aching piano in the background, the drums.

The second side of the album kicked off with a rollicking version of Sam Cooke's "Shake." The original version was light, with a sambalike beat, and Sam Cooke sang it like a guy clad in a coat and tie, playing a teenage twist party where nothing stronger than cherry Kool-Aid was being served. Otis took a different approach, singing it like a guy in a hot and sweaty nightclub who is calling out encouragement to the finest-looking woman he's ever seen in his life as she struts on the dance floor. Otis once again used the "Got-ta! Got-ta!" lines over and over during instrumental breaks in the song.

Much of the rest of the second side couldn't compete with the incredible heights reached on the first half. There was a wonderful cover of the Temptations' classic, "My Girl," that replaced the Motown strings with punchy Memphis horn lines. There was a workmanlike version of Sam Cooke's "Wonderful World" that failed to capture the lovely innocence of the original. There was a down-and-dirty version of B. B. King's blues classic "Rock Me, Baby" that featured the only guitar solo on the entire record and horns that chime in like katydids at twilight. There was a halting version of William Bell's "You Don't Miss Your Water."

The revelation was the arrangement of "Satisfaction" they recorded late that afternoon. Otis had never actually heard the Rolling Stones' version until Steve Cropper played the record so Otis could grasp the melody lines and write down the lyrics, some of which he changed. (Years later, Steve wanted to use the version for a movie soundtrack album and some clueless bureaucrat at the Stones' publishing company called, telling Steve he couldn't change the song's lyrics. Steve rolled his eyes. "You don't understand," he replied. "It's already been out and been a *hit*.")

Otis cutting "Satisfaction" was a moment filled with irony. The Beatles and Rolling Stones and the other British rock groups had started out playing American R&B and blues covers; in fact, the Stones had just recorded an Otis Redding song, "That's How Strong My Love Is," which appeared on *Out of Our Heads*, the same album that featured "Satisfaction." Now an American soul singer was covering one of *their* rock 'n' roll songs.

The song's sexual undertones were strongly implied in the Stones' version; Mick Jagger attacked the lyrics as if he was wearing a leer as he sang. Otis brought the sexuality right to the forefront—there was little doubt about exactly what *kind* of satisfaction he was trying to get. About two-thirds of the way through the song, Otis threw down the lyric sheet and began improvising lines at a frenzied pace. And he also pronounced "satisfaction" as "satis-*fashion*" throughout the recording. "Why change him?" said Steve Cropper. "That was Otis. We called it 'the dictionary of soul.' I loved it. That's what made him so unique; he'd just barrel right through that stuff unaware of anything."

The album was called *Otis Blue—Otis Redding Sings Soul* and the Stax staff went all out to make sure people understood this record was different. There were literate, informative liner notes on the back. The cover was downright radical—a blue-hued photograph of a white woman with blonde hair and puffy lips, eyes closed and the look of orgasmic bliss on her face. *Otis Blue* quickly shot up to the #1 spot on the R&B album charts and produced three Top-Five R&B singles: "I've Been Loving You Too Long," "Respect," and "Satisfaction." It rose only to #75 on the pop charts, although it charted for a remarkable thirty-four weeks.

But the numbers don't explain the breadth of influence that *Otis Blue* attained through the years. Despite the great rush to record it, it was cohesive. It felt complete and whole. It had balance and vision. Most critics consider *Otis Blue* one of the great R&B albums ever recorded, perhaps *the* greatest. Duck Dunn approaches that assessment with understatement. "Yeah," he says. "I'd say it's up there." But there also was an unmistakable pleasure in his voice; he does, after all, strive to be a meek and humble man.

10

Respect

Otis Blue also announced Stax Records as a new force in R&B music.

Up until the spring of 1965 the label was still a minor player in the music business. Of the hundred-odd singles released by Stax/Volt (Otis recorded for the Stax subsidiary Volt Records during his entire career), just eight had entered the R&B Top Ten and only "Green Onions" had topped the charts. Jim Stewart didn't even have enough confidence in Stax's shaky existence to quit his day job at the bank until "Mr. Pitiful" hit the charts. Stax's biggest cheerleader in the early days was Jerry Wexler of Atlantic Records. From the moment he first heard Carla Thomas sing "Gee Whiz" in 1960, Wexler was captivated by the sound captured inside the little studio, and he had even traveled to Memphis to meet Jim Stewart, Carla, and her father, Rufus. Wexler wanted to take them all to dinner, then discovered that was out of the question in the segregated South. Instead they went to Wexler's hotel—sneaking in through a back alley and then up a freight elevator—and ordered room service. Later that night Wexler was awakened by a loud banging on his door. It was the local vice squad demanding that he let them in because they suspected he "had a woman" in his room. Wexler had instant visions of being thrown into a car trunk and dumped somewhere across the river in Arkansas, and refused to let them in. He did agree to meet them in the lobby but before he went downstairs he dashed off a note to Atlantic Records president Ahmet Ertegun explaining the situation and dropped it in the mail slot . . . just in case he mysteriously disappeared.

As Stax slowly gained its footing, Jerry Wexler was paying close attention. People were already talking about "the Memphis Sound"— music that was funky and soulful and sweaty and unmistakably *Southern*. At the same time, he was growing disenchanted with

Atlantic's own in house studio in New York City. For years the studio was under the stewardship of Jerry Leiber and Mike Stoller, the songwriting combo who had produced and/or written many of the classic Atlantic hits—"Charlie Brown," "Along Came Jones," "Poison Ivy," "On Broadway," "There Goes My Baby," "Spanish Harlem," "Stand By Me." But when Leiber and Stoller left the label in 1963, they took much of the Atlantic magic with them and Wexler knew it. "The arrangers were out of ideas, the songwriters out of material, the session players out of licks," he said. "I was out of inspiration. Inspiration was on the boil at Stax. I'd watch the MG's arrive in the morning, hang up their coats, grab their axes, and start to play. It was effortless, easy as breathing. Here were four men with rapport as close as a classical string quartet's. The feel was everything—the feel was real, right, and tight in the pocket. It knocked my dick in the dirt."

Wexler began to envision Stax as much more than just a record label; he wanted the studio to become the epicenter of Atlantic's R&B division. It was no coincidence that Wexler began to bring new Atlantic artists to Memphis to record with Booker T. and the MG's. The first, was a singing duo from Miami: Sam and Dave. As a gesture of goodwill, Wexler even "gave" Sam and Dave to Stax even though they were signed to Atlantic. The second act was a former gospel singer from Prattville, Alabama: Wilson Pickett. Sam and Dave didn't pay immediate dividends, but Pickett did. Steve Cropper knew nothing about Pickett except that he had sung lead on the 1962 hit "I Found a Love" by the Falcons, so he went up to the record shop and gathered up every Falcons single he could find. On one of the songs, Steve noticed that Pickett began singing "I'm gonna wait till the midnight hour" on the vamp. He thought it was a marvelous tag line for a song and wrapped the phrase around a guitar lick he'd been playing around with for a few weeks. When Pickett got to town in early May of 1965, Wexler put him in a hotel room with Steve and a bottle of Jack Daniel's and told them to write. Steve offered his "midnight hour" idea to Pickett; they wrote it and then recorded it on May 12. Jerry Wexler's hunch paid off. "In the Midnight Hour" was an immediate hit, going to #1 on the R&B charts but only #21 on the pop.

It is strange to consider that one of the classic songs of a generation made such a benign impact on the pop charts, but it was a situation routinely faced by Otis and all the Stax artists. They were becoming wildly popular in the South, but were still barely known in the North. The very same attributes that attracted Wexler turned off many radio programmers, on both white and black stations. While radio embraced the pop sophistication of Motown, the Stax sound was viewed as too "country" and too overtly sexual. When Pickett sang about waiting till the midnight hour, there was little doubt of just what he was waiting for. "Midnight Hour" might have scorched the R&B charts, but it sold only about 300,000 copies. "These Arms of Mine" had sold approximately 59,000 copies. "I've Been Loving You Too Long" and "Respect" each sold in the neighborhood of 200,000 copies. And Otis's album sales were even more minute: *Pain in My Heart* barely sold 12,000 copies and *Otis Blue* sold only about 50,000 units in the initial weeks after its release despite going to the top of the album charts.

But Jerry Wexler believed in it. He knew there was something special going on at Stax and that, sooner or later, it was going to find an audience. Five days after the Wilson Pickett session, Jerry Wexler and Jim Stewart formalized a relationship that had operated on a handshake deal from the earliest days of the label. It was a five-year contract that kept everything as it was—Stax would continue producing records and Atlantic would continue distributing them. At least that's what Jim Stewart thought. And so, Jerry Wexler insists, did he.

Atlantic almost immediately began to assert itself in Memphis. One of the first things Wexler did was convince Jim to update his equipment. Stax was still using the same modest recording machinery they had purchased when the studio first opened. It was a mono unit that couldn't record music in stereo, the new industry standard. Jim was wary that changing the equipment would change the sound, so they cut a deal: When Atlantic's recording engineer, Tom Dowd, came to Memphis and installed the new recording gear, he hooked up it up so that every Stax recording could be captured on the new stereo recorder, but still be mixed on the original mono machine. The reason was simple; Jim Stewart didn't trust stereo yet. People listened to singles on car radios and little record players, both of which usually had just one speaker. And the stereo technology was so new—as much a breakthrough as the change from vinyl records to compact discs years later—that no one had mastered recording music in stereo. At Stax, the mix was completely unnatural; the mixing board was set up so the vocals and drums and guitar went to the right speaker through an effects device for echo; the horns and bass had no effects and they were sent to the left.

Everyone thought the stereo mixes at Stax were just plain weird-sounding, distracting, and virtually unlistenable. Jim relented on using stereo on full-length albums, a concession to the theory that audiophiles wanted stereo for their fancy new hi-fi systems, but he refused to mix singles in anything but mono. The mono recordings were so superior to the stereo mixes that when the Stax catalog was reissued on compact disc the original mono versions were almost always used.

The improvements weren't just in the studio equipment. With financial help from Atlantic, Stax also hired its first promotions director, Al Bell, a former Memphis disc jockey and civil-rights activist who was working at a radio station in Washington, D.C., where he championed Otis Redding and Booker T. and the MG's and Carla Thomas to a group of listeners more accustomed to East Coast doo-wop. "When I left Memphis to go to work in radio in Washington, I went with all the Stax product under my arm and Otis Redding was on top of the stack," Al Bell said. "Stax had a tough time winning acceptance above the Mason-Dixon line. They called it ' 'Bama music' and even R&B stations didn't want to play Otis Redding records."

Al not only helped expose Otis's music to Northern ears but he also had helped Otis land gigs at the prestigious Howard Theatre in Washington, D.C. Over the years, Otis began to call Al regularly to chat and to let him know he appreciated his efforts and they became quick friends. When Al joined Stax in early 1965, Otis's original contract was up and rumors were rampant that he was mulling over a $50,000 offer—huge money in that era—to jump to another label. Otis was on the road and had called Al to tell him not to worry, that he was going to re-sign with Stax as soon as he came back to Memphis. (It was like Elvis spurning RCA to stay with little Sun Records.) "That blew my mind," Al said. "He called to reassure me, and that stays with you in this competitive business. Otis was incredibly loyal."

About a month later, just before he recorded *Otis Blue*, Otis signed a new five-year contract with Stax. The two-page document was straightforward. He agreed to record at least eight new songs a year, and received a 5 percent royalty rate on singles and albums—up from the 3 percent he had received under his first contract. Stax had the right to approve all of his material and they owned the finished recordings. At the same time, Joe Galkin signed a new deal with Jim Stewart that continued the deal he had made when Otis first recorded in Memphis: half the money received by Stax from Otis's recordings.

As soon as Stax inked the deal with Atlantic Records and Al Bell came on board, the hits began to roll out with increasing frequency. Pickett followed up "In the Midnight Hour" with "634-5789 (Soulsville U.S.A.)." Sam and Dave hit with "You Don't Know Like I Know" and quickly released "Hold On, I'm Comin'" as a follow-up. Don Covay had a hit with "See-Saw." But Otis was the cornerstone of Stax—the heart and soul. "In a way," said Jim Stewart, "he epitomized Stax."

Al Bell took it even a step further. "You talk about *soul*, Otis epitomized it. The very essence of soul was in Otis Redding."

Stardom changes people. It can turn them paranoid. Make them put up walls. Swell their egos to uncontrollable proportions. Shape them into bullies. With Otis, it seemed the exact opposite. As his fame grew, so did his sense of himself and his place in the world. He was about to turn twenty-four years old and was maturing into the man everyone now remembers. Everything about him seemed larger than life. He was big physically, stocky and tall. He had big, expressive doe eyes. His smile was big, effervescent, and embracing. His pencil-thin mustache gave him an air of impish mischievousness. Most of all, Otis Redding had charm to spare and he knew how to use it. When Otis was home in Bellevue, he was still very much the person he was growing up. But outside of his home turf, he embraced the best parts of his personality and emphasized them, his wit and his native intelligence and his warmth. Whites perceived in Otis the personification of the self-actualized black man who was assured and proud but carried no chip on his shoulder; they had no idea he

embodied some of the very traits they most feared in black males—
the street, gangs, violence.

"Stardom never changed him," said Jerry Wexler. "He had a strong
inner life. He was emotionally centered. His manners were impeccable. His humor was sly and roguish; he relished calling my partner
Ahmet Ertegun 'Omelet' and always with a straight face. He had a
positive sense of racial identity. He was one of those rare souls beyond color; he dealt with you as a human being, not as a white or a
black or a Christian or a Jew."

When someone once read Steve Cropper a quote where Otis used
the word "motherfucker," Steve objected and insisted that Otis would
never have used such a term. "Otis was the nicest person I ever met,"
he said. "He didn't have any vices, and he didn't have any faults.
Which is very unusual and sounds like you're making it up. Everybody
loved him. Kids gravitated toward him. Women just worshiped the
guy. His fans were unbelievable. He was a tall, good-looking guy and
he sang his gazoo off, so why not? There are all these stories about
artists. They're always firing people and doing these crazy things. Otis
wasn't one of those kind of people. He was always working, always
on time, always together, loved everybody, made everybody feel
great. He was like a country preacher, always wanting to help people
out and always paying people compliments."

Every Otis Redding recording session at Stax was treated as an
event, greeted with gleeful anticipation. It often seemed as if Stax
was rolling out the hits like a factory assembly line, and with the
pressure mounting to produce hit after hit after hit, that's exactly
how recording sessions began to feel to some of the musicians in the
MG's. And then Otis would show up. "It got to be a little like work
there for a while," said Duck Dunn. "Jim Stewart got to the point
where . . . the old saying was we were cutting a hit a day down there
and if you didn't give him a hit a day, then he got mad. You could be
out on the floor playing and thinking you were playing your butt off
and you could see Jim in the control room through that window. He'd
have his head on his chin, kind of like, 'Well, when y'all gonna play
something that's *good*?' You know, that's hard. And you never got a
pat on the back too many times. But when Otis was there, it was a
revitalization of the whole thing. He brought out the best in you. He

made a better musician out of you. By his feeling, his energy. Particularly his energy. He was just a happy person. When Otis walked in, you wanted to be his best friend."

Even Tom Dowd saw it and he had recorded a who's who of legendary Atlantic artists, including Ray Charles and John Coltrane. Dowd was the recording engineer for the *Otis Blue* album and he told Phil Walden flat out that he thought Otis was a genius. "I've only been with two other people in that category," he said. "Bobby Darin and Ray Charles." Phil was astounded. He had never been in a professional studio with anyone other than Otis; he thought *everybody* did it that way.

Otis returned to Stax on November 5, 1965, with only a vague outline for his next single. He had the tempo. He had the coolest and most irresistible horn riff of his life. He had one piece of lyric, "Hip shakin' mama, I love ya." And he had the title: "I Can't Turn You Loose." He and Steve spent a couple of hours working out the rest of the song on the floor of the studio. They had a unique synergy— Otis could show up at the studio with only snippets of ideas, and Steve would immediately lock in on his train of thought and take it forward until there was a finished song. "Otis would walk in with his acoustic guitar and sit down and bang away on it, playing the ideas and things that he had worked up for songs," said Al Bell. "And he and Steve Cropper would go back and forth, back and forth, until they became as *one*. I always viewed that as a phenomenon, how the two of them would work on a song and become as one. He was that way with the entire band. It was like everyone was an extension of Otis. Al Jackson would look into Otis rhythmically in a manner that was uncanny to witness. If Otis dropped to his knees, Al was on him. If he shrugged his shoulders, Al was there."

Otis used to tell Wayne Cochran that to make a word in a song sound sad, you had to "worry it." At first, Wayne didn't have a clue what he was talking about. "You've got to stay on it," explained Otis. "Don't get off it. You can take the word 'happy' and make it sound sad by *stayin'* on it, *worryin'* it." And Al Jackson was the whole key to that. "Otis would sing rhythmically," said Wayne. "If you listen to Al Jackson on drums, he and Otis did some really unique things in drum breaks and Otis doing that, [singing] 'Good god! G-g-got-ta, g-g-goot-ta, gotta *have* it.' Listen to that. He was imitating the drums. And nobody else did that."

Otis was the person most responsible for establishing the fabled horn sound that is associated with Stax recordings. Because Otis always hummed the melodies to the horn players, they often sounded like a sophisticated choir singing behind him. Time after time he came up with riffs so inventive that the horn players would scratch their heads as they tried understand what he was trying to get them to do. Then they would play the notes over the rhythm section and suddenly everything would make perfect sense. Otis sometimes seemed self-conscious about his lack of musical training, almost going out of his way to keep from describing the riffs in musical terms. But his lack of training freed his imagination. He was bound by no rules because he didn't *know* the rules. He was free to put together combinations of notes that no one had ever considered before.

"Otis always had the hardest horn arrangements," Floyd Newman, who played baritone sax, told Stax historian Rob Bowman in his authoritative book, *Soulsville U.S.A.* "They were different and super difficult. He'd always work his things out on the bus when he'd be traveling. He knew every line in every place. He knew where he was going, what beats he wanted the lines to fall on. He could walk right in and sing it. Otis always did things in keys like E-sharp, A-sharp, F-sharp, the keys that nobody else was playing in. The sharp keys are brilliant keys, but people just don't mess around with them much. It gave his songs a lot of punch and drive and made you want to pop your fingers. He would always say, 'Floyd, if you listen to the song and your shoulders don't move, there's no groove to it.' "

The studio was set up inside the main theater. The control room was up on the stage where the screen used to be. Jim Stewart usually sat behind the board, with the tape machines to his right. Looming behind them was a huge set of "voice of theater" speakers salvaged from the movie house that they used for playbacks. "We'd crank the music up, play it back, and let it boom like crazy," said Duck. "It sounded great." The studio floor was on the graded slat where the seats used to be. They recorded everything live, with the musicians and singers all in the same room. The drums were in the middle, with the other musicians spread out around. There was no overdubbing;

it wasn't possible because the equipment was too primitive. But they turned it to their advantage. The setup gave the musicians a sense of great intimacy. They could look into one another's eyes as they recorded. They could watch Otis, react to his movements and cues.

Otis always sang in the studio as if he were performing before an audience—dancing and gesturing and moving his body to the beat. It was the only way he knew to summon the emotion and feeling and energy, not only from himself but also from the musicians recording with him. "Man, you better believe he was physical," said Wayne Jackson, the Stax trumpet player. "Otis had to have two cans of Right Guard to keep him down. The man was physical. Emotional and physical. We all loved him. God, we really did. He loved the horns. He would run from his vocal mike down to where the horns were and go (*sings the "I Can't Turn You Loose" horn lines*). He'd shake his fist at you and be singing those parts. It was just electrifying. He'd get right in front of you with that big fist up in the air and strut and sing that stuff at you until you were just foaming at the mouth. He'd just have you so excited."

Yet he never became overbearing in the studio. If someone flubbed a line, Otis was quick to shrug it off and offer encouragement for the next take. "Some artists are so intense about what they're doing that they make everybody feel kind of negative," said Floyd Newman. "When Otis came in, he brought happiness and smiles. He was laughing the whole time."

"Otis Redding was like a magic potion," said Jim Stewart. "When he walked into the studio, the studio lit up and all the worries and problems just sort of vanished. You knew something good was going to happen."

Newt Collier had used his connection with Otis to land occasional gigs at Stax, including the session for "Security," and he also wound up playing trumpet in the Sam and Dave road band. Watching Otis work in the studio was an unforgettable experience. "He was headstrong in his own ideas," Newt said. "He could play guitar, and Steve would pick up what he was doing. He'd tell Steve, '*Dang-a, dang-a, dang-a, da-da* . . . now remember that.' And then Booker T. would put the chords down over that. They'd just go from one person to another and keep adding. And when they'd get through, there'd be a song.

Otis was great in the studio; he could work miracles. He had that unorthodox style and everybody would wait to see what was coming next; it wasn't going to be common, so you'd just wait to see what else was going to come out of that mouth!"

William Bell had an even more unique perspective—he'd watch Otis write a song on the road, then see it take shape at the studio. "Sometimes we'd travel together in the same car on tour and he would sit with an old acoustic guitar and a tape recorder and just hum most of the stuff," William said. "He'd have an opening line of a verse and then just hum through it. If you're a conventional writer like I am, you're going, 'Okay, now, where's the story going to go?' Otis didn't do that at all. If you listened to him, you'd think, 'Hmmm, that's weird; how's that going to work?' But it was just uncanny. Nothing was written down. He'd come in and give the bass line, the notes, and he might strum some chords on the guitar and the keyboard player would pick it up and get the chord structure. But the horn lines and everything, he had it all up here (*points to his head*). It was just amazing how he did that."

Every person in the MG's was active in offering ways to refine Otis's ideas, especially Booker T. He would sometimes "edit" Otis's horn ideas and write out the lines for the other musicians. By then, he was about to graduate from Indiana University with a music degree; he'd worked at Stax on a part-time basis as he attended college, with Isaac Hayes handling much of the keyboard work in his absence. To many, Booker T. was an unsung hero of the studio band. "I remember him doing something one time that blew my mind," Newt Collier said. "They had some violin players in the studio one day and they weren't playing something correct. Booker T. got up from the keyboard and said, 'Can I see your violin for a second? Let me show you something. See right here? Play such-and-such and then come down off it like that. Then use this E string like this and come down off it. Okay? That'll be good for what we're playing.' He gave it back to the violin guy and the guy just *looks* at him! I've seen Booker T. take trumpets from guys and scare them to death. Booker T. was just amazing."

"I Can't Turn You Loose" was one of those collaborative efforts. The song was one of the hallmarks of Otis's career, with horn riffs that remain in the repertoire of seemingly every high-school and college marching band in America. And before Otis and Steve finished writing the song on the studio floor, those riffs were just about all he had. When Duck Dunn heard them, he began playing a slight variation of the bass line from the Four Tops hit "I Can't Help Myself (Sugar Pie Honey Bunch)." Duck's idea fit perfectly underneath the horns, and it gave the song a driving energy. "That bass line came from Motown," he said. "There's also a little horn line at the end of that song. Wayne and I played in the same nightclub together and that vamp is the way we used to play 'Night Train' at the club. If you listen to that, you'll hear a little bit of 'Night Train' in the horns even though the rhythm is different."

The song kicked off with Duck and Steve Cropper playing the Motown lick. Seconds later there was a fierce drum roll and then the horns came in with a four-note burst that soared over the melody. The song was solid groove, start to finish. Otis's voice settled over the rhythm section and rode it like a man at the wheel, steering a sleek and powerful automobile. The lyrics were incidental, almost nonsensical. It did matter. "You didn't have to understand any of the words Otis was singing to understand *what* he was saying," Duck Dunn said with a chuckle. As William Bell noted, Otis didn't tell stories with his lyrics; he conveyed emotions. Elemental and universal emotions: sadness, jealousy, fear, joy, lust. That's what mattered to Otis—the *feel*, not the specifics. When Alan Walden once voiced concern about his lyrics, Otis turned and replied, "Red, you worry about the damn lyrics; *I'm* gonna worry about settin' the groove. I get that groove going, they don't care what I say."

"I Can't Turn You Loose" was an instant hit, climbing to #11 on the R&B charts. It was backed with a charming and gentle ballad called "Just One More Day" that was a hit in its own right, peaking at #15 on the R&B charts. Steve Cropper was livid when he picked up the single and saw that Otis was credited as the sole songwriter of "I Can't Turn You Loose." Steve had helped write the song and when he demanded credit (plus his fair share of the songwriting royalties) Phil Walden managed to pull a fast one: He gave Steve a writing credit on the single but set it up so that Steve never received any credit (or royalties) on any versions of the song released on albums, including the lucrative compilations and reissues and boxed sets that came years later.

The same thing happened with Speedo Sims on "Respect." While Otis would take full songwriting credit, "Respect" actually was someone else's creation. Otis certainly wrote parts of the song and devised the arrangement, but the concept and the title and many of the lyrics were given to him by Speedo Sims; and some say that Speedo isn't even the actual author. It's worth noting that Speedo often seemed to carefully avoid ever actually saying that he wrote "Respect." "It was a song that came from a group that I was singing with at one time," he told writer Peter Guralnick. "We were going to record it but we never did. I found out that singing onstage live, I had no problem. But in the studio I just couldn't hold the tune. So finally Otis said, 'Why don't I do the song?' "

In its original form, "Respect" was a ballad. Otis turned the song into a scorching rocker, rewrote some of the lyrics, and took the song to Memphis. He also wound up with sole authorship. "He told me I would get credit," Speedo said. "Him being a friend and all, I took him at his word. But as time went on—and when I say this I'm not discrediting him or anything like that—I didn't think about it, nor did he think about it. I just consider that water under the bridge and move on. A lot of people have said I should sue, and I can listen to what they're saying but I make up my own mind. And I believe that to learn, well, I guess you have to pay for your own learning."

According to Percy Welch, there's a reason Speedo might seem to sidestep claiming outright credit for writing the song. "See, 'Respect,' it didn't belong to Otis in the first place and Speedo didn't write it neither," Percy said. "I know who wrote it. One of the boys with a little group we were recording down at Macon Recording Studio, Bobby Smith's place. One of the little guys who played guitar. We had Speedo down there trying to record it. Every time Speedo would get in the studio, his voice would crack up. We'd done recorded 'Respect' five or six times, and each time it'd get worse and worse. So Bobby told him, 'Just take this tape and the tape recorder. Go home and play this tape and listen at it. Listen at where you're getting weak. And come back tomorrow and we'll see what you can get.' Instead of doing that, he hauled his ass straight on up to Phil Walden. Played the tape. Otis was sitting there listening to it. Otis was the big man: 'Speedo, you don't need to do that tune; *I* need to do it. You let me cut it, I'll give you credit; I'll give you writer's credit.' Speedo should've made him sign a contract."

Whatever the origin, it is clear that Otis did with "Respect" what he essentially had done with "I've Been Loving You Too Long"—he took the genesis of somebody else's song and made it completely his own. The difference was that Jerry Butler received his writing credit and only Otis received credit for "Respect." Whether that was at Otis's directive or at Phil Walden's initiative is unknown.

Phil was a pit bull when it came to looking out for Otis, ruthless and single-minded. He had a quick temper and used it to his advantage, unafraid to intimidate when flattery didn't work. He was a master at looking for every possible angle to play, anything to squeeze out just a little more money even if it came at the expense of someone like Steve Cropper or Speedo Sims. If Phil made the decision to cut Speedo out of his royalties as the co-writer of "Respect," Otis certainly allowed him to get away with it. Same thing with Steve; Otis could have righted things with the wave of a finger. But everything Otis knew about the music business he learned from Phil, and he could be every bit as fixated on the bottom line when it came to money.

Percy Welch—who had first performed with Otis at Hillview Springs with Gladys Williams—had promoted Otis's first two Homecoming Shows at the City Auditorium; by the third one, he found himself squeezed out of the picture by Otis. As the next Homecoming was being planned, there was a meeting between Alan Walden, Mr. Walden, Otis, and Percy; Phil was still in the Army and away in Germany. Otis announced they could promote the show themselves without Percy's help. "Pops," Otis told Mr. Walden. "We give Percy all that money? We don't need him. You can do what he's doing." Alan offered up a spirited defense on Percy's behalf. It didn't move Otis and he told Percy he wasn't needed any longer. Percy stood up and looked at him. "Otis, well, I'll tell you this," he said. "It doesn't make any difference getting fired. Shit, I been fired a million times. I was Percy Welch when you first seen me, and I'll be still Percy Welch when you last see me."

Otis Redding was the entire focus of the two Walden brothers. He was their first act. They didn't want to make mistakes. They wanted to do everything right. The three of them usually worked well together. If Otis was wrong, Phil and Alan would go to him and tell him. If Phil was wrong, Alan and Otis would go to him. And if Phil couldn't get something across to Alan, he'd go get Otis to straighten him out. Phil and Alan had heard all the horror stories of their heroes who had recorded hit records and then turned up broke and destitute. And just as Phil and Alan wanted Otis to be the guy who retired with money in his pocket, they also wanted to make sure *they* could retire with a healthy chunk of money in the bank. If they had to step on people occasionally—as Otis had put it to Benny Davis when he was challenged about taking "These Arms of Mine"—it was simply done. They considered themselves underdogs from the backwoods competing against the city boys. "What gave us that special edge," Phil said, "was that we *had* to be better than anyone else because if we weren't, we couldn't compete."

They all reveled in the trappings of success. Otis's press releases (usually written by Phil) bragged that he owned two hundred suits and four hundred pairs of shoes. Otis, Phil, and Alan each bought brand-new Cadillac El Dorados and cruised around Macon like kings. "We'd go out in our El Dorados clubbing it," Phil said. "We'd go down Broadway and go up Cotton Avenue and they were just *full* of clubs. It was too good to be true. You couldn't make up a story like ours. To take all these people from diverse backgrounds, different cultures, different races, mix them all together in a little Georgia town, it's a helluva story."

At the end of the year, Otis bought a 270-acre ranch just outside Macon in Jones County, calling it the "Big O Ranch." It was as far away from the projects as a person could get, a big and sprawling spread with a red brick ranch house as the main house. Otis moved his parents out to the property and Alan moved into a log cabin down the road. "I was able to teach him how to ride horses and fish and things that he had never been able to learn in his childhood," Alan said. "He loved the woods once he moved out to the country. He literally fell in love with it. He loved sitting out in the back watching rabbits and squirrels."

Whatever success they achieved, there was an unquenchable yearning for more. Phil revived his agency, Walden Artists and Promotions, and was quickly managing and booking many of the current and future Southern soul stars: Otis, Sam and Dave, Percy Sledge, Johnnie Taylor, Clarence Carter, Eddie Floyd. They bought a two-story brick building on Cotton Avenue—a former chicken restaurant—to headquarter Redwal Music. Their ambition was encapsulated in the incorporation papers of the company: "Music publishing, record production, either as principle (sic) or as agent for musicians and artists, publishing sheet music, manufacturing records and managing careers." In short, the plan was to someday build their own version of Stax Records right there in Macon, Georgia. And the headquarters of the empire was going to be 535 Cotton Avenue.

It was a dream that would eventually come true, only in a way that Phil Walden had never imagined.

Try a Little Tenderness

Just a year after Alan Walden had nearly closed down the shop, Otis Redding was firmly established as an R&B star. He had hit the Top Ten with four different singles and the magnitude of his talent seemed to grow with each new recording session. His songwriting abilities had blossomed and the arrangements he devised were increasingly inventive. They were intended to accent every trace of emotion within a song and there was almost nothing like it in popular music—not Sam Cooke, not James Brown, not Motown, not the Beatles. The only person who exceeded Otis's gift for arrangements was Ray Charles.

Like Ray Charles, the core of Otis's talent was his believability as a singer. When you heard him sing a song, whether it was a pleading ballad or an up-tempo rocker, you never doubted that the performance was coming from the heart. His voice had a haunting quality, as if he wasn't singing to you so much as *confiding* his deepest secrets. It was expressive and rich and compelling. "When he recorded *Otis Blue* after the death of Sam Cooke, he had become a master," said Atlantic's Jerry Wexler. "When he sang Sam's 'A Change Is Gonna Come,' it was clear that the torch had been passed; the tradition was alive."

Yet Otis couldn't begin to compete commercially with the Motown artists who were regularly crossing over into the lucrative white market with #1 pop hits. A hit single by a Motown group could sell a million copies; *all* of Otis's singles in 1965 combined had sold just 800,000 copies. And his *career* album sales had yet to hit the 100,000 mark. Phil was acutely aware that the ultimate goal was to find a way to cross over into mainstream radio. And to do that, he had to get Otis in front of white audiences. He knew Otis would win them over. That wasn't the problem; he'd seen Otis win over redneck college kids in the outer reaches of Alabama. The problem was getting him there, creating the exposure.

For Phil, the ultimate sign of success was simple: *The Ed Sullivan Show*. That was about as mainstream and white as it got, the top prime-time variety show on television. To get there, Phil liked to say, Otis needed a "career song," one for the ages. Phil and Alan and Otis spent many a night hanging out at the office in Macon, dreaming aloud and plotting strategies for his career. "With Otis, it was, 'Hey, we're gonna conquer the world; we're gonna let 'em know who you are all over the world!' " Alan said. "I can safely say we sat down at several meetings and figured out how to conquer the music industry. After those meetings we could all walk out of that room and say, 'You know, if we decided to do anything, we could do it.' Because there was that much love between the three of us. With Otis, it was just family."

Otis went back to Stax in March to finish recording tracks for his fourth album, *The Soul Album*. The sessions captured a singer who had hit his stride. It was Otis's second straight album that stood on its own merits, that didn't act as a haven for stray singles. "Just One More Day" was the only hit on the album; surprisingly, "I Can't Turn You Loose" was not included even though it had yet to appear on a full-length record. Still, *The Soul Album* was full of solid originals and smart covers. There was a Sam Cooke song, a lively and romping version of "Chain Gang." There was a rare Stax cover of a Motown hit, "It's Growing," originally recorded by the Temptations. There was a version of Wilson Pickett's "634-5789" and the standard "Nobody Knows You When You're Down and Out," which Sam Cooke had covered on his *At the Copa* concert album. A highlight was Otis's aching and melancholy take on Jerry Butler's "Cigarettes and Coffee." Jerry himself wasn't impressed by this version ("On the scale of one to ten, I'd give him a four"), but Otis's voice was utterly convincing and the recording still ranks as one of Duck Dunn's favorites.

Besides co-writing "Just One More Day," Otis contributed a ballad called "Good to Me" that he wrote with a fellow Stax artist named Julius Green. He sang with a group called the Mad Lads and was hanging around the studio one afternoon when he heard Otis playing a melody on his guitar. He asked to hear the words and Otis said he hadn't written the words yet. So Green pondered for a moment and then began singing the first thing that came to mind: "I don't know what you got, baby, but it sure is good to me." Otis liked it, and they sat there in the studio and hammered out the lyrics; Green also got a writing credit.

Even without hit singles to drive it up the charts, *The Soul Album* was carried on the momentum of *Otis Blue*. It quickly rose to #3 on the R&B charts and #54 on the pop charts. The same month Otis recorded *The Soul Album*, the Beatles quietly sent their manager, Brian Epstein, to Memphis. The group had just completed its second American tour and wanted to do with a rock 'n' roll album what Otis had done with *Otis Blue*—make the record as an artistic statement unto itself, with or without Top 40 singles. The Beatles were huge fans of the Stax sound and were toying with the idea of recording in Memphis the album that would become *Rubber Soul*. Estelle Axton picked Epstein up at the airport to take him on a tour of Stax. But word got out and they were besieged by Beatles fans when they reached the studio. Epstein quickly realized security would be a nightmare and the Beatles eventually recorded the album at the Abbey Road Studios in England. But *Rubber Soul* did open with "Drive My Car," the obvious homage to Stax that featured the bass line inspired by "Respect." *Rubber Soul* was even mixed in stereo like a Stax album—the vocals came out of one speaker and much of the instrumentation came out of the other.

The encounter with the Beatles was an exhilarating moment for everyone at Stax. It wasn't just the possibility of brushing arms and working with them, it was the validation; here was the most popular rock 'n' roll group in the history of music, grooving on what they were doing in Memphis. For Phil and Otis the timing was especially encouraging: Phil had taken the bold step of booking his star for a three-night stand at the Whisky à Go Go, *the* hottest rock club in Los Angeles, California. It was the initial foray of breaking Otis to white audiences, a gamble of no small magnitude. There was no guarantee that white rock fans had any interest in Otis Redding. There was no guarantee they even knew who he was. And there was certainly no guarantee that anyone would bother to show up to see him perform. Still, it was not an uncalculated move. If Otis was going to get over with whites, Los Angeles was the logical jumping-off point because it was developing into a hotbed of new music. Music fans didn't tie themselves to prevailing commercial winds and they listened with religious conviction to the underground, free-format FM radio stations that played Otis Redding records.

The Whisky à Go Go gigs were to be a moment of truth, easily the most important performances of Otis's life. Stax raised the stakes even higher, deciding to record the shows for a concert album. They hired Wally Heider, the premier engineer on the West Coast for live recordings, and dispatched Al Jackson, Jr., to produce the record. Atlantic showed its support by sending Nesuhi Ertegun—Ahmet Ertegun's brother—to supervise and coordinate. And the man Otis loved to call "Omelet" flew out himself to hear his rising star perform.

Otis played three nights—April 8, 9, and 10—a total of seven shows; two sets on Friday and Sunday, then three sets on Saturday. Backing him was a ten-piece band: Elbert "Woody" Woodson on drums, Ralph Stewart on bass, and James Young on guitar; a horn section that featured Clarence Johnson, Jr., on trombone, Sammy Coleman and John Farris on trumpets, Robert Holloway and Robert Pittman and Donald Henry and Al Brisco Clark on tenor saxes. Otis clearly understood the magnitude of the moment, what was at stake. He rehearsed the band relentlessly the day before the gig, starting at two o'clock Friday morning and working until ten A.M. They took a sleep break until four P.M., then went to the club and rehearsed until nearly exactly the moment they opened the doors to let people come inside.

Any fear that Otis might be ignored was quickly erased; the club was packed. But then came a greater concern: The crowd sat on its hands when saxophonist/emcee Al Brisco Clark came out to introduce Otis. Clark used the old R&B trick of shouting out a roll call of a star's hit records before bringing them out. It usually worked a crowd into a frenzy; but not with the stoned kids at the Whisky à Go Go. " 'Pain in My Heart'!" Clark cried out. He was greeted with scattered applause. " 'I'm Depending on You'!" he shouted. Less applause. " 'Respect'!" Even less applause. " 'Security'!" Almost dead silence. There were a few fans in the crowd, but the vast majority seemed clueless. Just because they were there to see what all the buzz was about, they weren't convinced yet that they were going to like it. The emcee plowed ahead, ignoring the silence: "Let's welcome to the stage, with a great big round of applause, the star of the show! The one and only Volt recording artist, Otis Redding!"

Otis walked out as a rippling drum roll rang out. There were no deafening cheers, no standing ovations. If Otis noticed the skeptical reception, he paid it no mind. Instead he strutted out onstage with the grin of a magician who knows something you don't—that he holds the keys to the universe up his sleeves. "Now watch this!" he called out off-mike. Then he turned to the band. "Hey!" he exclaimed. The drums immediately shifted to that classic Stax backbeat while the horn section instantly kicked in beside it. Moments later, Otis launched into a driving version of "I'm Depending on You."

Otis had their attention that quickly. He was wild and exotic under the spotlights, unlike anything they'd ever seen before. Few in the audience had any firsthand experience with R&B music. For many, Otis was nothing less than a revelation—they were held spellbound by the intensity and depth of emotion in his voice, just as they were charmed by his effervescent smile and teased by his stage banter. "It's so good to be here, ladies and gentlemens," he said at one point. "We're recording our album now. Yeah, we're recording an album right now! So just holler as loud as you wanna! We gonna eat next week!" There was laughter in the background. Then Otis began to exhort the crowd like a Southern country preacher. "You know, just let your hair down! Holler as loud as you wanna! Stomp hard as you wanna! Just take your shoes on off. Get soulful! We'll get into a thing, you know?"

Later Otis told them, "We're gonna do a song that you've never heard before."

From the crowd, someone called out, "Says who?"

Otis giggled. "Says me," he shot back, launching into a slow and searing version of "Chained and Bound" that stretched for almost seven minutes. Otis was breathless by the end of the song. "Sure was a groove that time," he gasped once the applause began to die down. "Man, you see how hard we have to work to eat? Man, we have to work *hard.*"

By then the crowd was screaming out his name. Between songs, one woman kept calling out for "These Arms of Mine." She finally got his attention during a lull. "Otis!" she cried. Then her voice grew softer and it turned from a request to a plea: "Would you *please* do 'These Arms of Mine'?"

There was a moment of silence as other voices from the crowd seconded her. Otis grinned. "Yes, I would," he replied with a playful edge in his voice. He paused for a moment, then began singing the first lines of the song before the band fell in behind him.

The Whisky à Go Go shows caused an instant sensation. The Hollywood elite were in the audience, movie producers and music-industry people. Bob Dylan showed up on opening night; he made his way backstage with an acetate of a new song called "Just Like a Woman," gave it to Otis, and suggested he record it. When Otis listened to it, he turned to Phil and said, "I like it but it's got too many fuckin' words. All these pigtails and bobbytails and all that stuff."

Another music legend who sought out Otis was Phil Spector, the eccentric genius behind the hits of the Ronettes, the Crystals, and Darlene Love. Ahmet Ertegun took Otis out to Spector's mansion, and the two of them immediately hit it off. "Phil Spector sat down at the piano and Otis picked up a guitar and they went through virtually every song Otis had ever written," Jerry Wexler said. "Phil knew the changes on everything, and Otis was absolutely astonished. I don't think Otis had ever heard of Phil Spector. He was just amazed by this thin, little gray boy who knew all his tunes."

Just as important as the shows at the Whisky à Go Go was the buzz they created. Booking Otis into a white establishment in Los Angeles ensured attention in the mainstream media. At that point there was no *Rolling Stone* or *Spin* or any general-interest magazine devoting any serious attention to music. And the big-city newspapers weren't exactly clamoring to give ink to black R&B artists. Even back home in Macon, the *Telegraph* had published all of one story devoted to the topic of Otis Redding. Otis's first real exposure in the white media came when the *Los Angeles Times* printed a positively fawning review of the shows. "His gig at the Whisky à Go Go was probably the most exciting thing that rock-worn room has ever harbored," wrote critic Pete Johnson. "He was a magic singer with an unquenchable store of energy and a great flittering band. Crowds never sat still when he was onstage nor could they stay quiet when he asked them for a response, because he gave them too much to leave them strangers."

By every measure, the Los Angeles shows were a triumph and everyone was ecstatic because everything was on tape. When they began to listen, there was even more cause for celebration. The sound was pristine; Wally Heider had miked everything expertly—the drums were alive; the bass resonated; the guitar shimmered at just the right level. Then the smiles quickly turned to grimaces: one of the trumpet players was consistently atonal, completely out of tune. And it wasn't just one night; it was that way *every* night of the *entire* gig. The trumpet couldn't be taken out of the mix. They couldn't cover it up. The tapes were useless. Stax never released them.

The intense rehearsals Otis put his band through before the Whisky à Go Go gigs weren't unusual. Otis loved to rehearse, to nail every part of the show, and he had to do that because the lineup of his road band was in constant flux. Sometimes a musician would find a better-paying gig or get tired of the road and go home; sometimes Otis would decide they weren't up to snuff and find someone to replace them. Many of the musicians who backed him on the road were old friends from Macon. Ploonie, the drummer from the Pinetoppers, went on the road with Otis in 1965 shortly after "Mr. Pitiful" was released. "He was serious about rehearsing," said Ploonie. "It was just like he was doing a show. He'd work you. He'd say, 'It's gotta be right; it's gotta be right.' He'd change some of the material around. And he'd tell you what he wanted you to do. He'd come around and show you. He'd sit behind the drums and try to show you what he was talking about, and he could fool around with a guitar, too."

Ploonie used to tease Otis about using Al Jackson in the studio. "Take me down to Memphis with you sometime," Ploonie told him. "I want to see Al Jackson. I think I can cut him."

Otis just looked at him like he was crazy. "Uh-huh," he said. "I'll tell you what, Ploonie, that boy's *something* else."

One of the mainstays of Otis's road bands was a tenor saxophonist, a kid from Macon nicknamed "Shang-a-Lang." His real name was Harold Smith and he'd picked up his nickname in high school when he played the cymbals in the marching band. Shang had studied under Macon's best sax player, Jessie Hancock, and traveled with Little Richard before joining up with Otis. He was tall and lean as a string bean, his body almost mirroring the long and willowy saxophone that he played onstage. Because Otis couldn't dance, Shang was allowed to show off during the concerts and they even named a dance in New York, the "Shang-a-Lang," in his honor.

His selection of musicians wasn't the only way Otis stayed connected to Macon. Every year around Christmas, he'd fill up his trunk with half-pint bottles of scotch. He'd drive over to Bellevue, park at a curb, pop open his trunk, and people would line up to pick up a bottle of scotch out of his trunk. One time someone asked Otis to bring him back a gift from a road trip. Otis, of course, quickly forgot all about it. A few weeks later, Otis ran into the guy and he asked about his gift. Otis grimaced and said, "Aw, man!" And he took the watch off his wrist and gave it to the guy.

"That was the kind of person he was," said Newt Collier. "Otis never forgot where he came from; he never forgot Tindall Heights. He was basically a common man, even in his talking because his diction was poor. Otis was always real nice to me. When he would give the Homecoming Show at the City Auditorium every year, that would be a dynamic package. And he'd throw a party at his ranch around that time. You'd say, 'Hey, man, how much does it cost to get to your party?' He'd say—and he talked real fast—'Well, find your way out there and find out!' You'd get out there and Otis would be sitting there saying: 'Yeah, man! Come on in! Come on in! Go on back there and get you one of those drinks!'

"See, most people in Macon didn't realize Otis was as big as he was. Know why? Otis would park right out there on Broadway, come in and get his hair cut in Walter Johnson's barbershop, then sit out there on his car all day long talking to everybody that came around. You'd see Otis up at the liquor house, in the pool room shooting pool. You'd wonder: 'When the hell is he on the road?' Otis could be playing New York tonight and have a plane to catch at six o'clock and you know where he'd be right now? Down on Broadway shooting the shit with the boys. And Huck would be: 'Hey, Otis, it's time to go.' Then he'd be racing like a bat out of hell to make all his connections, running through the airport. That's the character of the man. He never forgot home."

David Tharpe—who idolized Otis and had, by then, signed a song-writing contract with Phil and Alan—echoed that sentiment. "People say fame changed Otis. It never changed him. He was the same Otis. We'd be out at Perry Hill's barbecue place playing pinball and Otis would come out and hang around with the guys. Success, what it did for Otis, it gave him a better life. He moved from the projects. The bigger Otis got, the better he got, the more humble he got. He was never nasty. He was the same Otis Redding that drilled wells with Bubba Howard, the same Otis Redding that I saw sign his first autograph. To me, Otis never forgot where he came from."

After the Los Angeles gigs, there was less and less time to spend at home. Otis seemed to always be on the road; when he wasn't, he was up in Memphis at the studio. No longer did he go months without recording—Otis was stopping by Stax every few weeks now and rolling out the hits. A session in early May produced "My Lover's Prayer," a single that hit #10 on the R&B charts although it did no better than #61 on the pop. The song was written from the viewpoint of a man who is away from his lover and is pleading for her understanding. That was something Otis always had from Zelma—even when rumors were ripe around town of dalliances Otis had had on the road with adoring women. She seemed to take the attitude that so long as he never threw them in her face, she wouldn't voice her displeasure. "When he wasn't on the road, he wouldn't be around the house because he'd go to the office and work down there and they might sit around until two in the morning," Zelma said. "But I had no problem with that because he respected me. It was never a problem with what he was doing with me because I supported him. I never got mad because he was gone and didn't get a chance to spend time with the kids. Wherever he was, I felt very secure so I had no beef about what he was doing and how much time he spent."

In mid-June, life became even more hectic when Otis hooked up with Sam and Dave for his biggest tour yet. Expectations were high. Otis was now an established star and Sam and Dave were nipping at his heels, having accomplished in less than a year with Stax what Otis yearned for and had yet to accomplish—a #1 hit single on the R&B charts. The bill for the thirty-seven-date tour was packed with talent: Percy Sledge, Patti Labelle and the Blue Belles, the Ovations, Garnet Mims. But the show was sparked by what quickly blossomed into an intense, and not always friendly, rivalry between Otis and Sam and Dave. The tour kicked off at the Apollo Theatre and Otis found himself in danger of being upstaged on the very first show. "Otis could not dance," said Newt Collier, who was playing with Sam and Dave's band. "And he didn't like Sam and Dave, because they were theatrically good. They would come out doing this James Brown thing. Sam would be doing cartwheels and flipping onstage. Otis would be standing there, smoke coming out his ears, saying, 'Get them sons-of-bitches off that stage.' They would scorch Otis to death. Otis just couldn't deal with that."

Alan Walden arrived at the Apollo midway through the seven-day stand and found Otis backstage sucking on lemons and eating honey, hoarse and as nervous as he'd ever seen him. "These motherfuckers are killing me," Otis told him. "They're killing me! I'm going as fast as I can, but they're still killing me. Goddamn!"

The next day, Alan took Otis over to the Atlantic Records offices to have lunch with Jerry Wexler. Otis was still obviously worried— he was losing his voice and he was being upstaged nightly by Sam and Dave. They reassured him, and both Alan and Jerry Wexler suggested Otis slow down the tempos of his songs. Otis declined their advice; he liked to play his fast songs at a breakneck pace in concert, far ahead of the tempo on the recordings. He thought it energized the music and he wanted to do it that way and that was final.

That night, just before Otis took the stage, Phil walked up to him. "Otis, you *are* the star," Phil said. "Now go out there and *star* the motherfucker like you should."

"And that's what he did," said Alan. "Sam and Dave were history that time."

By the time the seven-day stand at the Apollo was over, Otis had had all of Sam and Dave he wanted. "Goddamn, we got thirty-seven days of this?" he complained to Phil. "I ain't gonna put up with them right in front of me for another thirty dates. Let them close the first half of the show, and then let it build back up to another climax when I close the second." That lasted all of three days. Otis went back to

Phil and said, "Put those motherfuckers right in front of me. They're making me work harder than I ever did in my life."

They were locked in a duel for the entire tour. Who won and who lost is a matter of debate, but it certainly left the audiences all the richer. Afterwards, Otis sat down with Phil and Alan and laid down the law: No more shows with Sam and Dave. Ever.

Phil cleared his throat. "I just signed a contract for thirty days in Europe with them in Europe with the Stax/Volt tour."

Otis sighed. "Okay, I'll do that one," he said. "But after that, I don't ever want to see those two motherfuckers again."

One new member of Otis's road band was a twenty-one-year-old kid named Johnny Lee Johnson, who used the exotic spelling of Jai Johanny Johanson and carried the nickname of "Jaimoe." He was a drummer from Gulfport, Mississippi, who had come to Otis's attention playing drums for soul singer Ted Taylor. He was green, still learning his craft, but his deep wealth of talent was obvious and he would go on to be a founding member of the Allman Brothers Band. "I joined that band about nine days after they cut the Whisky à Go Go album," said Jaimoe. "The first thing Otis told me was: 'Play all the fast songs twice as fast as the records and play the slow songs twice as slow.' He liked that energy. And, man, those fast songs would go *fast*. We had a great band with Otis. We had thirteen pieces. Woody [Elbert Woodson] was the other drummer and we played double drums sometimes. I made a deal with him: 'You play behind Otis and I'll play behind all these other people.' I played behind every act on that tour except Sam and Dave. That was a gas. You learn variety by doing that; you get a lot of experience. Otis was into that rock 'n' roll type thing way back then. I'm talking about *energy*. It was really heavy. And I didn't know how to play it. We'd be playing so loud, I'd hit my cymbals so loud, man, I couldn't hear the horn parts to punctuate them."

One night, Jaimoe was at the hotel before a gig and spied Otis walking around singing something that made absolutely no sense: "*Fa, fa-fa-fa-fa, fa, fa, fa.*" "What is *that*?" he asked.

"That's my next record," said Otis.

Jaimoe crooked his head with a look of puzzlement. "*That's* your next record?"

"Yeah, man, it's gonna be a hit."

Jaimoe grinned broadly and paused as he told the story. "Two weeks later, I turn on the radio and there it is: '*Fa, fa-fa-fa-fa, fa, fa, fa.*' Man, I couldn't believe it. But there it was."

Otis had stopped by Stax in late August for a quick recording session and they had whipped up a song called "Fa-Fa-Fa-Fa-Fa (Sad Song)." It grew out of a horn riff that Otis had written that was based around the theme song of the television show *The $64,000 Question*. The "fa-fa" in the title represented the horn lick—"fa-fa" was Otis's sound for a saxophone. But his voice sounded so cool as he sang it that they decided to incorporate it into the song. It was another collaborative effort between Steve Cropper and Otis that was composed on the studio floor. "He always came in with fourteen ideas," Steve said. "He would run them down and there would be little bits and pieces, never songs. Little hooks and little rhythms. The greatest example of that is 'Fa-Fa-Fa.' He was humming me a horn line and I said, 'Hey, that's a good idea.' My trick with Otis, if you look at the songs that have my name on them, was that just about all those songs are about Otis himself rather than some obscure subject: 'I'm the Big O,' 'They call me Mr. Pitiful,' 'I keep singing these sad songs.' He was the easiest guy in the world to write about."

With its bouncy beat and irresistible horn line, "Fa-Fa-Fa-Fa-Fa (Sad Song)" became one of his biggest hits but in a way that was not quite expected. It peaked at #12 on the R&B charts, failing to match the #10 reached by his previous single, "My Lover's Prayer." But while "My Lover's Prayer" had stalled on the pop charts at #61, "Fa-Fa-Fa-Fa-Fa" climbed all the way to #29. It was his most successful pop single since "I've Been Loving You Too Long" and yet another sign that Otis was beginning to make inroads on the white market.

Stax planned to release a new Otis Redding album in October, and a week after he cut "Fa-Fa" Otis went back to Memphis to record four more songs. As usual, Otis didn't have enough material. He mostly had scraps. They kicked around ideas. Finally Otis mentioned a song that Sam Cooke used to sing. Why not work it up? Give it a try and see what happens. What happened was the "career song" that Phil Walden had always hoped for, Otis Redding's masterpiece: "Try a Little Tenderness."

Written in the 1930s as a torch ballad, the song was a warhorse, recorded by artists ranging from Bing Crosby to Frank Sinatra to Ella Fitzgerald. Sam Cooke had included it on his *At the Copa* album, combining two verses of "Tenderness" into a medley of songs that also included "For Sentimental Reasons" and "You Send Me." Phil thought it would be a perfect showcase for Otis and nagged him to record it. Otis shrugged off the suggestion until he got to that studio and needed songs to record. Once they began messing around with it at Stax, they basically approached it as just another one of Otis's weeping ballads. Then, on the second verse, Al Jackson unexpectedly began to tap out a double-time lick on the side of his snare drum. Suddenly eyes began lighting up; everyone saw the song from a whole different perspective. What if they used Al's drum part as a springboard, to take the song and build it from a soft ballad to a wild and frenzied ending? "When Al did that drum thing, it just wailed everybody," Duck Dunn said. "We didn't know he was gonna do that. When it went into that double-time thing, it was just amazing. That song's got to be Al's. If Al ever created one, it's that one."

Al played the drums with a complex simplicity. He traded bombast for subtlety. And he mastered the art of what musicians call "playing behind the beat." A basic song has four beats to a bar. A drummer usually accents two of them: the two and the four. Al would play the four right on the beat. But he would slightly delay playing the two and it would give songs an extra punch, a distinctive *feel*. "When I started playing with the MG's, it was just a treat to be in the same room with Al Jackson, Jr.," said Duck. "He was the most respected drummer in Memphis. He had the secret to that groove—that big pocket with the delayed feel. If there's any secret to my playing, I think it comes from what Al used to tell me: 'Just wait on the *two*.' With him, it could be an awfully long wait! Al just had this amazing sense of time, and he knew how to shape a song. A lot of what he did sounds so simple, but nobody else could play that way."

Al influenced every musician in the studio and was a key architect of the overall Stax sound. "Al would make you want to play very simple because he played simple," Steve said. "It sounded complicated when you backed off from it and listened from the outside, but when you got in the inside, he was playing very basic, simple stuff. It just had this incredible feel. He's definitely the greatest drummer I ever worked with."

As often happened in the studio, it was Al's drumming that opened up all the possibilities for "Try a Little Tenderness." The version recorded by Otis Redding is a study in nuance and dynamics. It started with a gorgeous three-part horn introduction. Isaac Hayes is generally credited with writing the intro, although Duck Dunn said he remembers Otis coming up with it and humming the lines to the horn players. As the horns faded, there was a heart-stopping silence before Otis began to sing the famed first lines: "Oh, she made me weary / Them young girls they do get wearied / Wearing that same old shabby dress." The accompaniment was muted and soft—an occasional gentle guitar chord, a discreet bass line, Al's hushed hi-hat. Then the piano (Isaac Hayes) darted through with a quick lick. A few seconds later, it was Booker T. doing the same thing with a resonating church organ.

For the second verse, the band kept the same slow tempo. But it was deceptive because Al had begun to play a double-time tap that sounded like someone had turned on a ticking metronome. It gave the music a sense of tension that was amplified when the piano and organ begin darting in and out with a steady frequency, almost sparring with a sorrowful single saxophone that played softly in the background. As the song veered to the bridge, it began to gather steam and going into the third verse everything quickly picked up speed: the guitar chords turned funky; the organ and piano began swirling in and out; the horn section played long, sustained single notes. Yet even as the band seemed to be going at full throttle, Al had not budged from that simple *tick-tick* backbeat. Finally, as Otis approached the end of the verse, it all meshed together. Al executed a quick drum roll and began to pound his drums with fury as the song soared with the power of a humming engine that is suddenly downshifted and revved.

The final minute of the song was a furiously charged performance.

The band played a powerful series of ascending notes that rose up and up and up while Otis breathlessly screamed out: "Squeeze her! Don't tease her! Never leave her!" The song reached a climatic moment, then briefly hovered on a series of chords before leaping back into another round of the ascending notes. They did it a second and then a third time before the unexpected happened; the song stopped cold except for Al playing a slinky series of licks on his hi-hat while Otis stuttered out nonsensical words as if he was too beside himself for coherence: "Got-ta! Try! My-my-my! Try! Try a little tenderness!" And even as the song faded, they were scaling up the heights yet again.

It was a breathtaking performance. And the constant was the emotion conveyed in Otis's voice and the way it transformed itself. At the beginning, over the quiet music, his voice was as weary-sounding as the lyrics. It was quiet, aching with a sense of defeat and resignation, as if he was having a conversation with himself about a true love he had lost forever. But by the bridge, his voice had gathered strength and resolve because he'd found the way to win her back: Try a little tenderness. By the end, it was as if his only hope was that the pure passion of his pleas would be enough to sway her into giving him one last chance to make things right.

It took just three takes to nail the song and the musicians put down their instruments with the instant understanding that they had just recorded the best song of their lives. Otis called Phil down in Macon late that night. "You know that fucking song that you've been on my ass about recording?"

Phil was caught off-guard; he didn't catch the reference. "What song is that?"

" 'Try a Little Tenderness,' " Otis said with a proud glee in his voice. "I cut that motherfucker. It's a brand-new song now."

Everyone had high hopes when "Try a Little Tenderness" was released as a single. They knew this was *it*, the song that was going to make Otis a star. For Jim Stewart, it was the most magical moment ever captured at Stax. "If there's one song, one performance that really sums up Otis and what he's about, it's 'Try a Little Tenderness,' " he said. "That one performance is so special and unique that it expresses *who* he is. That to me *is* Otis Redding. And if you want to wrap it up, just listen to 'Try a Little Tenderness.' " They were all shocked when the single seemed simply to run out of steam. It stalled at #4 on the R&B charts and topped out at just #25 on the pop. Phil Walden had thought it would be Otis's career song, the one that would land him on *The Ed Sullivan Show*.

Ed Sullivan's people never called.

Satisfaction

The album that included "Try a Little Tenderness," *Complete and Unbelievable . . . The Otis Redding Dictionary of Soul*, was released in October of 1966. It was anchored by two hit songs: "Fa-Fa-Fa-Fa-Fa (Sad Song)" and "My Lover's Prayer." One of the highlights was a swinging song called "I'm Sick Y'all" that was written by Otis, Steve Cropper, and David Porter. Another gem was an out-and-out rocker called "Sweet Lorene" written by Otis, Isaac Hayes, and Al Bell. And Otis came up with a funkier-than-they-ever-could-have-imagined version of the Beatles' "Day Tripper." The album also included one other song from Sam Cooke's *At the Copa* album and it was a decided departure for Otis: a country standard called "Tennessee Waltz."

Despite its rather gaudy title, *Dictionary of Soul* lacked the cohesion and power of Otis's two previous albums. It reached just #5 on the R&B charts, and breaking Otis in America, especially in white America, remained a problematic proposition. Black acts still couldn't play in most white clubs, often by both custom *and* law, and there was nowhere else to perform before white audiences. With that obstacle before them, Otis and Phil and Alan decided to look to another direction: Europe. In many ways it was even the more logical move. Otis was already big overseas. *Otis Blue* had hit the top of the charts in England. The young white audiences in that country loved black music and yearned for the chance to see their heroes in the flesh. The guys in the Beatles were in heavenly bliss when Little Richard toured England in 1962 and they served as an opening act. The Rolling Stones revered Muddy Waters and Howlin' Wolf. And they all worshiped the first poet of rock and roll: Chuck Berry.

With the help of Polygram Records, which distributed Atlantic's products in Europe, Phil set up a short ten-day tour overseas in late 1966. Jaimoe was left behind because he didn't have enough identification to receive a passport; he soon migrated to Macon where Phil would later team him up in a trio with Johnny Jenkins. Otis arrived in London on September 8 and immediately went to a press reception at the airport set up by a former British intelligence officer named Roger Cowles who had joined Polygram as a public relations man. Otis seemed to charm every single person he met. He was bright. Witty. People followed his smile across the room. It often seemed as if every eye was riveted to him. No one had known what to expect out of this black singer from the Deep South, but no one expected something like *this*. "To have come out of the woods of Georgia, Otis was just phenomenal," said Roger Cowles. "He was very gracious. He was very warm. He was very approachable. He was very articulate. Otis was colossal, not only as an artist but as an ambassador of the United States and for black people."

It was only a brief tour, a way for Phil to stick his toe in the water and gauge the conditions. And conditions were ripe. Crowds packed Otis's shows, and he gained nationwide exposure when he appeared on the British television show *Ready, Steady, Go!* "Try a Little Tenderness" may not have done the trick, but Phil could still smell it coming. The breakthrough. And he knew exactly when it was going to happen: in the spring of 1967 when Otis headlined the Stax/Volt tour of Europe. But Phil was wrong. It began even sooner, when he opened his office door one afternoon and found Bill Graham standing outside.

A thirty-five-year-old Jewish refugee from Berlin, Germany, Bill Graham had escaped the Nazis as a child by crossing Europe on foot. A failed actor, he wound up in San Francisco and began producing rock 'n' roll shows featuring local bands such as the Grateful Dead and Jefferson Airplane. It didn't take long for Graham to become a guiding force behind a fundamental change taking shape in the concert business. Prior to that, music fans had basically two choices: They could seek out clubs and hear full-length shows by bands that were either on the way up or else on the way down. Or they could catch their favorite groups on the concert circuit as part of the package shows that featured five or six acts, each performing sets that often lasted less than thirty minutes.

When Graham opened the Fillmore Auditorium in 1966 he was able to combine the ambience of a club with the size of a concert hall. It was a brilliant concept—the money was good enough to attract big-name bands and the audiences were treated to full-length concerts. In a world of sleazy, fly-by-night music promoters, Graham gained the reputation of treating the groups who performed at the Fillmore with respect and personal attention. He'd actually pay them the money he'd promised to pay them. He'd take care of them backstage with furnished dressing rooms full of good food and beverages. And his booking acumen was extraordinary. Graham would headline a show with a hot rock band and then hire artists *he* wanted to see to open for them: blues musicians such as Freddie King and Lightnin' Hopkins and Howlin' Wolf; jazz musicians such as Rahsaan Roland Kirk; gospel and R&B groups such as the Staple Singers. Graham liked to compare himself to a mother making her children eat all the food on their plates: You want the ice cream? Then you've got to eat your meat and vegetables.

Graham often relied on Bay Area musicians for booking suggestions. He wanted to know who *they* admired. "Who do you want to see at the Fillmore?" he'd ask Jerry Garcia or Paul Butterfield. Again and again, one name kept coming up: Otis Redding. "Everybody told me, *this* is the guy *Otis*," Graham said in his autobiography, *Bill Graham Presents*. "Otis Redding. He was *it*. For everybody that talked to me."

If nothing else, Bill Graham was a man who understood the importance of the grand gesture. He didn't telegram Phil Walden with an offer. He didn't call Otis on the telephone. He hopped on a plane and flew to Atlanta, then drove down to Macon. The last thing Graham wanted to do was come off as some stereotypical arrogant music promoter. Instead he used the soft-sell approach. He explained what he was trying to accomplish at the Fillmore, and he talked about the appreciative audiences who actually *listened* to the artists. "Everybody tells me that it's not right unless I get you to do this," he told Phil and Alan. "Myself, I'm a Latin-music fan and I don't really know of you. I'm a Carmen McRae fan." The Waldens looked at him with skeptical eyes. They had heard stories about San Francisco. They asked if the audience was made up of hippies and whether they took drugs in the auditorium. "They thought it was like voodoo rites out there," Graham said. "The lights, the paints, the crazy clothes. It was *strange* for them. Which was another reason my going to Macon helped. Because I was a pretty straight guy and I didn't dress fancy. Finally, they agreed to come."

Otis traveled to San Francisco for a three-night stand at the Fillmore in December of 1966 and every musician and every music fan in the Bay Area seemed to have come out to celebrate the event. Even thirty years after the fact, Graham still remembered those gigs with a sense of awe. "Every artist in the city asked to open for Otis. The first night, it was the Grateful Dead. Each night, Janis Joplin asked me ahead of time, she said, 'Bill, please, please, can I come there early before anybody else so I can make sure I see him?' She idolized Otis. To this day, no musician ever got *everybody* out to see them the way he did. He was *the* man. The *real man*. I had expected something special but not this. This sheer *animal*. By *far* Otis Redding was *the* single most extraordinary talent I had ever seen. There was no comparison. Then or *now*. He was a black Adonis. He moved like a serpent. A panther stalking his prey. Beautiful and shining, black, sweaty, sensuous and passionate."

After the show, Graham rushed up to Otis's dressing room. Otis was drenched in sweat, sitting with towels all around him. When he looked up and saw the promoter, Otis grinned broadly. "Bill! Bill!" he said breathlessly. "I *love* these people!"

Graham was beside himself. "Otis, I can't tell you. Jesus. That was . . ."

Otis listened politely. Then he grinned. "Very nice ladies here," he said. "*Very* nice ladies."

The promoter nodded in assent and continued his fawning. "My god, two more nights . . . is there anything I can get for you?"

"No, no," Otis said softly. As Graham turned to leave, Otis called out after him. "Wait! We just got back from England and when you tour over there, you can't get no ice. Can I get me a big thing of ice and some 7UP?"

"No problem," said Graham. He raced downstairs to only discover there *was* a problem: The ice machine was broken. Graham was almost beside himself. Here was the greatest performer he'd ever seen in his life and all he wanted was some ice and 7UP and, by God, Graham wasn't going to let him down. He headed for the doors and ran like a madman down Geary Street to a little store about a block away. He grabbed a bag of ice and hustled back to the Fillmore. He sat the ice on a counter, broke it up, and finally caught his breath as he put it into cups and poured the 7UP. As he walked back to the dressing room, Graham decided to seize the moment. When he reached the door, he stopped for a moment to gather himself and then he summoned up his acting skills. As Graham stepped inside the dressing room, he was suddenly out of breath and panting desperately for air. "Here's the 7UP," he gasped. "Enough ice for you?"

Otis looked at him as if he feared the promoter was about to have a heart attack. "What's the matter?"

"Nothing," Graham responded. "I had to . . . *we* . . . never mind."

"Hey, what happened?"

Graham pretended to catch his breath. "It's no big thing," he said. "I . . . *we* . . . the ice machine broke. I had to run down the street to get you the ice. Hey, no big deal."

Otis reached out and grabbed him by his shirt. "You did *what*? You went down the street for ice for *me*?"

"Yeah. So what?"

Otis gave him a big, warm hug. When he pulled away, he looked at Graham. "Let me tell you something, man. When I play this town from now on, I play for *you*."

Graham may have taken advantage of the opportunity, but his desire to please Otis was genuine. He'd just witnessed the performance of a lifetime and all he wanted to do was give Otis some small gesture of thanks. "With every passing year, those shows get better and better in terms of all the other people I've seen onstage since then," Graham said. "It was where his voice came from and how he put *everything* into a song. He was *impassioned*. He hasn't been equaled. There's nothing close. That was the best gig I ever put on in my entire life. I knew it then. No 'maybe' about it. Good sex with somebody you really love is great stuff. So was that."

Although Jerry Wexler had hoped to establish the Stax studio as the new headquarters of Atlantic's R&B division, Jim Stewart eventually turned down the chance and Wexler instead took his studio business down to a fledgling little studio in Muscle Shoals, Alabama. Jim's rationale was simple; he didn't want Stax to diminish itself to uplift Atlantic. Jim wanted Stax to succeed on its own merits, not as Atlantic's studio band. For just as Otis was positioning himself to go after the white audience, Stax Records was gearing up to take on Motown and even Atlantic as the premier R&B/soul label.

Motown and Stax were natural rivals. Motown was the established hitmaker; Stax was the new kid in town. Motown was North; Stax was South. Motown was Hitsville U.S.A.; Stax was Soulsville U.S.A. Motown was urban, with a pristine sound that strove for cool perfection; Stax was rural and raw, emotional and often blatantly sexual. Motown was teenage love; Stax was adult lust. There was a romantic and innocent quality to Smokey Robinson's "You've Really Got a Hold on Me"; when Wilson Pickett sang, "All you wanna do is ride, Sally, ride," it didn't take a vivid imagination to know just *what* Sally was wanting to ride. Motown sent its performers to finishing school; the mere thought of "The Wicked" Pickett in finishing school would have been enough to send the guys at Stax rolling on the floor in laughter. "We were real different from Motown," said Phil Walden. "They were slick in every way. They sounded it, too. They played these white Las Vegas shows. I remember going to see the Four Tops. They started with 'There's No Business Like Show Business' and I thought, 'What in the world is that?' It was awful. How about 'Sugar Pie Honey Bunch'?"

Motown had enjoyed tremendous success pairing male and female vocalists, especially Marvin Gaye with Kim Weston. So Jim Stewart decided Otis should pair up with Carla Thomas. "One of my contributions was to put them together," he said. "I had to fight to do it. They really didn't jump overboard about the idea, but after it was done they liked it. I thought it would be helpful to both artists' careers. Carla was always sort of special to me because she was my first artist and I felt she needed a boost. I thought the combination of his rawness and her sophistication would work."

At the time, Carla was attending Howard University in Washington, D.C., studying for an M.A. in English. When she came home for her Christmas break, she and Otis went into the studio to record one song and find out how well they would work together. Otis suggested they work up a version of Lowell Fulsom's hit "Tramp." Basically, Otis set up the arrangement so that he and Carla spent the song verbally sparring—Otis as a smooth-talking ladies' man and Carla as the sassy city girl turning him away with flirtful insults about his country roots. "O-o-o-o, I'm a lover!" Otis protested. "Matter of opinion," Carla snipped behind him. "You know what, Otis?" she said. "You're country. You're straight from the Georgia woods."

It was a delightful exchange, played out over a classic Stax backbeat and a riveting horn riff. And much of it was ad-libbed on the studio floor. "I was surprised it came off as well as it did," Carla said. "I was so used to singing those little sweet ballads, I didn't know how I was going to stack up. Our styles were so different. I mean, from 'Gee Whiz' to 'Tramp'!"

Their chemistry was immediate. There was an obvious spark between Otis and Carla, and it was reflected in the way their voices meshed and the way they played off each other. Everyone quickly agreed to press forward and record enough songs for an album to be called *King and Queen*. They recorded "Knock On Wood," a song Eddie Floyd had originally written for Otis only to see it rejected by Jim Stewart. It turned out Eddie's instincts were on target. "Knock On Wood" was an ideal vehicle for Otis and he recorded a rollicking version with Carla. Another highlight was "Lovey Dovey," a remake of a 1954 hit for the Clovers. Otis and Carla sped up the tempo and used it as another showcase for their playful vocal sparring. Like all of Otis's recent albums, *King and Queen* included a Sam Cooke cover, "Bring It On Home to Me." The best track of all may have been a haunting ballad called "New Year's Resolution" that was penned by three Stax staff writers—Deanie Parker (who also did PR for the label), Randall Catron, and Mary Frierson. The two vocal performances are unforgettable, warm and intimate and captivating. Otis and Carla sang with all the passion of young lovers dancing slowly in the dark, tenderly holding each other and making up after a fight that nearly tore them apart.

At the same time Otis was recording the album with Carla, he also was laying down tracks for his own upcoming album. The first single was a ballad co-written by Eddie Floyd and Booker T. called "I Love You More Than Words Can Say" and it marked the first time Otis had ever used a string section on a song, owing as much to pop influences as it did his classic soul sound. It wasn't one of Otis's stronger efforts, and it was a testament to the public's growing appetite for Otis Redding that it managed to reach #30 on the R&B charts. There was a midtempo blues rocker called "Let Me Come on Home." There were two more ballads: "Glory of Love" and "Open the Door." He also used the sessions to cut his first Christmas songs. One was a souled-up version of the Charles Brown blues standard "Merry Christmas, Baby" that featured Booker T. playing a clever countermelody on the organ; the other was the most decidedly untraditional-sounding rendition of Irving Berlin's classic "White Christmas" since Elvis Presley had recorded it in 1957.

For the first time in his career Otis had a backlog of material waiting to be released. The Christmas songs, of course, wouldn't come out until the late fall. And unlike his other albums, which were usually put on the market within days of the recording session, *King and Queen* sat on the shelf for two months before it was released in March. The album was an immediate success, rising to #36 on the pop charts, making it his most successful album by far.

But there was little time to celebrate. By the time *King and Queen* came out, Otis and Carla and nearly the entire Stax crew were far, far away from Memphis: It was the Stax/Volt Revue and it hit Europe by storm.

The plan was perfect: Take nearly every major Stax star to Europe on a package tour and bring along Booker T. and the MG's to back them up. The MG's were strictly a studio band; aside from a very few gigs, they had never backed any of the Stax artists in a concert setting. At first there was considerable grousing about whether some of them would even make the trip. The guys had only recently been put on salary at $125 a week; before that, they were paid by the session and some of them supplemented their income by playing six nights a week at Hernando's Hideaway. Duck Dunn and horn players Wayne

Jackson and Joe Arnold each took home about $15 or $20 every night from their side gigs, and all three seriously considered not going to Europe for the simple reason it would mean losing that steady income. "I knew I needed that gig financially and that I'd need it when I got back," Duck said. "The manager was a guy who felt like he was doing you a favor by giving you a job."

Finally, they were swayed by the money—each member of the band was promised $5,000, and they'd be allowed to bring their spouses along. "Duck and I quit that job [at Hernando's] to go on the Stax/Volt Revue," said Wayne Jackson. "And, believe me, we had to think it over."

They didn't even own stage clothes, so everyone in the band was sent over to Lansky Brothers on Beale Street. It was a clothing store popular with musicians; Elvis had purchased many of his most outlandish suits at Lansky Brothers. Each of the MG's got two Continental mohair suits—one lime green and the other blue.

Deciding whether the MG's were traveling to Europe was just the first of several controversies that swirled around the trip to Europe. Phil was serving as the tour promoter and even though it was called the Stax/Volt Revue, two significant Stax artists weren't coming along—Rufus Thomas and William Bell. Instead Phil added one of Otis's protégés, Arthur Conley, Jr. Not only was Conley not a Stax artist; he was being billed above Sam and Dave. That left a sour taste in the mouths of many at Stax, and it wasn't helped when they arrived in England and found out that programs and ads for the opening night were billing it as the Otis Redding Show rather than the Stax/Volt Revue.

Whether it was a simple error or a deliberate act by Phil, Otis *was* the unquestionable star of the tour. He flew in ahead of everyone to do advance PR, arriving on March 11. Polygram's Roger Cowles once again set up a press party at the airport. "Otis must have met thousands of people on the first visit," he said. "When he came back, he walked into the lounge and he remembered at least half the people there: 'Hello, Dick; hi, Penny, how are you?' It just seemed to come naturally to him."

The London papers heralded the tour with nearly the same kind of hype and hysteria that had greeted the Beatles on their first tour of

America. There were headlines every day. Endless stories featuring the latest press releases about Otis and Sam and Dave. Everyone back in Memphis was oblivious to all the hype and hysteria; they had no idea. And nothing surprised them more than their arrival in London and the bedlam that greeted them at the airport. Fans were waiting for them. The media swarmed around them. The Beatles sent limos to pick them up and then tried to arrange a jam session that never came off because they were finishing up *Sgt. Pepper's Lonely Hearts Club Band.*

The reception they received surprised all of them. "Hell, we were just in Memphis cutting records; we didn't know," Steve Cropper said. "When we got over there, there were hordes of people waiting at the airport. I didn't know what it was all about. They treated us like we were the Beatles or something. It was a mind-blower. It pretty much overwhelmed everybody in the band."

"I was shocked when we got to Europe," Booker T. said. "We were living in a kind of cocoon, just going to the studio every day and making music. Not reading the trade magazines. Not knowing how the rest of the world saw Stax. It was really a surprise. I couldn't believe it—people knew my songs in Scotland and France."

Many of the British fans were just as shocked when they saw the MG's. The band stayed hidden away in the studio all the time and most British fans had never even seen pictures of the MG's; they assumed everyone in the band was black and were quite taken aback to see the pale skin of Duck Dunn and Steve Cropper. "Some people thought I was an English bass player that they'd picked up for the tour," Duck said with a laugh. "They thought 'Duck Dunn' was a black man who'd stayed home and couldn't make it to Europe."

Once they arrived in London, Carla Thomas performed a gig at a London club and the Beatles took a break from *Sgt. Pepper* to go to the show and meet Otis. He was sitting at a table with Jerry Wexler and Phil Walden when the Fab Four arrived. They each lined up and took turns sitting down and chatting with him. "He was the King and they were the peons," said Phil. "He really liked what they were doing and thought they were exceptionally clever."

After that, it was time to get to work. Just because the MG's had backed up all the artists in the studio didn't mean they knew all the songs. They didn't. A studio musician generally learns a song long enough to record it; then he forgets it and moves on to the next one—the life of a studio musician is essentially an assembly-line job and there's no reason to remember a song when they fully expect never to play it again. The MG's had to hustle to relearn much of the Stax songbook, and they had to do it quickly.

The first date of the tour was March 17 at the Finsbury Park Astoria in London before a packed house that matched all the fervor of the greeting they'd received at the airport. The crowd rose to its feet as Booker T. and the MG's walked onstage. The audience cheered the introductions. They cheered after the songs. Sometimes they erupted into spontaneous applause *during* songs. For the *whole* show.

It was a fast-paced revue. The MG's performed three songs, highlighted by "Green Onions," then brought out the horn section—Andrew Love, Wayne Jackson, and Joe Arnold—which performed as the Mar-Keys. With the MG's laying down a meaty groove, the horn players took their turn in the spotlight taking soaring solos on "Last Night" and "Philly Dog." Then came Carla Thomas, who first held the crowd spellbound with a slow and dramatic version of "Yesterday" and then rocked the house with "B-A-B-Y." Arthur Conley followed, singing his brand-new hit, "Sweet Soul Music," followed by Eddie Floyd doing "Knock On Wood" and "Something You Got."

Then came Sam and Dave, determined to make Otis work, to make him work *hard*. It was the Apollo Theatre all over again, except Booker T. and the MG's hadn't been at the Apollo Theatre and they'd never even seen Sam and Dave perform. They'd heard stories but nothing had prepared them for the reality. "Everybody on that show was good, and Sam and Dave was just *incredible*," said Duck. "And Otis had to follow them. He would be backstage peeking from behind the curtain, watching them. And he was a little nervous. But he'd come out there and bust their ass every night. In those days, it was competition. And you just wouldn't think he could follow Sam and Dave. But he did it."

"Every night you would feel sorry for Otis," Wayne Jackson told Stax historian Rob Bowman. "Sam and Dave had taken this audience to heaven and back. They would jump out in the audience and just go crazy like they were having a fit, and then jump back onstage and faint. They would have to carry Dave off like he was dead, and then they would carry him back on like he was resurrected. By the time that was over with, all the wax on the floor was gone, burnt up. Sam and Dave left that stage smoking. The audience was just frothing at the mouth when Sam and Dave left and then when Otis got through with them, it was just total chaos."

By the time London disc jockey Emperor Roscoe came out to introduce Otis, the audience was almost out of control and the Emperor was enough of a showman to milk it. He demanded the crowd spell out Otis's full name, from the "O" in Otis all the way to the "G" in Redding. The crowd shouted out each letter with gusto; in the background women could be heard screaming out, "Otis! Otis!" in swooning voices. When he finally hit the stage, people began rushing forward just to be close to him. "It was like Elvis," said Wayne Jackson. "We had guards along the stage who actually had to keep people off the stage. I mean, drag crying women away. First time I had seen that in person. It was scary. They were crazed, their eyes were glassed over, and they were wanting to be involved with Otis so bad. Otis was amazed by it. He loved it. Of course he egged them on, holding his hand out. He was a master showman."

Steve Cropper was no less astounded. "Very few people I ever met, one of them being Elvis Presley, when they walked into a room all heads turned. And Otis was that dynamic; he was that kind of guy. And when he was onstage, he was just bigger than life. I mean, he was like a god."

The reviews bordered on worship. The *Manchester Evening Post* called Otis "the undisputed King of an outfit which produces music at its richest and earthiest." The *Bristol Evening News* said: "Otis Redding topped it all. 'Satisfaction,' 'My Girl,' and finally 'Try a Little Tenderness' were the pile-drivers that smashed in the final blows of an evening not to be forgotten." *Melody Maker* called it "the rave show to end them all." When a critic at the *Record Mirror* dared to offer the lone voice of dissent, readers flooded the newspaper's office with complaints.

Polygram's Frank Fenter (who would later help Phil Walden found Capricorn Records) had suggested they record a live album in Europe, so Tom Dowd was flown over to tape the opening-night show in London. He had to find equipment and managed to track down two 3-track tape recorders, hardly state-of-the-art machines. He used both recorders simultaneously; he started one of them five minutes after the other so that he wouldn't miss any of the show when a reel of tape ran out and he had to change it. He also recorded a follow-up show in Paris (the only two shows of the tour featuring Carla, who had to return to the States to guest at a civil rights fundraiser).

As Jim Stewart listened to Otis's show, he grew livid—everything was too damned fast! All of it. The MG's tried. They'd come out playing the standard tempo and Otis would stand there with one hand on the microphone and the other hand behind his back gesturing for Al to speed up the pace. And it was killing Al because he didn't like to rush; he liked to set a groove and keep it in the pocket. But Otis insisted—as he told Jaimoe, he wanted all the fast songs played faster and all the slow songs played slower and playing with the MG's in Europe was going to be no exception.

After the show, Jim stormed into Otis's dressing room and demanded that he keep the songs at the same speed as the original recordings. "Otis, you've got to drop those tempos and drop them right now," he said. "We're taping this and trying to make a record."

Otis wasn't about to let someone else dictate how he conducted his concerts. "I'm over *here* playing a fucking date," he shot back. "I make *records* in Memphis, Tennessee. Don't tell me about my tempos. I'm out here entertaining these people. They don't know shit about this record we're making and the tempos are gonna stay. That's my career out there."

Jim Steward looked at him and said with disdain, "You're a fucking *star*."

It was the only time Duck Dunn ever saw Otis get angry. It's no wonder Steve Cropper couldn't imagine Otis using a swear word— he *never* used them at Stax. "After that little conversation in Europe about tempos, I knew he'd lost his temper; I heard him come back saying, '*Fuck him*,'" said Duck Dunn. "Otis told him, 'Jim, this is the way it is. *You* run the record company and *I'll* perform live.' And that's the way it came down. We picked up the tempos and that was just fine with me. I'll tell you, I didn't know I could play that fast."

Stax released no fewer than three concert albums from the Stax/Volt Revue of Europe: *Otis Redding: Live in Europe* and then two others that each featured the other Stax artists on the bill along with one song by Otis. The recording quality was nowhere near the pristine sound of the Whisky à Go Go shows captured by Wally Heider, and they featured that odd Stax stereo mix with Otis's voice, the bass, and the guitar coming out of the left speaker; the drums, the horns, and the organ coming out of the other. But the tapes nonetheless vividly captured the vibrant energy of the tour, especially Otis's set. It was the document that his growing legion of fans had been waiting for—a live concert recorded under the most optimum of circumstances, Otis backed up by Booker T. and the MG's. It quickly became Otis's strongest-selling album, buoyed by the buzz caused by both the Fillmore concerts and the European tour, reaching all the way to #32 on the pop charts.

Triumph that it was, the European tour created ripples that ushered in changes at Stax. On the final chorus of "Try a Little Tenderness" during every show, all of the Stax stars would walk out onstage and sing harmonies with Otis. But at the Paris show, Otis thought Sam was trying to imitate him, show him up. He walked over and grabbed the microphone away from Sam. Otis came back to Macon and told Phil: "Don't bring those monkeys in front of me in no kind of way. I don't want to see them again."

"Sam tried to communicate with Otis a couple of times and got no response," said Newt Collier. "Otis would not acknowledge anything. Otis didn't want to be dealing with Sam and Dave no more and they pulled out from Phil's office and booked themselves in the Apollo Theatre. And then 'Soul Man' came out. Their bookings were unbelievable from that point on. Then they picked up the best musicians they could find. Drove me from playing lead trumpet to playing trombone. Couldn't handle pressure of all those trumpet players. They were scorching me; I used to be the one scorching the other horn players. It even got to the point that Sam and Dave did *The Ed Sullivan Show*. Otis never got that far."

The tour also strained relations between Phil Walden and Jim Stewart over Arthur Conley, between Otis and Jim over tempos. Besides that, Otis and Phil weren't as tight anymore. Phil's intensity was sometimes too overbearing for Otis, and the hassles produced by Phil's rift with Jim Stewart didn't help since everyone thought Jim had a very valid point—Arthur Conley *didn't* belong on a Stax/Volt revue.

Otis also faced lingering resentment from the star treatment he had received in Europe. He got the suites in the top hotels; everyone else stayed in single rooms at the cheaper places. He traveled in better cars. He got the bulk of the press attention. "Everybody got mad at Otis for a while," said Stax songwriter Joe Shamwell. "It all kind of went to his head, and Otis started to grandstand and act like they were his peons. It was like he was the sole architect of Stax's success."

Steve Cropper found himself faced with similar kinds of resentment. In the middle of the tour, the Stax brass convened a meeting. The agenda was limited to a single item: Al Bell was threatening to leave unless there were changes. Specifically, he wanted Steve removed as the label's A&R man, the chief talent scout and coordinator. "I got singled out," Steve said. "I was doing a lot of interviews and there was a lot of animosity. I thought I was doing the guys a favor. We had a meeting in Al Bell's room one night. Some things were said; there were some bad feelings that I never, ever got over. I was given in no uncertain terms: 'Change your ways or else.' Well, change what ways? We're all in this together. They seemed to take it like I was in it for myself. All of sudden, I wasn't A&R director anymore. I was still a member of the band. I was still making the same money. But I had no stick. My stick was taken away and given to Al Bell."

In many ways, no one had enjoyed the trip. They were completely unsophisticated, unaware of the ways of the world and experiencing new cultures they didn't understand or appreciate. Rather than feasting on the exotic food, they detested it because it was different. Faced with a particularly stuffy waiter at one restaurant, Duck Dunn looked up from the menu and dryly asked if they had any fatback cacciatore. "The food was terrible," said Duck. "Just horrible. All I could eat was boiled eggs and baked potatoes. The rest of it, horrible. The lettuce was like wet newspapers. It was a great time. But it was also the longest five weeks of my life."

Would he trade the experience? Never. "I was just twenty-seven years old," he said. "That was when I was at my absolute best. And Otis did it. He caused it; he made me do it. I know it's me, but he made me do it. He made all of us better. He wore that halo. There ain't too many people who wear that crown. Elvis wore it. Frank Sinatra. And, boy, Otis wore it. He knew it. He *was* a goddamn star."

Shake!

Otis had only been home from Europe for a matter of days when Phil got a phone call from Andrew Loog Oldham, the manager of the Rolling Stones. Oldham said he was helping to organize a music festival in Monterey, California, that they expected 100,000 people to attend. He told Phil that everyone wanted Otis on the bill; his performances at the Fillmore were reaching legendary status around the Bay Area and this could be his finest hour. In fact, Oldham promised that Monterey was going to be the defining moment of the sixties, a three-day celebration of peace, love, and great music.

Phil got right to the point: "How much money are we talking?"

Oldham explained that all the bands would perform for free. This was an event that transcended financial considerations. Yes, they would charge admission but all the profits would be donated to charity. Phil listened to the pitch and told Oldham that he'd have to check with Otis and look at the schedule, then get back with him. In other words, he brushed Oldham off.

In truth Phil smelled a rip-off, and he wasn't the only one. The Monterey Pop Festival had been a hard sell from the moment it was conceived by a rock promoter named Ben Shapiro. Music festivals were a growing tradition in other styles of music, most notably the Newport Jazz Festival and the companion Newport Folk Festival in Rhode Island. And there was the famed Monterey Jazz Festival. But nobody had ever tried to pull one off using rock 'n' roll bands.

Shapiro saw it as an event to celebrate the burgeoning hippie movement blossoming out of San Francisco's Haight-Ashbury district. The concept was nice enough but the Grateful Dead and other Bay Area bands—groups the promoters were counting on to legitimize the festival in San Francisco's hippie community—were every bit as suspicious as Phil. They feared they were going to be flimflammed by capitalistic promoters who saw the hippie movement as nothing more than a potential cash cow. The idea of donating all the profits of a festival to charity was appealing. But nobody would say *which* charities or *how much* money. And even if that was legit, the promoters still stood to make a mint on film and album rights while the musicians themselves would walk away with nary a penny for their efforts.

After the hippie bands failed to embrace the concept, the leadership of the festival was handed over to John Phillips of the Mamas and the Papas and his manager, Lou Adler, on the theory they would be better equipped to win the confidence of their contemporaries. They enlisted Derek Taylor, the former publicist for the Beatles, who signed on as the festival's press agent. One of the first people the new organizers contacted was Bill Graham. They wanted his advice in booking the event. Even more, they wanted his presence to lend Monterey a much-needed air of credibility. Graham listened to their plans and agreed to help, eventually putting up $10,000 to help finance the festival. With that, Monterey was finally rolling forward and building a sense of momentum.

Phil was both intrigued by and skeptical of the idea of Monterey. If it went like the Fillmore gigs, it could be an immediate and powerful entree into the world of white rock 'n' roll. If it didn't—if Otis got in front of thousands of hippies flying on psychedelic drugs and failed to connect with them—it could be a devastating blow to his career. He might never get another chance, forever tainted by the failure; something like that would simply destroy every trace of forward progress they'd worked so hard to achieve. And it certainly didn't escape Phil's notice that every other soul act the promoters had contacted about Monterey had turned them down; they saw it as too much of a risk, performing before a culture that was completely alien to them. It was Bill Graham's involvement that made Otis and Phil feel easier about the whole deal. And then Jerry Wexler called and urged Phil to go for it.

There was just one hitch—Otis had broken up his road band before going to Europe because he planned to take some time off. If Otis was going to perform, they'd have to get Booker T. and the MG's to back him up. It wasn't as simple as it sounded because Phil and Jim were barely speaking to each other. Phil had to ask Jerry Wexler to call Memphis to find out if the MG's could take time off from the studio to go play with Otis at Monterey. Jim agreed, but only two of the three horn players made the trip—Joe Arnold had gone back to playing at Hernando's Hideaway and the owner wouldn't let him have the time off.

By then the festival was beginning to take shape. Otis was in. Jefferson Airplane had signed on. So had Country Joe and the Fish. The Byrds agreed to be there. But the Grateful Dead still refused to perform until the organizers agreed to appoint a board of governors that included Mick Jagger and Paul McCartney to oversee the distribution of profits to suitable charities. With that, the Dead at last relented, signaling that the hippies of Haight-Ashbury would embrace the proceedings.

The Monterey International Pop Festival was *on*.

Monterey was the first rock festival and, with all due apologies to Woodstock, quite possibly also the best.

"So much of Monterey had nothing to do with logistics or planning," Bill Graham mused. "The bird just landed there. No rules, no instructions. It also said a lot to me about northern California. So much of it could *never* have happened anywhere else." Much of what happened at Monterey was dictated by the times. The audience was a group of kids who believed they were going to change the world. They shared a bond and that bond united them—ending the war in Vietnam, fighting the military machine with flower power. To the kids, this was a force far greater than a three-day music festival. It was an event dripping in symbolism, taking the legacy of the Monterey Pop Festival to mythical proportions. This wasn't just some rock concert—it was the Summer of Love's Grand Ball.

The three-day festival, held at the Monterey fairgrounds, began on June 16, 1967. The hippies came by the thousands. Conservative estimates put the crowd at 55,000 although some say it went closer to 100,000. Some had tickets, some didn't; after a while, it didn't seem to matter. The kids began gathering the day before the festival and the fairgrounds became an instant commune of tents and trailers and multicolored buses. The organizers flew in 100,000 orchid blossoms from Hawaii and everyone entering the festival on Friday was handed a flower. People were clad in their most outlandish clothing of bold colors and psychedelic patterns, expressions of liberation and freedom. Famed LSD guru Augustus Stanley Owsley III showed up with hundreds of tabs of "purple acid" that were discreetly passed around the crowd, perhaps one reason that couples could be seen breaking out in spontaneous dance. The cops made the decision to turn the other way when they saw someone toking on a joint. And the kids responded by overwhelming the cops with kindness. The Monterey Police Department had feared mass riots; they had put the local National Guard on alert and imported in over two hundred police officers from surrounding areas. By the second day of the festival, half of the imported cops had been sent home—the crowd was that tame, that well-behaved.

Most of the musicians had rooms at a strip of low-rent motels behind the fairgrounds and it quickly developed into a free-form party. At some point Jerry Garcia mentioned that a jam session might be nice. The idea quickly gained enthusiasm and the Dead's road crew began setting up a makeshift stage and a PA system out where many of the kids were camping out. Later that night, the lights came on and out walked Garcia and Jimi Hendrix, along with musicians from Jefferson Airplane. There was a second jam Saturday morning featuring musicians from the Grateful Dead, the Byrds, and the Who. Kids were waking up in their sleeping bags to the sounds of Eric Burdon singing "House of the Rising Sun" with Pete Townshend on lead guitar—trying to figure out whether this was real or some strange acid hangover.

The first night of the festival felt like a warm-up for what was to come. Simon and Garfunkel, who had just scored a hit with "Sounds of Silence," headlined. The Animals performed. Representing a more pop sound were Johnny Rivers and the Association. Lou Rawls was one of the few black performers on the bill and seemed to turn off much of the crowd when he began playing Vegas-styled songs such as "On a Clear Day I Can See Forever."

Otis was handed the coveted closing spot for Saturday night and arrived that afternoon with what seemed a big entourage: band members, girlfriends, friends. Janis Joplin trailed Otis all day like a devoted puppy. Ever since the Fillmore shows, she had walked around telling anybody who'd listen that "Otis is God, man." Most of the musicians were too intimidated by Otis and his entourage to try to approach him. But they couldn't take their eyes off of him. It was like watching a king parade around with his court. And they were all amused by Janis Joplin's obvious worship, how she lustfully fawned over Otis.

Pigpen, the Dead's piano player, couldn't resist teasing her: "So," he asked, "does God have a big dick?"

"Only if you believe in him," Janis shot back.

In the hours before his performance, Otis was understandably nervous. He fully understood the stakes, that his entire career was riding on this one show. When he arrived backstage, he began to focus. Everything was fine. This was just another gig. He'd just spent a whole month in Europe having to walk on stages freshly scorched by Sam and Dave, every single night. Now, *that* was pressure. This? This was *nothing*, man.

The music began early on Saturday afternoon. Electric Flag performed. So did Janis Joplin, with Big Brother and the Holding Company. Steve Miller was there. Paul Butterfield. Canned Heat. Country Joe and the Fish. The Byrds. Laura Nyro. The last act before Otis was Jefferson Airplane, riding high on the strength of "Somebody to Love." Otis was standing in the wings, quietly watching the Airplane wrap up their set, when Phil walked up and asked if he'd given Steve Cropper a set list. Otis shook his head and Phil gave him a look of consternation; by now, Phil was even more tightly wound than Otis. As always, there was too much to worry about. There hadn't been time for a rehearsal—just Otis, Steve, Duck, and Booker gathering in a hotel room to quickly go over the set and try to knock off some rust before they went out there before the biggest crowd and most important gig of their lives. On top of that, Phil had had to listen to static from some of the MG's because they had flown all the way to California and thought they deserved to perform an entire set before Otis took the stage. Phil's opinion was that he was being more than generous in giving the MG's and the Mar-Keys one song each. Then a light rain began falling just before Otis went on and there was fear that the performance might have to be abbreviated or canceled altogether because of concerns the musicians could get electrocuted. And now here was yet another crisis: Otis was spacing out and had no idea what songs he was going to perform. Phil couldn't believe it. "We're going on in about ten fuckin' minutes," he snapped. "Don't you think we ought to have a set list?"

"Yeah, sure," Otis calmly replied. "What do you want us to do?"

Phil thought back to Europe. They'd only had about twenty or so minutes onstage. Otis needed to make an immediate impression and then follow it up hard. Phil suggested starting with "Shake." If the energy behind that song didn't grab the crowd, then nothing would. From there, they quickly came up with a five-song set.

The MG's took the stage to perform "Green Onions" and the contrast with the groups that had preceded them was striking. The most immediate difference was their look. All the other bands were clad in hippie attire—bell-bottoms, buckskin jackets with fringe, multicolored serapes and shirts. Everyone's hair was long and flowing, often wrapped with streaming headbands or resting under funky-looking top hats. And then came the MG's, looking as if they had gotten lost on the way to play a senior prom at the country club. Their hair was slicked back and neatly combed. They were clad in the lime-green mohair suits they had purchased at Lansky Brothers for the European tour; Al Jackson was the lone holdout, and he wore a pastel yellow suit jacket and a green turtleneck sweater. Even their amplifiers seemed out of place, tiny and toylike compared with the huge stacks of sound equipment the other groups had used.

If anyone in the crowd was tempted to ridicule them, that impulse quickly evaporated. They were suddenly confronted with a band that could *swing*, that could effortlessly lay down a groove the rest of the bands at Monterey could only envy. The MG's were men among boys. They knew what to do, and how to do it. The beat was aimed at the feet, and it was absolutely irresistible.

In the spirit of the festival, Otis pulled out a joint and lit it up while the MG's performed. Phil turned around and couldn't believe his eyes. "Man, don't smoke that shit now! Not before we go on."

"Aw, fuck, don't worry about it, man," Otis calmly responded. By now, he was *ready*. He was in a space where nothing intruded, focus on nothing but the task at hand. "Everything's all right. It's just a fuckin' show."

It was about one o'clock in the morning when comedian Tommy Smothers came out to introduce Otis. A light drizzle was falling and some of the crowd was beginning to leave. Then Otis bounded out onstage and groaned, "Oh!" to the dramatic flurry of horns pumping out the introduction to "Shake." Otis grooved his shoulders to the sassy beat, wrapped in the effervescent glow of a star being born. He was dressed in a dark green silk suit. His shoulders bounced to the beat of the drums. His smile seemed to cover the entire stage. And then he did something no one in the MG's expected—instead of going into the first verse as he'd always done, Otis sang just one word— "Shake!" There was a moment of confusion, but Al quickly fell in behind him and softly held the beat.

Otis used those first few moments to do what few others had done that day—he bonded with the crowd. He pulled the microphone off the stand and sang out, "Everybody say it, 'Shake!' " He picked up the mike stand, set it off to the side, and the message was clear: Gotta have some room to *move* up here. "Let me hear the whole crowd!" he demanded, raising his left hand and pointing his index finger at them like a magician waving his wand and weaving a spell. " 'Shake!' " By then the response was a loud roar. Otis was bouncing on the balls of his feet in time to the beat. His glee and excitement were intoxicating, impossible for the crowd to resist. "A little bit louder!" he teased them.

"Shake!" they screamed back.

"Early in the mornin'!"

"Shake!"

"Later in the evenin'!"

"Shake!"

"In the midnight hour!"

"Shake!"

"When the times goin' bad!"

"Shake!"

"Shake with the feelin'!"

"Shake!"

"Shake with the feelin'!"

Otis gave the band a subtle cue and finally went into the first verse. And just like that, he *had* them. The crowd had been there all day and hadn't seen anything like this. Otis prowled the stage as if it was his territory, his domain. People in front of the stage pushed forward, wanting to be close to this man, to touch him and to *see* him. Even the crew filming the festival under the direction of D. A. Pennebaker was transfixed. "Anywhere after Booker T. and the MG's, the film is completely red," said Chip Monck, a member of the crew. "I just said, 'Go to frame six, guys—wow, this is fucking groovy.' Pennebaker was *not* pleased. Everybody went to frame six, we took off the headsets, and we sat there, just sort of gazing at the stage."

If Jim Stewart had been upset that the tempos were fast in Paris, he would have had a complete stroke in Monterey. "Shake" moved at breakneck speed and Otis kept pushing the tempo faster and faster. By the end, Al's eyes were glued to Otis. The faster Otis jumped up and down, the faster Al pushed the beat until finally it seemed as if the song didn't end so much as it erupted. Otis was as breathless as a sprinter after a 200-meter dash as he caught his breath and thanked the crowd.

He introduced the next song, "Respect," with a gentle tease of Aretha Franklin. She had released her own heavily rearranged and anthematic version of "Respect" while Otis was in Europe—it had gone straight to #1, not just on the R&B charts but on the pop charts as well. "This is another one of mine," Otis said. "This is a song that a girl took away from me, a good friend of mine." He laughed as he said it, as if he recognized the irony of kidding someone else about stealing "Respect." "This girl, she just took this song. But I'm still gonna do it anyway." With that, the MG's kicked off a stampeding version of "Respect." Otis threw things off when he forgot the second verse and instead jumped straight to the bridge. The MG's hung with him and Otis quickly adjusted the melody to make the mistake all but unnoticeable. By the closing vamp, Otis was pulling out all the stops. With Duck Dunn playing a throbbing series of bass runs, his demand for respect became a clarion call to the audience of young white kids. "Got-ta! Got-ta! Have it! Respect! Got-ta! Got-ta! Respect! Everything I want, give it to me! Respect!"

Otis had worked the crowd into a frenzy, and backstage there were nervous cops breathing down John Phillips's neck. They may have been sympathetic to peace and love but when they saw the kids rushing the stage area and dancing they saw a potential riot threatening to break out. They told Phillips they were going pull the plug on the show unless people got back into their chairs and calmed down. As the ovation for "Respect" died down, Phillips called Otis over to the side of the stage. "We've got a problem," he said. "We've got to get everybody in their chairs again."

Otis smiled incredulously. "I thought that was the whole idea, to get 'em up!"

"Otis, they're going to pull the plug on the electricity if we don't get everything down again."

Otis didn't bat an eye. "Okay, I can take care of that."

As he approached the crowd again, Otis was still catching his breath. "This is the love crowd, right?" he said. "We all love each other, don't we? Am I *right!*" The crowd responded with an enthusiastic "Yeah!" Otis knew exactly how to play them, how to make a crowd feel as if they were an integral part of the show, as if this wasn't so much a concert as a private party. He flashed another big smile. Then he dipped his knees, cupped his hand to his ear, and called out, "Let me hear ya say, 'Yeah!' " Once again the response was boisterous.

His smile suddenly faded. His eyes shut and his face turned sorrowful as he began singing: "I've been lovin' you too long, to stop now." The words came slow, lonely, and aching until the first verse concluded with that emphatic three-note horn burst. There was a brief, dramatic silence and Otis was supposed to begin singing the second verse. Instead he threw yet another curve ball at the MG's. A mischievous smile appeared on his face and he turned around to Al. "Can we do that just one more time, Al, just like that?" The drummer executed a drum roll and as the horns again rang out that dramatic triplet of notes Otis rolled his body to the beat. Again the stage was quiet. Otis's grin grew bigger. He looked over his shoulder at the horn players. "Do it just one more time. One more." They played the riff a third time. The crowd was screaming and Otis's grin was even wider.

"Do it just one more time!" he called out. Then, as suddenly as he had broken the mood, he slipped right back into the song and began singing the second verse with an aching vulnerability that was at once touching and entrancing.

When the song ended, Otis hardly paused for a breath before he cried out, "Jump again!" He began snapping his fingers and shouted, "Here we go!" and they launched into "Satisfaction." Like "Shake," the song zipped along at a frenetic pace. Just when the song seemed to be moving toward a climax, Otis hoarsely and almost awkwardly yelled out, "Bring it down!" Al brought the beat to a leisurely stroll while Otis ad-libbed over the quiet backbeat. After a moment, he put his left hand behind his back and began gesturing for Al to pick it back up again. Al slowly drove the beat faster and faster and faster and faster, until Otis at last turned and signaled for an ending.

"Satisfaction" whipped the crowd into a second frenzy and Otis only encouraged it by waving and walking offstage as if the show were over. He quickly returned for the finale: "Try a Little Tenderness." Otis walked to the microphone and dedicated the song to "all the miniskirts." The audience sat enchanted and entranced. Brian Jones of the Rolling Stones was one of many in tears. Jimi Hendrix, who would make his own American breakthrough the following night when he set his Fender Stratocaster on fire onstage, watched in quiet reverence. So did members of the Grateful Dead. By the climax of the song, the crowd was rising to its feet to scream and cheer. After singing the vamp four times, Otis put down the microphone, stretched out both hands, and walked offstage. The crowd kept on screaming and he quickly returned to sing it one last time.

Backstage, John Phillips rushed up to Phil Walden: "God, that was just so incredible! *So* incredible!"

Phil just smugly looked at him. "John," he said, "he does that every single night."

By all measures, it was a triumphant performance. In just twenty minutes onstage, Otis had taken the crowd at Monterey on a musical roller-coaster of emotions that left them exhilarated and drained. "Hendrix and the Who were our personal favorites," said Rock Scully, the Dead's co-manager. "But when Otis Redding showed up, he put

Townshend and Hendrix in the shade. Forget about the flaming gui-
tars and exploding drum kits. Otis was a force of nature, just a living
blur of energy."

Rock critic Jon Landau, who would go on to write for *Rolling Stone*
and later become Bruce Springsteen's manager, wrote that Otis represented rock's "past, present, and future . . . Otis Redding's performances constitute, as a whole, the highest level of expression rock
'n' roll has yet attained. . . . Otis Redding *is* rock 'n' roll."

Even considering the excitement of the European tour, Monterey
was still a revelation for the MG's. Europe wasn't home; this was.
"Monterey was a wake-up call," Booker T. said. "We'd just come back
from Europe and we had acceptance there. We had never had acceptance from [a white] audience in the United States. It was like Monterey should have been in Germany or maybe Holland, *but it was
California.* It was our first announcement that something new was
happening culturally and musically in the United States. The police-
men were gone. We were led into the concert by Hell's Angels. They
were protecting us! It was a completely different feeling. History was
changing at that moment and we knew it."

The next day, Otis and Phil rented a car and drove down to Los
Angeles for a couple of days before they had to head back north to
San Francisco for another stand at the Fillmore. When they got to
L.A., they went to eat breakfast and Phil bought a copy of the *Los
Angeles Times.* His eyes widened when he read the review: "The Fes-
tival really took off when Otis Redding got up onstage," it said.

Phil read it aloud, then looked up. *"Otis.* We fucking *killed* them
up there."

Otis didn't need to read a review to know what had happened—
you'd have to have been deaf, dumb, and blind to have missed it. Phil
could get wound up quick, and Otis enjoyed teasing him. "You're
shitting me," he said innocently. "That little ol' show? You mean we
did okay?"

"Yeah," Phil said, his voice growing in excitement. "It says so right
here. We were the *best* thing there."

"Wow," Otis said with a straight face. "You believe that?" And he
chuckled at Phil all the way to San Francisco.

Sittin' on the Dock of the Bay

Otis was intrigued by the new rock 'n' roll scene he had encountered at Monterey. While the drug use had shocked Phil and the guys in the MG's, it didn't faze Otis much. No matter how much it seemed to surprise Phil, it was nothing for Otis to smoke pot. Otis was, after all, from Bellevue. His best friend was Huck. And Huck was the man when people around Bellevue wanted to get their dope. Besides, musicians were always around drugs and Otis's backup bands were no exception. His longtime saxophonist, Shang-a-Lang, was hooked on heroin. Sometimes when Shang would wear sunglasses to hide the smack-induced glaze in his eyes, Otis would embarrass him and make him take them off. But he also showed moments of compassion, understanding the power heroin can have over people. They were playing in Texas one time when Shang ran out of smack; rather than watch his friend suffer through withdrawal, Otis sent someone to New York City to score a bag for Shang.

The psychedelics and free love and free spirit of Monterey amused Otis as much as anything else; but the music—the music had absolutely captivated him. He was intrigued by the way the white kids weaved tapestries of sound that stretched the definitions of rock 'n' roll. After listening to the Beatles and Bob Dylan, Otis began to question his long-held belief that the words didn't matter so long as you had the groove. The Beatles had released the groundbreaking *Sgt. Pepper's Lonely Hearts Club Band* a couple of weeks prior to Monterey, and Otis wore out his copy, playing it over and over and over. "He dissected the *Sgt. Pepper* album, trying to figure out what they were doing," Phil said. "I'd get him Bob Dylan albums and stuff like that. It was an awareness of people like Dylan and the Beatles that made him much more conscious of the importance of lyrics."

While Otis was in San Francisco for his gig at the Fillmore, he and
Speedo Sims stayed on a rented houseboat on the Bay in Sausalito.
It was an idyllic setting, peaceful and reflective, and Otis began writing a song there that offered the first tangible sign of a modern rock
influence on his music. He didn't have it all, but he had a melody and
he had a title: "(Sittin' on) The Dock of the Bay." He also had the
first couple of lines: "Sittin' in the morning sun / I'll be sittin' when
the evening comes." It wasn't much, but it was enough to know it
was a completely different song, unlike anything he had ever written.
It couldn't even be described as R&B. In fact, it was even closer to
folk than it was to rock 'n' roll. Every afternoon Otis would sit on
the boat and play the chords on his acoustic guitar while Speedo kept
a beat by slapping his legs. "We must have been out there three or
four days before I could get any concept as to where he was going
with the song," Speedo said. "I just didn't understand it. And, lyrically,
it sounded weird to me. He was changing with the times, is what was
happening. And I was looking at the times change."

Otis didn't talk about it with very many people, but the new song
also was a reflection of a growing inner turmoil, both personally and
professionally. Everything in his life suddenly seemed to be swirling,
and Otis was contemplating essential changes in his life. In a way he
felt as if he was being reborn. And in being reborn, he felt an overwhelming need to shed everything from his old life. It began with
Zelma. Otis had come to the realization that he had outgrown his
wife. While she stayed at home raising their children, he had traveled
the world and experienced things she could never understand. Her
worldview didn't travel very far outside the city limits of Macon. It
was no secret there were women on the road; they threw themselves
at him in ways that few men could have resisted. Otis was even
known to have a white girlfriend in Macon. Now things had changed.
Otis told Huck and other friends that he had fallen in love with another woman. And that other woman was Carla Thomas.

The discontent didn't stop with his marriage. Otis was beginning
to feel constrained by Stax Records. Part of that was Otis's ambition
to be more than just a recording star. It wasn't enough to merely
make it as a singer. People could attribute that to natural talent, as
if he had nothing at all to do with it. He wanted to prove that he

could be a success at whatever he wanted to do in music; that it wasn't a fluke of nature, that it was *him*—high-school dropout or not, kid from Bellevue or not. As his career progressed, Otis had slowly developed his skills as a businessman. He had studied Phil. He had listened and learned. Like Phil, he had the nerves of a poker player. One afternoon not long after the release of "Mr. Pitiful," Otis happened to be at the office and answered the phone when someone called to book a gig. Otis sat down on the desk and listened, then shook his head and said emphatically, "No, no, no; my price now is a thousand dollars."

The other person protested. "What? You think you're James Brown?"

"No, baby," Otis shot back. "I'm the Big O." And he hung up the phone.

Otis and Phil hadn't started Jotis Records as a goof. Otis was serious. He wanted to discover new talent, write songs for them, and produce their records. And Arthur Conley had proven that he could pull it off. Arthur was nineteen years old when he was signed to Jotis Records in 1965. He recorded his first single. It flopped and Jotis Records was quickly retired. The label was distributed by Stax and it seemed as if Stax never lifted a finger to promote the record. When Jotis folded, they didn't move Arthur's contract to Stax; instead they signed with Atco Records, a subsidiary of Atlantic Records. One of two things had happened: Either Jim Stewart had just slapped them in the face by refusing to sign Conley, or else they had just slapped Jim in the face by taking Conley to Atlantic. Neither scenario allowed for pleasant relations.

Arthur Conley seemed to personify the growing friction between Memphis and Macon. And it went far beyond the fact that Phil had placed Conley on the bill for the Stax/Volt tour. It had begun months earlier when Otis had written a song called "Sweet Soul Music." He had thought it was going to be a huge hit; Jim didn't like it and his contract with Otis gave him veto power over the material Otis could record. Otis was not to be deterred. Not only did he give the song to Arthur Conley; he went with Conley to record at Stax's new rival— the studio in Muscle Shoals where Jerry Wexler was now taking all of Atlantic's soul acts, from Aretha Franklin to Wilson Pickett. And it didn't help matters that Jim was completely wrong about the song. "He believed in that song and Stax refused to put it out, told him he'd have to get somebody else to sing it," said Wayne Cochran. "Boy, he had that touch. Listen to that song. The introduction and the harmony in the middle come from a classical song. But nobody relates to the fact they heard it every single day on the radio and TV, a thousand times a day. It was the Marlboro theme song."

"Sweet Soul Music" was a huge hit and also raised an old ghost for Otis—accusations of plagiarism. Otis not only lifted the horn riff from the Marlboro commercials; the song's melody was pretty much directly lifted from an obscure Sam Cooke album cut. Cooke's publishing company promptly filed a lawsuit, and there was a quick settlement that gave Cooke partial songwriting credit and a share of the royalties for his estate; Otis also agreed to record more of Cooke's songs—hardly a concession considering he'd included at least one Sam Cooke song on virtually every album he had ever recorded.

If taking Arthur Conley to Muscle Shoals sent a not-so-subtle message to Stax, Otis took things a step further when he recorded there himself. Even though his contract with Stax specifically required him to record exclusively in Memphis, he cut a rough demo of an original called "You Left the Water Running" at Muscle Shoals. It was a spartan production, with Muscle Shoals owner Rick Hall drumming on a box, Phil keeping the beat with a tambourine, and Otis playing acoustic guitar. Still, Otis didn't take the song to Stax; he offered it to Atlantic's Wilson Pickett, who recorded it in Muscle Shoals for his *Wicked Pickett* album.

None of that went unnoticed in Memphis. "I heard he was actually thinking about parting ways with Stax," said Duck Dunn. "He did 'Sweet Soul Music' and he started producing. He was thinking about starting a label—that's a guess, but there's no doubt that Atlantic would have backed him. There's no telling what he had in the back of his mind after his contracts were up. Because the man was a genius. He could do anything. He could produce. He could write. He could sing. He could just do anything."

Meanwhile Otis was telling friends that he planned to leave Stax; even though he was contractually bound to the label through 1970, loopholes could always be found. Late that summer Otis performed in Miami. Wayne Cochran was living there and went to see his old friend, who was staying in the Presidential Suite at the Fountaine-bleau Hotel. "He told me that he had just agreed to sign—him and the artists he managed—with Atlantic," Wayne said. "The front money was something like $6 million. Nobody had ever done such a thing. He was about to transfer it all to Atlantic, and Stax would basically exist no more because Otis [and Phil] managed all their artists."

Otis also called Jerry Wexler and asked him to produce his next album. He said he wanted to move to a more polished sound, something on the scale of Ray Charles. Jerry was flattered, but openly wondered about the political implications with Jim Stewart at Stax. "No sweat, Jerry," Otis told him. "I'll take care of that part of it."

And a move away from Stax wasn't the only change in the air. Otis also was kicking around the idea of severing the very relationship that had helped catapult him to stardom, with Phil Walden. He told friends he was growing disenchanted. There were money issues, even rumors floating around that Phil had ties to gangsters. Johnny Jenkins saw the changes in Phil from his first days as manager for the Pine-toppers. "Back then, Phil was like a brother. He was somebody that cared and he was somebody that would stand by me," said Johnny. "I think another organization got into him, financing, and they didn't know how to handle it and didn't know where he was coming from. You know, it's like a person who's been without—all of sudden they get it and they don't know how to handle it. They don't realize there's always an end to every beginning. Yeah, he was like a brother. We all drank together. We played and sung and if we needed anything, we'd go to Phil to get it. And then all the people started taking over, dressed up in them black suits. They come to see you and then they got different ideas."

Johnny is cryptic about identifying the people he is referring to. "I don't really want to get into it. That's a long time ago. You asking me what he was like and I was just telling you. He was like a brother. And all this other stuff that took place, it really wasn't the Phil I knew. Success can change you. You get that kind of money, you get involved in them kind of people, then you can't turn back."

Success certainly had changed Phil. He always had a quick temper. He could be guided by his ego. He didn't take "no" easily. His and

Otis's relationship had begun to falter as far back as Phil's return from the Army. When Ploonie was playing in Otis's road band in 1965, he walked over to the new office Phil and Otis had bought on Cotton Avenue. As he drew close, he heard loud voices coming from the alley and realized that Phil and Otis were arguing. Phil wanted to buy the rest of the block, from the alley on up to the traffic light, and Otis thought it was a bad idea. "I just turned around and walked out," Ploonie said. "When we had the Pinetopper band, they were just like this (*two fingers twisted together*). They got along good. Phil was a nice guy. Then when he got big, I don't know, it wasn't like it used to be. You could see things; you could hear things. It was a business thing with those two. And it's a complicated business."

One person Otis confided in was his father. Mr. Redding had begun taking an active interest in his son's career; no longer could he argue that Otis Jr. was on a fast road leading nowhere. And there were no more comments about Otis being his "worst" son. In August of 1966, Otis had formed a company called Otis Redding Enterprises and given 60 percent interest to his father and another small percentage to his brother, Luther Rodgers. And eventually Mr. Redding began telling close friends that he was going to become his son's business manager.

"I think that was one of the Reverend Redding's shortcomings," said the Reverend Moses Dumas, who had helped Mr. Redding enter the ministry. "He was worried down until the boy started to making money. Then he saw, 'This ain't so bad after all!' He told me he was going to resign from pastoring to manage his son's business. That's something I couldn't quite comprehend, that he'd want to resign to manage something that he at one time thought was the 'worst' thing! But the money starts. [Otis] gave his daddy that car and that house. You take a person who comes up rough, has very little, and starts living with the upper class, it's bound to have some effect. There ain't no *ifs*, *ands*, or *buts* about it. There's no need for me or anybody else to try to crucify him for that because that's just life."

Before he could go back on the road, Otis needed a new band since he'd broken up his old group before the European tour. He didn't have to look far; a young six-piece group called the Bar-Kays was serving as the second-string studio band at Stax and looking for steady work. They were a William Bell discovery, students from his old junior high school. William began using them on his weekend gigs and at a little club he owned in Memphis. They had auditioned at Stax several times, but Steve Cropper always turned them down. Then Jim Stewart heard about them and suggested they stop by the studio on a day Steve wasn't around. They showed up on March 13, 1967, and recorded an instrumental called "Soul Finger" that turned into a monster hit for Stax, reaching #3 on the R&B charts and #17 on the pop. But being the MG's understudy at Stax essentially meant they got to sit around and watch a lot more often than they actually got to play. When Otis found out a hot rhythm section was standing handy at Stax, he quickly grabbed them up.

Otis was eager to build on Monterey, and to do it quickly. But it didn't happen. The years of singing night after night after night on the road had taken a toll and his voice had simply given out. Otis was worried for months; his voice grew hoarse and his throat always seemed sore. "Otis kept talking about his voice a lot, whether he was gonna *have* a voice," Ploonie said. "He was really worried about it. He'd say, 'I'm a little worried about my voice. I don't know how long it's going to last.' You can tell the difference in his songs. Like 'Your One and Only Man' and 'That's How Strong My Love Is,' the voice was strong. And after that, you can tell the difference. The 'Fa-Fa' song, you could tell it there. It's not strong like it was on the other tunes: The range wasn't there no more."

His throat had especially bothered him on the Stax/Volt tour in Europe. He'd often spend the hours before a show sipping hot tea with honey and lemon. And in Monterey his voice had seemed to give out altogether during the vamp on "Satisfaction." Otis was suffering from a common malady for singers with no formal training. Stage and opera singers learn to draw their voices from their chest and belly; untrained singers typically sing from the throat, which can tear the soft tissue in the larynx. Then, when the wounds heal, they create calluses. Otis finally went to a doctor and found out he had polyps in his larynx. Left untreated, the condition could ruin his voice—it also was potentially cancerous.

Rest wouldn't help. The prognosis was surgery. Otis was terrified. There was a chance he could lose his voice altogether. How cruelly ironic that would be—a singer poised to become a star just as he learns he can no longer sing. Phil found a throat specialist in New York City who assured Otis that surgery would cure his problem; all he had to do was stay silent for about six weeks afterwards to give his larynx time to heal. No singing. No talking. Nothing. While they were waiting for test results, Otis told the specialist about his life in Georgia and how much he enjoyed hunting. The doctor was so charmed by Otis that he offered a deal: He'd waive his fee if Otis would give him a 30.06 rifle with a scope.

Otis finished up his concert commitments and then cleared out two months beginning just before Labor Day. Before he went under the knife, he threw a massive party at his farm in Round Oak. There was a disc jockey convention in Atlanta that drew a slew of R&B music-industry people, and Otis invited four or five hundred of them to a backyard barbecue. It was hardly a convenient time—Zelma was in the midst of overseeing a remodeling of their house, including a new swimming pool in the backyard. Otis was frantic to get everything done in time, even though he didn't get home from a tour until the day before the party. That also was the day they put the finishing touches on the swimming pool; it held 90,000 gallons of water and there just wasn't time to fill it up before the guests arrived. Otis was frustrated. He told Zelma that he was going to call the fire department and ask them to bring out a truck to fill it up.

"Otis, please," she replied. "It'll be all right. They might not *want* to swim."

It was an elaborate affair. They cooked five hogs and two cows for dinner. Otis had the guests bused in from Atlanta. He set up a huge stage behind the house for a full-blown backyard concert that featured Sam and Dave, Percy Sledge, Arthur Conley, Bettye Swan, and the Bar-Kays. Otis himself never took the stage, claiming exhaustion from his final road trip. "He was so tired he was just sitting there out in the middle of the front yard," Zelma said. "He spoke to everybody, but he just couldn't move."

A few days later he flew to New York City to go under the knife.

Otis turned twenty-six years old on September 9 and for a man accustomed to action, to spending most of his time out on the road, six weeks at home was an almost impossible adjustment. He couldn't sing. He couldn't record. He couldn't even go into town and hang out because he couldn't speak until his throat healed; he had to communicate by writing notes. "That was the most time we ever spent together," Zelma said. "And I wasn't used to him being around every day. So I would say, 'Oh God, when are you going to get well and leave?' Because he'd make me crazy. It was always, 'Would you please go get me a glass of water?' 'Would you please make me some Kool-Aid?' And I wasn't used to that. He sat around and moped and worried about whether his voice was going to be all right. He was scared at first. Everybody around him was scared to death that he was not going to be able to sing again. He stayed home most of the time writing songs with his guitar and writing the words down."

Otis also got to know his kids. Dexter was now five. Karla was four, and Otis III was three. Otis loved chocolate ice cream, and he would take the kids into Macon to the ice-cream parlor. One afternoon, he decided he wanted some food and stopped by a barbecue restaurant in Gray, a little town a couple of miles from his farm. Otis had bought barbecue there before with no problem because the owner liked his music. But when he walked inside, he saw no familiar faces. A woman behind the counter openly scowled at him. "You know we don't serve niggers," she snarled.

Otis didn't make a scene; he couldn't even speak because of his throat. He simply turned around and walked out and found another place to pick up food. "There was a note from that woman waiting when we got home," said Karla. "She said she was sorry and didn't know he was Otis Redding. She had sent him a pint of Brunswick stew and some barbecue. He picked it up and threw it in the trash."

For Otis, the fall of 1967 was further time for reflection and contemplation. There was nothing else to do. He had a room at his house where he could retreat, write songs, and work. When he wasn't there, he was out on the farm. He rode his horses. He loved to hunt. He worked around the farm. Otis used the solitude to think about his life and where he wanted it to go. And he confirmed the decisions he'd already made. He was definitely going to seek the divorce from Zelma. There also was going to be a divorce from Phil. Otis was going back to Memphis for three weeks of recording before going out for three dates that would mark his return to the stage following surgery. After that, he told friends, he was going to fire his longtime manager.

And, finally, he was going to make a break from Stax and start his own label with the financial backing of Atlantic Records. That was one of Otis's strongest dreams, running his own record company and building a studio in Macon that would challenge Memphis and Muscle Shoals for supremacy. His first choice for the studio band was the Bar-Kays. And if they didn't work out, then there was plenty of local talent around Macon. Not long before his surgery, Otis had approached Ish Mosley, his old buddy from the Pinetoppers, to see if he was interested in playing at the studio. Otis had purchased the house next door to Ish's mother's house and stopped by one afternoon to chat. He mysteriously told Ish he was going to use the house for "musicians coming through town," then asked Ish if he could still read musical charts.

"Yeah, man, I can still read," Ish responded.

"Would you be interested in being a studio musician?" Otis whispered.

"Yeah, I'd love to be a studio musician."

Otis nodded and smiled enigmatically. "Well, okay." And he promised to be in touch.

For the previous ten years, the British music magazine *Melody Maker* had asked readers to vote for the world's #1 vocalist. And for the previous ten years, readers had cast their ballots for Elvis Presley. But in October of 1967, Otis learned that he had dethroned the King. Riding on the strength of the Stax/Volt tour, *Melody Maker* named Otis Redding the top male vocalist in the world.

This wasn't exactly an opportune time to be sidelined. Otis was on the brink. He was poised for a breakthrough to the white audience, on the verge of superstardom. He was bringing in a reported $35,000 a week from concerts. He had agreed to play the Fillmore again at Christmas for a whopping $15,000. He had just purchased an airplane, a twin-engine Beechcraft. His absence hadn't hurt his career, but people were clamoring for new material and expecting nothing less than his first #1 record. Otis finally made his long-awaited return to Stax in mid-November, armed with dozens of fragments of songs and eager to get to work even though his voice wasn't fully healed. He couldn't bear to wait any longer; patience was never his virtue. "We went through sitting in the hotel room and just strumming the guitar, testing his voice and seeing how the stress would be," William Bell said. "He took a softer approach vocally, mainly because he was just beginning to test the waters with his throat. For about three weeks, he was coming in and out of Memphis. He had to write everything down on a pad because the doctors wouldn't allow him to talk."

Once he was sure he could sing, Otis leapt to work as if he'd been freed from prison. Even though his voice was fragile, Otis sounded so good that they decided to go back and recut some of the vocal performances of unreleased songs he had recorded prior to the surgery. By then Stax had upgraded its studio equipment and now had the capacity to overdub instruments and vocals. It opened up tremendous opportunities to sweeten songs and add layered instruments as the Beatles had done on *Sgt. Pepper*. The MG's and Otis still recorded "live" in the studio but Steve Cropper now had the opportunity to record a second guitar track to add to the mix. It also gave Otis the opportunity to recut his vocals if he flubbed a line or two, or if he thought he could offer a better performance. "We went back and listened to the things that had been cut," Steve Cropper said. "Things that he didn't sound all that good on, we recut. There was only one reason . . . he was singing better than he ever had in his life; it was just obvious."

Otis was so eager to work that he sometimes returned to the studio after dinner even though the MG's had long gone. Armed with JB scotch and water, Otis and Steve and engineer Ron Capone would stay there all night recording songs. Steve called them "the Midnight Recorders sessions." Ron would play drums; Otis would play the acoustic guitar; Steve would play electric guitar and maybe the bass and keyboard parts. Then the rest of the MG's—sometimes with Carl Cunningham of the Bar-Kays on drums—would come in the next day and overdub their parts.

For a while, Otis stayed at Jim Stewart's estate outside Memphis with a white soul singer named Johnny Daye, whom he had met in Cleveland and brought to Stax. Johnny's manager, Joe Rock, also stayed there and he happened to be an accomplished songwriter, the author of the Skyliners' hit "Since I Don't Have You." Otis didn't let that opportunity go to waste; he and Joe began writing together at night, coming up with five new songs, two of which Otis wound up recording. "One night Otis couldn't sleep," Joe Rock said. "It was winter [and] there was a fireplace going. Otis got the guitar and said, 'Joe, we ought to write some songs.' He would tell me what he wanted to convey. I was trying to articulate his feelings as he expressed them to me. Simply said, he wanted to do a real hurting song like 'Since I Don't Have You.' He said, 'This woman has to know the hurt she's left behind.' " The idea evolved into "Gone Again," a ballad Otis cut the next day at Stax.

Rock also collaborated with Otis on one of his most beautiful and well-crafted songs, "I've Got Dreams to Remember." It actually started as a poem Zelma had written while Otis was in Europe for the Stax/Volt tour. "He was away for a month, which was a long time," Zelma said. "He was usually away for a week or ten days. I was sitting one night in the den. My kids were very small and I had put them to bed. I thought, 'Well, I've got dreams to remember.' It was just a poem. I was thinking about him. I said, 'Oh God, he's been gone so long, maybe I'll just start getting involved.' I was just missing him so bad—that was my way of trying to get involved in something he was doing."

Zelma showed Otis the song as soon as he came home. "Look at this song I wrote," she said proudly.

"Yeah, I bet you did," Otis scoffed. "You don't know how to write songs."

As he read it, Zelma noticed a change in her husband's face; she could tell he liked it even though he said nothing. Otis stuffed the poem in his pocket and stashed it away and never mentioned it again. Zelma didn't even know he had taken it to Memphis. "I guess he just wanted me to be the housewife and the mother," she said. "He would kid around with me all the time like that. So many things were happening at the time, he never got to express his feelings about the song directly to me."

As Zelma wrote it, "I've Got Dreams to Remember" was a plea to a faraway love whose devotion is doubted: "I dreamed you got the message / But you still wouldn't come to see me." It was one of the first songs Otis cut with the MG's once he reached Memphis, but he wasn't happy with the way it turned out. He was right: Zelma was no songwriter; sometimes the lyrics rhymed and sometimes they didn't. But she *had* come up with a great title and hook for a song, and Otis had put a gorgeous melody behind it. So he played it for Joe Rock and they rewrote it, using the perspective of a man who is watching a relationship slowly slip away and has no power to stop it. He is devastated when he goes to a bar and sees his woman sitting with another man: "I know you said he was just a friend / But I saw him kiss you again and again and again." It was the first "adult" song Otis had ever written, addressing issues that went beyond the swaggering songs of lust or heartbroken songs of lost love that had dominated his earlier material.

That trend continued on one of the initial up-tempo tunes Otis recorded after his surgery, a song he'd co-written with Steve called "Happy Song (Dum-Dum)." It opened with one of Otis's most memorable horn lines, an obvious play on "Fa-Fa-Fa-Fa-Fa (Sad Song)." Otis sang like a man giddy with his very first taste of mature, *real* love. The sentiments are tender, even romantic.

Another change of direction was a finger-snapping song called "Hard to Handle" that began as a conversation between Otis and Al Bell. "We were talking about the concept of being a particular kind of guy," Al said. "Not hard to handle in a negative way, but hard to handle because he's *bad*! Allen Jones [a Stax songwriter] came into the room and started banging away on the piano. And we continued to tell this story and fashion these lyrics, and Otis started singing it. We were laughing as we came up with the lines. We were telling stories and the stories would give rise to a line in the song."

It was driven by a classic soul backbeat but also featured guitar riffs that veered close to pure rock 'n' roll. Writer Stanley Booth— who would go on to write the groundbreaking book *Dance with the Devil*, a backstage chronicle of the Rolling Stones, leading up to the tragedy at Altamont that many believe was the symbolic death of the sixties—showed up at the sessions on assignment with the *Saturday Evening Post* and even though he was a native of Macon, he had no idea what he was about to encounter. "I was very ignorant," he said. "I was a jazz person and a blues person. This stuff was a little bit déclassé to me. Then I went over there. I saw Otis and I saw him cut

'Hard-to-fuckin'-Handle,' baby. And let me tell you, I was converted. Otis doing 'Hard to Handle' in the studio was just like Otis doing it anywhere. And I mean it was goddamned exciting."

Otis's intentions seemed obvious: Rock-flavored songs such as "Hard to Handle" were designed to reach out to the white audience. "I had this argument with him that week about Ray Charles," Stanley Booth said. "I was a big Ray Charles fan when I was a kid; then he did that country-and-western thing, which turned me off. I told Otis. And Otis said, 'I don't know, man. I think he know what he doing.' Now I realize I should have had bigger ears. Otis was looking at it from a business point of view, just like Ray."

Otis himself would face the same kind of heat after he finally re-corded the song he had begun on the houseboat in Sausalito. He had been at work at Stax for over two weeks before he finally sat down with Steve Cropper to finish writing it. They faced each other on the studio floor, Otis holding his battered red guitar and Steve holding his Fender Telecaster. Otis began playing the intro, then sang the first two lines: "Sittin' in the mornin' sun / I'll be sittin' when the evenin' comes." Then he stopped. "But I don't know why he's sitting," Otis said, shaking his head. "Wait. Wait a minute." While Steve sat quietly, Otis thought it over and then sang, "I left my home in Georgia / Headed for the Frisco Bay." They added a bridge, had it finished in twenty or thirty minutes, and then put it on tape.

Stanley Booth had a bird's-eye view of the "Sittin' on the Dock of the Bay" session. "When Steve and Otis have the outline of a song, they are joined by the rest of the MG's," he recounted in his *Saturday Evening Post* article.

Booker sits at the piano, Duck gets his bass, which has been lying in its case on the worn red rug, and they begin to pick up the chord patterns from Steve and Otis. Al stands by, listening, his head tilted to one side. Duck asks him a question about counting the rhythm, and Steve looks up to say, "In a minute he'll want to know what key we're in." Duck sticks out his lower lip. He plays bass as fluently as if it were a guitar, plucking the stout steel strings with his first two fingers, holding a cigarette between the other two. Booker sits erect, his right hand playing short punctuating notes, his left hand resting on his left knee. Otis is standing now, moving around the room, waving his arms as he conducts these men, his friends. He looks like a swimmer, moving effortlessly underwater. Then something happens, a connection is made in Al Jackson's mind, and he goes to the drums, baffled on two sides with wallboard. "One, two," he announces. "One-two-three-four." And for the first time they are all together, everyone has found the groove.

The Mar-Keys drift into the studio and sit on folding chairs behind another baffle. They listen . . . as Otis and the rhythm section rehearse the song. When Steve calls, "Hey, horns! Ready to record?" they are thrown into confusion, like a man waked in the middle of the night. They have nothing to record; there are, as yet, no horn parts. Steve and Otis develop them by singing to each other. "De-de-da-dee," Steve says. "De-de-da-*daah*," says Otis, as if he were making a point in an argument. When they have the lines they want, they sing them to the Mar-Keys, starting with the verse part, which the Mar-Keys will forget while learning the parts for the chorus. After a few tries, however, they know both parts, and are ready to record. "That feels good, man, let's cut it."

From that very first take it was clear this song was unlike anything ever recorded at Stax. It wasn't so much a soul song as it was a pop ballad, a lot closer to the Beatles than Sam and Dave. It featured Steve playing an acoustic guitar, an extreme rarity on a Stax recording. And on top of that, Otis wanted to use sound effects. There were seagulls everywhere when he had begun writing the song on the houseboat, and their cries were so ingrained in his concept of the song that he couldn't imagine it without them; to illustrate what he wanted to hear, Otis began the first take of the song by doing a dead-on imitation of a cawing seagull. That take also happened to be the first time Otis had ever performed the complete song; he was tentative and searching, refining the melody and playing around with his approach to the lyrics. There were lines that sounded awkward and would be fine-tuned. There were lines he flubbed outright. As it faded out, Otis began whistling but most of the notes sputtered out. By the end, there was loud laughter coming from the control room. "You're not gonna make it as a whistler," someone cracked.

The second take sharpened everything. Steve and Duck began the song together, Steve on acoustic and Duck playing a bass line he'd first used on the MG's instrumental hit of the Rascals' "Groovin'." Then Al came in and quickly established the backbeat. Otis found a weariness in his voice that shaped the song. You didn't have to listen to the lyrics to understand the song's underlying despair. But this time the lyrics *mattered*—Otis finally had something to *say*. Steve and Booker went back in to record overdubs. Booker played a striding piano that stayed in the background except for little gliding notes that snuck to the forefront every so often. Steve formed brilliant guitar fills that echoed the vocal melody and gave the song a sense of dimension.

When they gathered in the control room to hear the playback, everyone seemed spellbound. "That's it," Otis declared as the song faded.

Booker T. looked at him. "That's a mother," he said.

"I just knew this was *it*," Steve said. "It was a just a great song. We just knew we finally had the song that was going to cross him over to the pop market. We just *knew* it."

There was just one problem: Aside from Steve and Booker and Otis, nobody else much liked "(Sittin' on) the Dock of the Bay." Jim Stewart didn't even want to release it. "It was just too far over the border for Jim," said Duck Dunn. "It had no R&B whatsoever. I agreed with Jim. It just didn't impress me. I thought it was kind of out of context. Otis was soulful and for him to change over and go that way, it just wasn't as soulful as I knew Otis. I thought it might even be detrimental."

Otis headed back to Macon on Thursday, December 7, with a tape of the song in hand. He played it for Zelma, for Alan Walden, for Phil, and they all had the same basic reaction as Jim Stewart: It just *wasn't* Otis. There was no driving beat. No "Got-ta!"s No searing horn parts. No *energy*.

Zelma frowned when she heard it and looked quizzically at her husband. "Oh God," she said. "You're changing."

When Otis showed up at Alan's log cabin, he was visibly excited and wearing a Cheshire-cat smile. "Guess what I'm doing on the new record?" he asked.

"What?" Alan replied. "You screamin' your ass off? You gettin' down?"

Otis grinned again. "You ain't gonna believe what I'm doing on this record."

"Come on, goddammit, you going to tell me or not?"

Otis walked out to his car and came back with the tape.

"He played it for me and at the end of the song, of course, he's whistling. And, you know, all of his songs were famous for their strong ad-libs at the end and here he is whistling this one out! My first reaction was I didn't even like the song. I told him I liked a song called 'Think About It' better. I thought it would make a better record. And he told me, 'This is my first number one record; it's the biggest song I ever had.' "

That same afternoon Otis went to visit Bobby Smith, his old friend from the Macon Recording Studio. Otis stopped by Bobby's apartment on Vineville Avenue and asked if he had some time to talk. Bobby hopped in Otis's Cadillac and they drove over to a white woman's apartment, where Otis made himself at home. He broke open a bottle of tequila and offered some to Bobby; he didn't drink hard liquor, so Otis sent the woman out to pick up some beer. Then Otis got down to business. He told Bobby he didn't like what was going on with the money. Otis said he was about to go on a short weekend road trip; when he came back, he was going to fire Phil. Otis was going to manage himself, maybe with his father's help.

Afterwards, Otis stopped by the office on Cotton Avenue. He was getting ready to fly back to Memphis for some more studio work and then he was going to head out for his weekend gigs. There was something of a crisis: Huck couldn't go out with him to the gigs because his son was in the hospital. And Speedo had quit. He wasn't happy with his financial arrangements and had gone to work cleaning cars at a shop Percy Welch owned on Third Street. Percy hadn't spoken to Otis in three or four years, not since Otis had fired him as the promoter for the Homecoming Shows at the City Auditorium. But when he walked up Cotton Avenue and saw Otis hanging around outside Phil's office, he stopped and struck up a conversation. At first there was friendly chitchat. Then Percy decided to get into Otis's face. He was angry at the way Otis had treated Speedo. Otis had gotten rich off "Respect"; Speedo had nothing to show for it. "Otis, you know God ain't pleased with the way you done Speedo about his record," Percy told him. "You just take *everybody's* songs. It's just a damned shame. Here you are, driving a brand-new car, and the boy, Speedo, ain't even got a scooter to ride. You took that boy's record, promised him the royalties from it, and haven't given him a damned dime. God don't like the way you done Speedo."

Otis glared at him. Percy could see the anger in his face. "*Damn God*," he finally snarled back. "*I'm* God."

Otis was back at Stax the next day to work some more on "(Sittin' on) The Dock of the Bay." He still wasn't completely happy with the song. He had gotten a lot of criticism and lukewarm reactions back home, and he toyed with the idea of changing the arrangement. He thought he might take out the whistle at the end and come up with an ad-lib vamp of some kind. And maybe there was a way to make it more "soulful." There was talk of bringing in the Staple Singers to add background vocals.

By midafternoon, it seemed as if everybody associated with Stax had dropped by to say hello. They all wound up crowded into David Porter's office drinking Cherry Kjofa wine and eating fried chicken. William Bell was there; he was supposed to fly to Chicago for a show and heavy snow had closed the Chicago airport. So Otis tried to talk him into going on the weekend jaunt with him. They were going to Nashville, Cleveland, and then over to Madison, Wisconsin. They'd be back Monday. It was Otis's first live performance in over two months. He was nervous. He wanted to have a familiar face with him. "Why don't you go with us?" Otis asked. "I'll play the date and we'll hang out."

William shook his head. "No, I've got the weekend off," he said. "I'll just hang at home."

It was getting late and Otis got up to leave; he had to make the gig in Nashville. "We were standing up in the hallway," Duck Dunn said. "He always used to stand and kind of shrug his shoulders. And he said he'd be back next week because when he'd leave, you'd always want to know when he was coming back. He'd always kind of tug his pants up, like a fighter. And he'd shrug his shoulders. That meant he was getting anxious and ready to get out of there."

Otis's plane was waiting at the airport. When he arrived, he climbed on board with the members of the Bar-Kays—trumpet player Ben Cauley, bassist James Alexander, drummer Carl Cunningham, guitarist Jimmy Lee King, saxophonist Phalon Jones, keyboardist Ronnie Caldwell, and the valet, Matthew Kelly. The twin-engine Beechcraft was piloted by Richard "Dick" Fraser, a twenty-six-year-old pilot who had worked at the Air Force base in Warner Robins. He was rated as both a commercial pilot and flight instructor, and he had extensive experience—1,290 total hours in the air.

They performed in Nashville that night, a Friday, then stayed over and flew to Hopkins Field in Cleveland early the next morning. Otis appeared on Don Webster's syndicated show *Upbeat*, singing "Knock On Wood" with Mitch Ryder, and then did another club gig that night at a place called Leo's Casino. Otis was awake early the next morning and called Zelma around eight A.M. She thought Otis sounded depressed and asked what was wrong.

"Nothing," he said. "I'm just tired."

He asked to speak to the kids. Three-year-old Otis III was the only one awake; Zelma put him on the phone and Otis spoke to his son for a few moments.

"I'm sleepy," he said when Zelma got back on the line.

"I'm cleaning the pool for you," she said.

"Good. I'm going to buy you a new Buick when I get back. Hold on; there's someone at the door." Otis put the phone down, then came back a minute later. "It's Dick. I gotta go now. He's getting ready to leave. I'll call you when I get to Madison."

They said good-bye and Zelma was hanging up when she heard Otis call out her name; she raised the phone back up to her ear. "You know what I want you to do?" he asked.

"What?" she asked.

"I want you to be real sweet and I want you to be real good."

Zelma shook her head. "What are you talking about? I'm always good. I'm the best thing you know."

Otis didn't laugh. "Seriously, Zelma," he said. "I want you to be real good."

They said good-bye again. And Zelma hung up the phone.

The final stop on the weekend road trip was to be a gig at a white rock club in Madison called The Factory on Sunday night, December 10. Otis had two shows to play, the first beginning at six-thirty P.M. The opening act was a band called the Grim Reapers that later would become known as Cheap Trick. Otis and the Bar-Kays rode over to the airport in Cleveland late that morning. His plane could carry only six passengers; every time they flew, one of the guys in the band had to take a commercial flight. It was bassist James Alexander's turn, and he headed into the terminal to catch another flight. Dick Fraser began checking Otis's Beechcraft with a mechanic, who noticed the batteries on the plane were low; Fraser checked it out and decided it would be okay to fly. The weather in Madison was far from optimum. It was very cold, rainy and foggy; the same storm that had canceled William Bell's flight to Chicago was pushing south. There was even talk of canceling the gig and staying put in Cleveland. Otis said no. "I've never missed a job yet," he told them.

They climbed aboard and took off at twelve-thirty P.M. It was a three-hour flight from Cleveland to Madison, and it was uneventful. Some of the guys in the Bar-Kays were in the back trying to catch up on their sleep. Otis was in the co-pilot's seat. He was fascinated by planes and wanted to learn to fly, so he'd always sit up front with Dick and pick his brain for flying tips. Sometimes Dick would even let him fly the Beechcraft.

At 3:25 P.M., Dick Fraser radioed the flight tower at Truax Field in Madison. He reported the plane was about four miles south of the airport, above Squaw Bay, and asked for clearance to land. The Beechcraft was given permission and directed to Runway 36. The conditions were poor. There was a steady, light drizzle on the ground and low, misty clouds. It was a tricky landing, but Dick was rated for instrument flying and had landed in rainy weather dozens of times.

Ben Cauley was asleep in the backseat when he was awakened by a jolt. It felt as if the plane had hit a bump in the road. It began shaking and Ben suddenly felt a tremendous sensation of falling. One engine was grunting and growling; the other was dead altogether. There were no cries or screams, just an eerie silence as they all watched Dick Fraser fight to get the plane down. Time seemed to stand still. It was like forever. Then Ben Cauley heard someone scream out: "Oh, no!"

At that moment Bernard Reese was standing out in his yard in front of a house that sat on the shore of Lake Monona just outside Madison. He had heard the sputtering plane overhead and looked up in time to see it flash through the low clouds. Its left wing was dipping and the plane kept drifting lower and lower and lower until it hit the water with a loud thud. It rested on the surface, about a half mile off the southeastern shore, for a few minutes. And then it began to sink.

In the water, Ben Cauley could hear screams. He heard someone call out: "Help!" He thought it was Ronnie Caldwell. Seconds later, he heard another cry for help. This time it sounded like Carl Cunningham. Soon he heard nothing but the quiet splashes of water against his ears. He spent what seemed like an eternity in the freezing water, clutching a seat cushion and praying for help. His legs were numb; his entire body was numb. The water was cold, *so* cold. He held on for as long as he could, knowing his life was hanging in the balance. Finally, he could hold on no longer. He was slipping helplessly beneath the water when he felt something grasp his arm. It was a cop pulling him into a boat.

A while later, someone came up to him. "You're very lucky," he said.

"Why?" Ben Cauley asked.

There was a long pause before the man answered. "Everybody else is dead," he said.

A Change Is Gonna Come

The call came Sunday night.

Zelma was at the farm with Otis's mother. A friend of Mrs. Redding's was on the phone, all worried because she'd heard something had happened to Otis's plane. This wasn't the first time somebody had called Zelma's house with some wild rumor of a plane crash; they always turned out wrong, but they never failed to spook her. She decided to check with Diane Fraser, the pilot's wife, just to make sure nothing was wrong. Zelma dialed the number and her heart began to pound when Diane Fraser answered, in tears and barely able to speak. "Dick is gone," she gasped. "Otis, too."

Moments later, Zelma's phone rang. The man identified himself as Bud Chamberlain. He was the coroner in Madison, Wisconsin. He explained that her husband's plane had crashed into a lake. A body was recovered that they thought was her husband. "He's tall and dark and has on a black undershirt."

"That's not Otis," Zelma shot back as if she were suffering a fool. "He doesn't wear undershirts. He's not dead. He's a good swimmer. He's just lost. You find him."

Phil Walden was in Las Vegas attending an R&B convention. He was in a casino with his wife and Tom Dowd when he was paged over the intercom and went up to his room for the call. It was his secretary, Carolyn Brown, and she had grim news: Otis's plane had crashed and he was presumed dead. "I was real calm," Phil said. "I locked into this trance. I told her to book me a flight. I thought that I had to make some decisions and make sure everything was done properly."

Phil went back downstairs and found Tom Dowd. "Otis is dead," Phil told him, speaking in a dazed voice. He walked away, found his wife, and told her they had to go home. She asked what was wrong. "Otis is dead," he replied.

Phil left them to go back to the room to make some calls. When Phil reached the elevator, it was full of black disc jockeys and one of them started in on him. It was the same old song: What was a white man doing in a black man's world? "Hey, there's that Phil Walden," he said in a loud voice. "Him and Otis, they got all the money in the world. How many millions you making off that black man? What y'all doing with all that money? You got Cadillacs and mansions?"

Phil never responded. He could hardly breathe. There was a long, uncomfortable silence. Finally the elevator stopped and the doors opened. As he stepped out, Phil stopped and turned back to them. "Otis is dead," he said. Their faces fell ashen and Phil stepped off. When the door closed, Phil finally lost it, collapsing to the floor and weeping hysterically until a doctor came to give him a shot to calm him down.

Word of the crash spread quickly around Macon. Most of Otis's friends heard about it from radio bulletins. Bubba Sailor was at Bubba Howard's house when the news broke and they sat in stunned silence. Soon, Huck was with them. Bubba Sailor hadn't been tight with Otis's circle of friends since he'd failed to show up for the gunfight on Roy Street. None of that mattered now. "Everybody in the house was crying," said Bubba Sailor. "We all loved him."

Ploonie, the old Pinetoppers drummer, found out when his mother called him late Sunday afternoon. Only a few weeks earlier, he had run into Otis on Cotton Avenue. "Hey, man," Otis had said. "I've been trying to get in touch with you. You wanna go back out with us?" Otis told him he'd bought an airplane, so there would be no more grueling trips in buses and cars. Now they could fly out for a gig and then come back home the same night. Ploonie quickly agreed and when he mentioned it to his mother he was taken aback by her reaction. "I don't think you ought to go out there no more," she said. "You should find somebody to play with around here."

"Mom, I need to go," Ploonie replied.

"No, you don't need to go this time," she said. "I've got a funny feeling. Something's not right; I just can't put my hand on it."

Ploonie eventually backed out; he couldn't get his mother's reaction out of his mind. On the day of the crash, Ploonie spent the afternoon at a show starring an exotic dancer named Sister Wimbush who was known around Macon as a black Mae West. When he came home, his phone rang. It was his mother. "Did you hear about Otis?" she asked.

Ploonie didn't notice the edge in her voice. "No," he casually replied. "What's he done now?"

"His airplane went down and it killed all but one."

It was like someone had knocked the air out of Ploonie's lungs. "Where?" he managed to ask.

"Madison, Wisconsin." There was a long silence. "I told you," she said.

Like everyone else, Johnny Jenkins was glued to the radio waiting for updates. He said Otis also had asked him to rejoin him on the road, including the date that weekend in Madison. "We looked at that plane; it just wasn't sufficient enough," Johnny said. "I said, 'I'm not going up in that.' Everybody in his office was laughing because I was scared to go up in an airplane. But after that incident happened, nobody ever laughed anymore about Johnny."

Wayne Cochran was in Miami, where he was running his own nightclub, when he heard the news over the radio. At first he thought it was some disc jockey playing a sick joke. "I was going to the club," he said. "Had the radio on and they said, 'Otis Redding was just killed in a plane crash.' And it was such a shock to me that I went back to the house. I couldn't believe it. I thought, some idiot, some *prankster*, had the nerve to say Otis was killed in a plane crash! I decided it couldn't be real. So I got in the car and headed back to the club. Then came another announcement: 'Otis Redding crashed into a lake in Madison, Wisconsin, tonight; his body has not been recovered.' And I lost it. I just lost it. Went to the club that night and closed it. Said, 'I'm not going on tonight; you can forget it.' It was just devastating. So very painful."

He had seen Otis only two weeks earlier. "I was flying back to Miami and he happened to be at the airport in Atlanta," Wayne said in a voice so soft it could barely be heard. "We talked and he'd just got his new Beechcraft and he said he was going to take me up for a ride. He was all excited that he was getting his voice back. I said, 'Hey, man, you ought to come down to Miami and stay the weekend.' He said, 'I'm gonna do that, two weeks.' They had booked him on *Upbeat,* a show in Cleveland, and since he was up there, they got him that gig in Madison. That's why he didn't come here; otherwise, he'd been here that weekend."

Newt Collier was in Augusta that Sunday night, on break from touring with Sam and Dave and picking up some extra cash by playing a club date with an old friend named Leroy Lloyd. "I heard about it and called my aunt in Macon," said Newt. "She said, 'You know Otis swims real good so he's probably gonna get out of there.' I asked who else was on the plane. She started naming people and I just started crying. I don't remember too much about playing that night. At the club, it was like everybody knew what was happening. There was just a hush. I told Leroy afterwards, 'I'm going home.' I came back to Macon. There was a complete silence over this whole city."

Even though the *Macon Telegraph* seldom published news of the black community on the front page, the plane crash was too big to ignore and was played as the lead story in the following morning's edition. "Redding Feared Dead In Crash," read the headline. "Macon Singer," noted a smaller headline for the scores of whites who had no idea who Otis Redding was. The story quoted Madison officials as saying the crash had apparently killed everyone aboard except for Ben Cauley. Even more heart-wrenching were the ages of the Bar-Kays: the youngest was seventeen, the oldest nineteen.

In Memphis, there was chaos. When the news reports said, "Otis Redding and his band," many people naturally assumed that Booker T. and the MG's were on the flight and had perished. "Actually, we had a gig up in Ohio that night," Duck Dunn said. "There were people who were afraid to call June, my wife, because they thought *we* were out with Otis. They didn't know we didn't play with him on the road. In the meantime, we were en route home in an airplane. We heard about it when we got home."

Estelle Axton heard about it on television. "It was such a shock," she said. "Something like the day before, he had recorded 'Dock of the Bay.' It was a shock; it was so sad." Her brother, Jim Stewart, was in Las Vegas with Al Bell at the same R&B convention Phil was attending. Jim was numb, lifeless for days. He couldn't shake an image from the previous Friday. He had been up in his office and got a strange feeling that he should go down and see Otis before he left for the gig in Nashville. That had never happened to him before and the feeling was so strong that he went downstairs, only to find that Otis was already gone.

Steve Cropper dealt with it by working. While they were combing Lake Monona for Otis's body, Steve escaped to the studio to mix "Dock of the Bay." That afternoon he had gone over to a little jingle studio and found a sound-effects tape with seagulls and crashing waves. Then he worked for hours, subtly working in short bursts of the sound effects throughout the song. "That's probably one of the hardest things I ever had to do is mix that record," he later told a television interviewer. "The toughest part was they hadn't even found Otis yet. And there I am, working on a song, 'Dock of the Bay.' " Steve sighed and his voice began to break. "*Very* difficult."

Zelma flew to Madison early Monday morning with Otis's father and Twiggs Lyndon, Phil's assistant from Macon. She still held out hope her husband was alive, that he was somehow lost somewhere on the shores of the lake. Then she was taken to the lake and shown where the plane rested beneath thirty to forty feet of water. It was bitterly cold. The lake had yet to ice over, but it had started to freeze. As Zelma was briefed on what had happened, her hope plummeted into despair. The plane had gone down at 3:28 P.M., three miles from the airport. Exactly seventeen minutes later, a rescue boat had reached the site and found debris. They also found Ben Cauley floating with the help of a cushion, barely alive. Two others—pilot Richard Fraser and eighteen-year-old guitarist Jimmy Lee King—also were floating on the surface; both were found dead. Ben Cauley told them the plane had broken apart upon impact. He was thrown from the cabin, still buckled to his seat. Ben—who couldn't swim—had freed himself, grabbed the seat cushion, and held on until help arrived. They had searched for survivors until nightfall, then called things off until first light Monday morning. The chances of finding more survivors had grown faint. It was too cold to survive in the water.

Later that morning, divers went into the murky, gray water and found the fuselage. Using grappling hooks attached with heavy lines to a Coast Guard cutter, the plane was brought back to the surface. Inside, near the rear of the fuselage, they found the body of Otis Redding. He was still strapped his seat, clad in a dark silk mohair suit and matching shirt that was still neatly in place. "He looked as if he was taking a little nap," said one person who helped pull him from the wreckage.

It was December 11, 1967. Exactly three years to the day Sam Cooke had died. Otis Redding was just twenty-six years old.

The news was quickly broadcast in Macon. David Tharpe, who was with Otis the day he signed his very first autograph, rushed over to Huck's little duplex; it sat up on a little hill by Mumford Road. Huck was disconsolate, playing Otis records on a big stereo console. They were both crazy with sorrow and desperate to do *something*, find some way to express their grief. Finally, Huck and David carried the big stereo console outside and sat it down overlooking the street. They turned it up as loud as it would go and played Otis Redding songs deep into the night. For many who have lived in Bellevue all their lives, one memory of that long day is forever etched in their minds: No matter where you were, it seemed as if you could hear the haunting sounds of Otis Redding singing from someplace far off in the distance.

Zelma and Mr. Redding flew back to Macon on Tuesday aboard a commercial flight that also carried the body. Mr. Redding requested a funeral in the City Auditorium, the site of Otis's annual Homecoming Shows. Even though the Auditorium had not hosted a funeral since 1947, Mayor Ronnie Thompson quickly agreed and the service was scheduled for Monday, January 18, at noon.

The obituary for Otis Redding ran in the Negro section of the *Macon Telegraph* the day before the funeral. Published without a byline but likely written by Mildred Henderson, the section's editor, it was eloquent in its simplicity and reverence.

Last Sunday evening the citizens of Macon were saddened to learn of the passing of one of Macon's internationally known celebrities, Otis Redding, in Madison, Wisconsin. One could hardly believe the news casts, knowing that one so young and full of life could depart so suddenly without a word of farewell. Young, middle aged, old alike wept violently, hoping that somehow it would not be true. Now today, we are preparing to attend the final rites of Otis Redding on tomorrow, December 18, 1967, at 12 noon . . . The remains will lie in state at the Auditorium on tomorrow from 7 a.m. until hour of funeral. Private grave side rites will follow.

Mr. Redding was born to the parentage of Rev. Otis and Mrs. Fannie Mae Redding. He attended B. S. Ingram Elementary School and Ballard-Hudson Senior High School. At an early age he joined the Vineville Baptist Church where he was a member of the junior choir. Otis loved to sing, and started singing professionally with the Johnny Jenkins Pinetoppers Band, prior to recording his own numbers. In the past years, Otis and his manager of Phil Walden Promotions worked hard and made success in Macon and throughout the nation. Phone calls from far and near have been made concerning the tragic loss of one many had learned to love. Otis Redding's fans are at a loss, along with his dear family and Promotions associates . . .

A funeral for three of the victims—the Bar-Kays' Carl Cunningham and Jimmy Lee King, and valet Matthew Kelly—was held on Sunday, December 17, at the Clayborn Temple African Methodist Episcopal Church in Memphis. At the end of the service Duck Dunn walked outside to smoke a cigarette. "Been to one today," he said wearily. "Got to get up and go to another one tomorrow."

Macon was cold and gloomy that morning, overcast and gray. At six-twenty A.M., a woman aided by a cane walked slowly and deliberately to the front door of the City Auditorium. Her name was Mary Durham, and she had come to say good-bye. Then they all began to come—mourners from all over the city, from all over the state, from all over the country—forming a single-file line outside. The doors to the Auditorium were opened early, and the masses of people began slowly moving inside to pay their last respects. The dark copper-colored coffin was placed in front of the stage, covered with chrysanthemums and carnations and surrounded by dozens of floral arrangements. By the time the funeral began at noon, at least 4,500 people were crowded inside a building that was built to hold 3,500. On the floor, folding chairs were placed into neat rows. Once the seats were taken, people still poured in and lined up against the wall from one side of the Auditorium to the other until, at last, the doors were shut, leaving thousands of people stranded outside.

Among the mourners was a virtual who's who of soul stars: James Brown, Aretha Franklin, Little Stevie Wonder, Solomon Burke, Wilson Pickett, Percy Sledge, Sam and Dave. The MG's were there and Booker T. was stationed behind the organ, playing "Come Ye Disconsolate" as the Processional. The fifty-minute service was marked by frequent outbursts of emotion. Stax's Johnnie Taylor broke down as he sang "I'll Stand By," sobbing for a few long moments before he was able to continue. Then, as soul star Joe Simon sang "Jesus, Keep Me Near the Cross," Zelma suddenly began uncontrollably wailing and hysterically stomping the wood floor with her heels. Two nurses who had accompanied her to the service rushed up to aid her. Between the two hymns, prayers were led by the Reverend W. L. Reynolds and then the Reverend Moses Dumas. The Reverend C. J. Andrews, the Redding family pastor who had married Otis and Zelma, delivered a eulogy. Hamp Swain addressed the mourners. As Mayor Ronnie Thompson rose to call Otis the city's "ambassador of goodwill," Arthur Conley bolted from his seat. He made his way to the casket and stood for a moment, tears streaming down his face. Then he slowly turned, walked back, and collapsed into his chair.

Finally, Jerry Wexler walked slowly to the podium. He had been in shock since hearing about the crash—he had received a call at the airport as he returned from the R&B convention in Las Vegas, where he had been named Record Executive of the Year for the third straight year. He struggled to compose himself. His eyes were welled up with tears. When he began to speak, his voice was halting, often cracking with emotion. "Otis was a natural prince. When you were with him, he communicated love and a tremendous faith in human possibilities, a promise that great and happy events were coming. He was loved the world over. This year he was chosen by the British trade publications as the #1 male singer in the world, replacing Elvis for the first time in ten years. . . . Out of his character and dedication, he bought his beautiful ranch in Macon to make his home and base his business operations when he could have chosen any other place in the world. He thought it the obligation of educated or talented blacks to remain in their native South to help open the doors of opportunities for their race. Respect for his roots is another quality of the man whose composition 'Respect' has become an anthem of hope for people everywhere. Respect is something Otis achieved. Otis sang, 'Respect when I come home.' And Otis has come home."

As the service ended, Booker T. played the Recessional, a lonesome-sounding solitary version of "These Arms of Mine." One by one the pallbearers walked to the casket: Huck, Speedo Sims, Clark Walden (Phil's brother), Joe Simon, Johnnie Taylor, Joe Tex, Hamp Swain, and Arthur Conley. They picked it up, carried it down the aisle and out the front doors. Tears filled Booker T.'s eyes as he played the final notes. He turned to someone and sobbed, "I guess I'll never play for him again."

As they brought the casket through the throngs outside, Zelma followed behind, crying and screaming. When James Brown walked out moments later, there was sudden pandemonium. The crowd began pushing forward trying to touch him, and James dove for his car. Joe Tex stepped outside and the crowd swarmed him, tearing at his clothes before he, too, ran for cover. As James Brown's car began to pull out to follow the hearse, the kids surrounded it until the police finally drove them back.

Those invited to the private burial followed the hearse through downtown Macon, then east out Gray Highway toward Round Oak. Police cars were positioned at every traffic signal along the route; the procession moved without hindrance to the ranch. Zelma wasn't shy about it at all: The grave site was in the front yard, just a few feet to the left of the driveway and impossible not to see from the kitchen window or living room. "He wanted to be buried here at the ranch," she said. "There is an old cemetery in the back of the house, but I didn't want him to be that far away. It never bothers me having him there."

As Otis Redding was laid to rest in Macon, the Federal Aviation Administration was picking through the wreckage and trying to figure out what happened. They quickly surmised the victims were either trapped in the wreckage and unable to get out before it sank to the bottom of the lake or else knocked unconscious by the force of the impact. Otis suffered an abrasion in the middle of his forehead, indicating he had hit his head against the instrument panel; he also suffered other cuts around his face and neck, and press reports from the time stated his right leg was broken. He was wearing a Bulova watch. They found a black leather billfold holding $302 in cash in his pocket; they also found a bag of marijuana there.

What caused the crash was anybody's guess. The Beechcraft, first built to transport General Dwight D. Eisenhower and other Army brass around Europe during World War II, had a very good safety record. There was heavy fog, but that didn't seem to be a factor because the plane was under obvious duress—fog would not cause the sudden bump felt by Ben Cauley, nor the loss of the left engine and the sputtering right engine. There was no explosion and investigators found nothing in the recovered wreckage that spoke to what had happened. It could have been something as simple as running out of gas. The most tantalizing pieces of evidence—the left wing and engine—lay somewhere on the floor of Lake Monona. They were never recovered.

In many circles around Macon, there were unsubstantiated theories floating around that cast an accusatory eye on Phil Walden. With no real evidence, there are those who believe he hired someone to sabotage the plane. They'll tell you the logic is simple: Phil had a $1 million insurance policy on Otis's life. The plane was parked in Cleveland before the crash and Cleveland was a mob outpost; there were people to be hired who could cause a plane to go down. Phil had found out Otis was about to leave him. It would have destroyed him professionally. Did he react to the news in a cold rage, getting Otis before Otis got him?

"I'm not the only one to have views on the death," Newt Collier said. "That was a mysterious death, and everything just came into Phil's hands. I put two and two together quick. If your plane is going to crash, are you gonna be strapped in your seat? With a smile on your face? Wouldn't there be some kind of effort made to get out of that plane? If they'd found him loose, hands beat up where he'd tried to pound on the plane to get out, I could have gone with that. Maybe that's just me thinking. But I think the man was killed."

Bobby Smith has heard the same rumor. "Everybody seems to think that," he said. "I don't want to. I'm not here to put nobody down. But I've heard the same things you've heard. And I heard other things, too. I don't know whether they're true or not, but I've heard from some people that definitely, definitely think so. There's the million-dollar insurance policy. I know that for a fact. And I know what Otis told me before he died."

Others scoff at the suggestion that Phil, or anyone else for that matter, sabotaged the plane. "There were so many people that wanted to read into his death some sort of conspiracy, about him getting knocked off and somebody had tampered with his plane," Steve Cropper said. "As far as we could tell, it was just an accident. And that's all."

The Reverend Moses Dumas has considered all the possibilities and never reached a conclusion. "Otis had been up under Phil Walden and he was getting out from under that contract. From what Reverend Redding was telling me, he was going to resign as pastor and take over his son's business. Then, all of a sudden, his son's plane fell. And I'm sure that this thing stayed on his mind after his boy crashed: 'Was I doing the right thing? Was I the cause of it?' And some people feel that Phil Walden had it done. Now, *these* days you could do some investigating. Back in them days, it was just some Negroes killed. The book was opened and closed."

Repeated requests for the crash investigation file, made to the National Transportation Safety Board and the Federal Aviation Administration—which was charged with investigating crashes at that time—yielded one single page of paperwork. "Cause: undetermined," it says.

Two days after the funeral, Jim Stewart called a meeting at Stax. The message was simple: *Guys, we've got to keep it going.* The first order of business was getting Otis's final song, "Dock of the Bay," out on the market. Jim sent a copy of the final mix to Jerry Wexler in New York, who refused to release it until it was fine-tuned. Wexler thought it was heavy on the seagull and ocean sound effects. He also thought Otis's voice should be more out front. "That was my standing argument with Stax," he said. "The only thing I was in constant disagreement with Jim Stewart was on the mixes. Always the battle of the mixes. They always buried the voices, to my taste. He always prevailed, except this one time. That's the only one on which I really stood up."

Steve Cropper may have gotten orders to remix the song but he never actually did it. "I went back and tried, but I couldn't. I couldn't move a knob. Without saying a word, I put the same mix on another tape and sent it to Atlantic. That's the version that saw the light of day."

And Otis was right all along: "Dock of the Bay" was his breakthrough, his "career" song. Released on January 8, 1968, the record shot up the charts. It reached #1 on *both* the pop and R&B charts for the week of March 16 and stayed there four consecutive weeks. Jerry Wexler has always thought that Otis's death fueled the popularity of "Dock of the Bay." "I have a theory that it sold so well because the fans were taken with the mystical coincidence of the song and Otis's death," he said. "I think it was spiritually nourishing for them to project him seated in heavenly rapture on some big dock-of-the-bay in the sky."

And Duck Dunn still shakes his head whenever he hears the record. "It was almost like it was incomplete," he said. "That's the feeling I got from it. I think he whistled because he ran out of something to do. I might piss some people off with that but, you know, I think it would've been different if he'd lived longer. It was almost like it was just a demo. If he'd've lived, we might have done something there. He'd have maybe taken it somewhere else. Different rhythm or whatever—that, I don't know."

But most look at "Dock of the Bay" with wonder and admiration— it showed a side of Otis that was so unexpected and so unanticipated and so completely original. "I'd love to have the chance to talk to him again," said Wayne Cochran. "I'd really love to find out: Where did he come up with the idea for 'Dock of the Bay'? It was like nothing he'd ever done. 'Dock of the Bay'? He *wrote* that. He *wrote* it. Where did that come from in Otis Redding's life? I'm talking about the style. The melody. The structure. Boy, was it different. It was like night and day. It has a little Sam Cooke flavor. And the whistle. Jesus, man, what happened? Where'd that *come* from? Because that ain't like nothing he'd ever done before."

While some are convinced that Otis performed the whistle at the end only as a reminder of a horn melody he wanted to use for the fade-out, there are hints that it was actually quite intentional. Why whistle a future horn part when the horn players are standing ready right there in the studio? Otis did the exact same whistle from the first take through the last one. Perhaps he sensed that it would add a beautiful coda to the song's pensive, searching mood—the image of a man sitting alone by the water, idly whistling away and lost in deep contemplation. There's every indication that Otis Redding knew *exactly* what he was doing, knew *exactly* the sound he was after, knew *exactly* the message he wanted to send. He knew this was the record that was going to open a door long nailed shut; he just never got to step inside.

Epilogue

Two or three days after the crash, William Bell was sitting in Booker T.'s living room. "We were trying to think of something we could do to ease the pain," said William. "So we started writing this song about Otis." What started out as a few random lyrics turned into a sad and lovely gospel-flavored ballad they called "A Tribute to a King." The next day, William and Booker T. headed into the studio to record it with the sole intention of doing nothing more than sending a copy to Zelma. "I didn't write this for release," William told her. "I'm just sending it to you to have."

A couple of days later, Zelma called him from Macon. "You've got to release this."

William hesitated. He didn't want to upset Zelma, but he also didn't want people to think that he was trying to cash in on his friend's death. He declined Zelma's request, so she called Jim Stewart and told him, "I want this record out." William at last relented, but only if they put it on as the B-side of his next single. "Not a single jock played the A-side," he said. "They all played the Otis tribute. And to this day, people always request it. And I still feel a little weird about singing it."

A couple of months later, William was in Macon for a concert and Zelma came backstage and asked if he was going to sing the song about Otis. "Well, no, I don't have it on the list," he replied.

"Well, you've got to," Zelma said. "That's all they're playing down here."

He couldn't say no to Zelma and performed it for his final encore. The crowd went wild, standing to cheer as if they were offering their own final tribute to Otis. "His brother [Luther Rodgers] came backstage," William said. "And it was so funny because facially they almost looked alike. I was coming offstage after I sang it; somebody touched me on the shoulder. I turned around, looked at Rodgers's face, and for a moment it was like . . ." William's voice trailed off and there was a long silence. "It just took me aback," he said finally. "It was such a weird thing. That was a rough time. Stax never really recovered from that. It was like cutting the heart out of something."

For a while the hits kept on rolling at Stax. But it quickly became obvious the train was out of fuel and sputtering ahead on the embers. "The day Otis Redding died, that took a lot out of me," said Jim Stewart. "I was never the same person. The company was never the same to me after that. Something was taken out and was never replaced."

For Steve Cropper, the death of Otis Redding was the end of an era. "If Otis had lived, everything would have been totally different. The future of Atlantic Records would have been different. The future of Stax would have been different."

The changes began almost immediately. A month after the plane crash, word came down that Warner Brothers had acquired Atlantic Records for $20 million. Jim Stewart was naturally expecting to dovetail that deal and either sell Stax to Warner Brothers for big money (and, like Atlantic, maintain local autonomy) or, at worst, sign a more lucrative distribution deal. That was the moment Jerry Wexler dropped the hammer. He informed Jim that Warner Brothers already *owned* Stax. Jim had never really read the contract that he had signed with Atlantic back in 1965. Halfway through the thirteen-page document was a paragraph that clearly gave Atlantic sole ownership of each and every Stax record they distributed; in exchange, Stax received 10 cents for each single and 10 percent of the retail price for each album. That wasn't the only news Jerry Wexler had to offer: Atlantic also owned the contract of Stax's biggest remaining artists, Sam and Dave; they'd only been "loaning" them to Stax. In other words, Jim Stewart and Estelle Axton owned nothing more than the Stax name and the future work of a severely depleted roster of artists. Everything else—every single and every album that Stax had ever released—belonged to Atlantic. And the chips were being called in.

Jerry Wexler would later plead that the clause had been inserted by the lawyers without his knowledge. "I've got to tell you that we made a contract with him that probably was unfair," he told a skeptical writer. "I didn't know that until the end. It was a loaded deal, and I tried to give them back their catalog. But I couldn't because the lawyers had put it over. . . . What are you getting at, that we were slick? The name of the game was whatever the traffic would bear."

The people at Stax were devastated by this sudden cold infusion of "business" into something they had always held as a creative, even sacred, endeavor. "It was tough to swallow," Jim Stewart said. "It was a serious mistake I made. They obviously did not have the right or deserve [the masters] because they hadn't paid for them. They never paid for a session. Atlantic Records had a total investment of five thousand dollars in Stax Records. . . . That moment was my awakening; that was when I suddenly realized, 'Hey, I'm in the record *business*.' "

Even more, it was a betrayal. They had trusted Jerry Wexler. They had trusted Atlantic Records. Truth be known, they all felt Stax *had carried* Atlantic for a number of years, and it was an easy argument to make. The news was met with understandable anger. "Jim just felt like he was being totally taken advantage of," said Steve Cropper. "We kept [Atlantic] alive, and then they offered us so little for our endeavor. Jerry Wexler gave Sam and Dave to Stax. When we turned them down, they just looked at us with their Jewish eyes and said, 'Okay, we'll take Sam and Dave back.' It was real high-school. Then they went ahead and killed their career."

After the debacle, morale at Stax collapsed and the label struggled to stay on its feet. While Jim got an infusion of money by selling Stax to Gulf and Western for $4.3 million, it was too late; Stax was coming apart. Steve left in 1970 because of his falling-out with Al Bell, and Booker moved to California. "Al [Jackson] and I were the only remaining two when it was over with," said Duck Dunn. "By then everyone was going to Muscle Shoals to record because we didn't have Booker and we didn't have Steve. I'd always heard that Stax artists were treated fairly and Motown artists were always really screwed; they'd buy you a Cadillac but you'd never get a royalty check. And what did Stax do? They go out and get Motown's comptroller. I heard they were bringing him in and told myself, 'Well, I'm about to get fucked.' I think Jim tried to be as fair as he could with Al and me. Jim, he meant well. Stax was great to me but, you know, I left there owed a lot of money, like everybody else."

Jim Stewart and Al Bell would eventually buy back Stax; then Al bought out Jim in 1972 and became the sole owner. That's when things really turned ugly. Stax had borrowed millions from Union Planter's Bank (ironically, the same bank where Estelle Axton had worked as a teller when she and Jim had launched Stax). Union Planter's pushed a criminal investigation that ended with Al Bell under federal indictment for conspiring with a bank officer to obtain more than $18 million in fraudulent loans. Al was acquitted, but by then it was too late to save the company; Union Planter's also had forced Stax into receivership and then bankruptcy.

As that drama played itself out in 1975, tragedy struck again: Al Jackson was gunned down and murdered. Al had already been shot in the chest two months earlier by his wife, Barbara, after a heated argument. As Al recovered, he planned a divorce and a move to Atlanta to work with William Bell, who had relocated to Georgia to open his own studio and music production company. On the night of September 31, Al went to see the closed-circuit broadcast of the third fight between Muhammad Ali and Joe Frazier, the legendary "Thrilla in Manila." After the fight he was supposed to go directly to the airport and fly to Atlanta. Instead he dropped by his house. Hours later, an off-duty cop spotted a woman screaming on a front lawn, her hands tied behind her back. She identified herself as Barbara Jackson. She said she had come home the previous night and found a black male ransacking her home. She was tied up and when her husband arrived the intruder forced him to lie facedown on the floor and then shot him five times. Police went inside to find Al Jackson, shot to death.

The case was never solved, although police openly theorized that Barbara Jackson was behind her husband's murder. At one point, news reports said authorities were moving forward with indictments against her and three alleged accomplices, including the triggerman. The indictments were never handed up and, without explanation, authorities appeared to suddenly stop pursuing the case. Even today, police refuse to lift the veil of secrecy and release their case files, claiming it is still an "open" investigation.

For the surviving MG's, who still occasionally perform together and remain coveted session musicians, the losses of Otis and Al have become entwined emotions of sadness. "I remember on my twenty-seventh birthday, my wife threw me a surprise birthday party," Duck Dunn said. "Al took me to some mall and I was saying, 'Hey, I've got to get home.' So he finally said he'd drop me off. And I got home and it was a surprise party, the only one of my life. Otis was there. That was a treat. Otis was a sweetheart; you just wanted to be his friend. When we were recording and taking a break, you'd always want to walk up and hear his stories, hear his jokes. He was just so warm to be around. And I can't express how good Otis was. If I'm noted for anything, it was for playing with Otis. This isn't to slight anybody, but Otis Redding was just the best. And I don't think anybody can deny that."

Phil Walden's heart just wasn't in it anymore. One by one, he dropped all of his soul acts and began scouting for white rock bands. "Quite honestly, after Otis's death, black music just didn't seem the same for me," he said. "It became less rural as the seventies came around. Stax had been *very* rural. I don't know . . . it just wasn't near as exciting for me. And Otis had been so much more than just a client. I guess I just felt robbed that he had been poised, ready to seize the throne, and it all just went away in an accident." Phil vowed that he would never again get so personally involved with another artist. "And then," he said, "Duane Allman came along."

Instead of becoming the home of the Redwal Music empire, 535 Cotton Avenue became the headquarters of Capricorn Records. Phil's first act on the label was the Allman Brothers Band, and Capricorn spearheaded the Southern-rock phenomenon of the early 1970s. Ironically enough, the eventual collapse of Capricorn in 1979 echoed the fall of Stax—both labels reached the heights of popularity, then were decimated by death and egos before dissolving into lawsuits and bankruptcy.

Phil has publicly discussed his long period of cocaine addiction and alcoholism; after Capricorn folded, he eventually moved to Nashville and declared himself clean and sober in 1991. Phil then revived the Capricorn label and, before the label folded in 2001, created a niche in the alternative-rock scene with popular bands such as 311, Cake, and Government Mule. "I don't think about the bad times," Phil said. "Bad times come with the territory. There aren't things that plague me, that I worry about. I prefer to think about the accomplishments, the great times. I don't envy anyone in the world. I've had excitement, joy, and pleasure, everything anyone could hope for. I have some great, great memories."

Speedo Sims lives in the Atlanta area and maintains close ties to Phil Walden. Ask him about Otis and he might tell you about the night he and Otis arrived at the airport outside Macon and got into Otis's brand-new Cadillac to drive home. Once again, Speedo had forgotten to gas up the car and the gauge was sitting on empty. As usual, Otis wasn't carrying any cash and neither was Speedo. They managed to get to a gas station and Otis asked the white man inside if he could use the phone to call for help. The man refused. Otis asked if they could get some gas on credit; he even offered to leave his watch behind for collateral. The man still refused. He had no idea who Otis Redding was, and didn't care. They had to walk up a lonely highway for several miles to find a phone. Speedo told the story without bitterness; rather, he burst into laughter as if he *still* couldn't believe how dumb that white man was. Speedo then held up his left arm. On his wrist was a big, diamond-studded watch. "There were two of these in existence," he said. "Otis had one. This is the other."

Wayne Cochran is retired from the music business and pastor at Voice for Jesus Christian Center, his high-profile church in Miami, Florida. "Otis was probably the closest friend I've ever had in the music business," he said quietly. "When he died, my whole link back to Macon and the music there, it was gone. The last time I saw him, there was supposed to be an article about him coming out in a big magazine. He said, 'Man, I want to tell you before the article comes out, I don't want to embarrass you but I told them that you were my hero.'" Wayne stopped talking for a moment, still moved by the gesture. He shook his head slowly, then shrugged. "I don't know why, unless he remembered all those years . . . see, I never treated him like he was black and he never treated me like I was white. Maybe that was the issue for him; I don't know. And it's really strange because he was like an idol to me. And that's what he said about *me*. . . . I heard the story, I don't know if it's true, but I heard that the week before he was killed, they flew back into town and he got into his car, which I'm sure was a Cadillac or a Lincoln, going out to his farm. He stopped by a fireworks stand to get his kids some fireworks, and they wouldn't sell him any because he was black. Is that ignorant or what? He could have bought and sold that place a hundred times. To me, he had a hundred times more class than those people who acted like that. That was my first opportunity to pull up that curtain on society and say, 'This is stupid. This is bad.' "

Wayne was silent for a moment. There was a faraway look in his eyes; then they suddenly brightened. "Boy, Otis looked so proud in that '63 Ford convertible. Purple with black interior. He'd ride around Macon and all them people that knew him in Macon, they got to see it. I can always picture him wearing black mohair pants. Back then, the legs were tight and just a little short. He'd have on like a red V-neck sweater and red socks. And pants always pulled a little high. Yeah, that was the cool thing. And that smile of his. Great smile; *great smile*."

After a long career with King Records, Bobby Smith also retired from the business. His last big act was the masked Orion, an Elvis look-alike and sound-alike (real name: Jimmy Ellis) who became popular after Elvis died. His gimmick was clever. Trading on the theory that Elvis had faked his own death, Orion encouraged the notion that it might really *be* Elvis hiding under that Lone Ranger mask. He also recorded two surprisingly good rockabilly albums that were lost to the novelty of the act. "When I left Nashville," said Bobby, "everybody said, 'Bobby's not going to stay out of the music business; he loves it too much.' Shoot, the only way I'd get back into it was if I heard a rabbit or a squirrel sing or something. I'm too old to get back into those headaches."

It has always bothered Bobby that his role in Otis's early career was overshadowed, even forgotten. "Selling the contract on Otis was a mistake," he said. "But what's going to happen, you don't ever

know. I have a lot of respect for Otis. He was my friend. I was in bed
with the flu; wanted to go to the funeral and tried, but I couldn't. I
just couldn't. It hurt me. And, in my mind, I knew I'd had something
to do with his career. But nobody's ever said that. Johnny Jenkins
and the Pinetoppers, they were a big part of it and nobody's ever
taken care of Johnny Jenkins, either. I don't care if he drank every
day. If I had the money, the first thing I'd try to do is get him help.
Nobody's ever helped him. He's just kind of a forgotten part of it. I
heard Johnny was just drinking his life away. He had a lot of talent."

Johnny Jenkins's career never reached its promise, even though he
did turn out to be a very soulful singer in his own right. After Otis's
death, Phil Walden put Johnny together with Jaimoe and a bass player
in a power trio. It was an attempt to capitalize on the popularity of
Jimi Hendrix and it fizzled after a few months. In 1970 Johnny recorded an album for Capricorn Records called *Ton-Ton Macoute!* The
name, much to Johnny's shock and chagrin, came from a violent Hai-
tian "police" gang. The album featured members of the Allman Brothers Band, including Duane Allman on guitar, but Johnny never had
much use for it because it was too rock 'n' roll for his taste. Then,
twenty-six years later, in 1996, Johnny released his second album on
the revived Capricorn label—the wonderful *Blessed Blues*, which includes the funkiest version of "Statesboro Blues" you could ever hope
to hear.

To many, Johnny has always been viewed as a reclusive enigma.
He seldom gives interviews. He has a reputation for being cantan-
kerous and paranoid. Ploonie waved all that off. "He don't drink no
more, he don't smoke, nothing," said Ploonie, who remains in Bellevue and still plays drums with Johnny the occasional times he per-
forms. "Johnny's settled down a great deal. You can talk to him. His
story needs to be told anyway."

Johnny's cozy and comfortable little house is in East Macon, where
he lives with his wife. On the wall hangs an old battered Gibson
electric, once Johnny's main guitar and now retired from duty.
Johnny was warm and friendly and gave the impression of a man
who has found a certain peace with himself. "I never did want to be
no star, a bright-lights-and-big-city man and all that jive. I didn't care
nothing about that. I like to play my guitar and sing at home with my

family. I was raised up in the country and that's what we did. I know how to adjust to being poor. I wasn't born with no silver spoon, so if I got one I couldn't eat with it. Country folks back in them days ate with their fingers. Eating collard greens off the plate. So all that stuff didn't interest me at all. But Otis had seen other guys out there and he wanted to be just like them. Fast living. He was like that his whole life. He wanted to be a big star. He wanted people to notice him. He wanted to be seen and heard. That was his whole downfall. That's right.

"Like I say, all them guys who want to be musicians, they want to be where the women and liquor and the parties and the dope and the fashion clothes all are. I didn't want that kind of life. I always wanted a house, a wife, and a family. Breathe fresh air and live good and try to be good, try to treat people right. That's the only thing I wanted. It seemed like everywhere I went on the road there was some wrong, and I just got sick of it. And when it started happening to me, I got too sick. That's when I told them, 'To hell with it.' "

Of the other Pinetoppers, Poor Sam is living in California and Charles Davis is in Michigan. "The last time I saw Otis was about seven months before he died," said Charles. "I was visiting Macon; he was riding in a big station wagon and saw me walking up to Mann's Drive-In. When I heard that Otis had died, it threw me for almost a year. I'm fifty-eight now and whenever I hear 'Dock of the Bay,' I get that funny feeling all over again. Because I knew Otis personally. He was a friend. He was the one that started me to playing drums. I had more fun with the Pinetoppers than I ever had in my life. We were all like brothers. I haven't really kept in touch with the guys. But now—now I think I'm going to look them up."

His brother Benny also lives in Michigan and had a successful music career, going on to perform with the Moonglows (featuring Marvin Gaye), James Brown, and Etta James. While he spoke fondly of his old friend, he also still harbored anger that Otis stole "These Arms of Mine" from him. "I talked to him about it and he put it to me like this: In this business, sometimes you've got to step on somebody to make it to the top. I can put it to *you* like this: When you do people wrong, it'll come back to you. I'm fifty-seven years old and still living. And he's not. That's how I feel. He did dirty and he died a violent way. He knew the right way. His daddy was a preacher. He was taught right. He didn't have to do me like that. But he did it."

Many of the old band members are still in Macon. Ploonie's eyes lit up whenever the subject of Otis came up. "He used to kid around with me a lot," Ploonie said. "We drove over to Tindall Heights one day with Bubba Sailor. We took my car and when we went to leave, they pulled off and left me standing there on the curb! And then came back around the block, laughing. I was mad then! He just laughed. I said, 'Man, I'm gonna get you tonight!' People ask me sometimes, 'If Otis was living today, what do you think he'd be doing?' He'd still have it. Otis became a superstar in five years. A lot of people say he was living too fast or ahead of his time or however you want to put it. But the man was thinking. That's what he was doing, thinking about how to get up on top. And he got there."

Ish Mosley hasn't played the saxophone since 1969. When Otis's plane crashed, Ish was in Thailand working with the Air Force and made it back as far as San Francisco by the day of the funeral. "When I did get home, the kids said, 'Dad, Mr. Otis was by here last Monday looking for you.' I said, 'He was?' They said, 'Yeah, Daddy, he said he wanted to talk to you about something.' I *know* he wanted to talk to me about the studio he wanted to build. I'd talked to him in September about that. I was happy that he made it, you know? And it saddened me when I heard about the disaster. It was just the year before last that I . . . I didn't even know where his ranch was at. But I went out there. I saw where he was buried. Zelma, she saw me and sent out her son and then realized it was Ish. She hasn't forgotten me."

There is but a single photograph of the Pinetoppers, a black-and-white taken around 1961 at the YWCA in Macon. The guys are standing in a semicircle, in front of a wall that is covered by a large mural depicting a city street corner. They are all dressed in the same uniform: dark pants and slightly lighter shaded tuxedo jackets, bow-ties, and white shirts. Poor Sam is to the far left, on his knees and playing bass notes on a six-string guitar. Ploonie is next to him, standing up and hunched over his drum kit. In the center is Johnny, playing his Gibson with legs spread far apart in a split. To his left is Ish, down on one knee and wailing on his saxophone. Only Otis is dressed differently. He's clad in a cream-colored suit jacket and dark pants—

standing behind Johnny, almost hidden from view and with a large microphone in front of his face. Otis looks shy, almost afraid to be seen.

"There was some kind of big to-do down there that night and Phil got us to play it backing up Nappy Brown," Ploonie said as he looked at the photo. "That's me, right there. It was a real photographer. He asked us to take our instruments down and then set them up on the floor in front of that picture. And that's what we did. Then we backed up Nappy Brown that night. That man had so much money in his pockets, I never *will* forget that! Nappy Brown, is he still living?"

The Douglass Theatre, home to the old *Teenage Party* talent shows, went into decline and was eventually turned into a seedy porn house before its doors finally closed. The theater stood empty for nearly two decades; at one point a wrecking ball literally hovered outside before the city saved it at the last minute. In the late 1990s, the Douglass was restored to its original splendor and reopened as part of a planned rebirth of downtown Macon. Across the street from the Douglass stands the Georgia Music Hall of Fame, which opened in 1996.

Both hosts of the talent show at the Douglass—Ray "Satellite Poppa" Brown and Hamp "King Bee" Swain—are out of the radio business. Satellite moved to the island of St. Thomas and became a tour guide; Hamp is a manager at the Huckabee car dealership in Macon. "That was a special time," Hamp said. "Of course, when it was happening, you didn't think too much about it. But it's unreal what Macon has meant to R&B music. That was an important era, one of the most important eras, and I'm proud to have been a little part of that." He smiled broadly and chuckled heartily. "When I think about it now, I wish I'd held on to some of those things, all those old records; they'd be priceless, you know?"

The Hillview Springs clubhouse where Otis performed for the first time with Gladys Williams and her band burned to the ground around 1960. Even the lake is gone. All that's left is a concrete floor tucked away in the pines and overgrown by weeds. Gladys Williams died in the late 1980s; Percy Welch is still in Macon, as are dozens of other musicians who gained their first professional experience by performing with her. But others, such as Jessie Hancock, have passed away. "I wish Gladys would have lived so that people could interview her," Jessie said not long before his death. "She died without people realizing what an impact she had on Macon. Of course, it's another day now. Macon's quieted down now. I never would have believed that Macon would be as dead now as it is. It's so different, you can't even imagine how it looked then."

Two of Otis's closest friends from childhood—Bubba Howard and Sylvester Huckaby—are dead; Bubba Sailor and the Davis brothers are among the few people in his inner circle still living. Bubba Sailor is still haunted that he didn't show up for the gunfight Otis led on Roy Street back in 1964. Their relationship was never the same afterwards. "For a while, we were together 24/7 when he wasn't gone someplace," Bubba Sailor said. "We'd drink from each other's sodas. He'd break a hot dog in half. Whatever he had, I had it. Looking back now, I think Otis lived fast. Like he had to pack everything into one day. I didn't go to the funeral. I really didn't want to go. I miss him still. I'll hear a certain song and it'll bring back a lot. That hurt for a long time."

Huck seemed to lose hope after the plane crash. "I [could] see myself rising as he moved up in life," Huck told writer Peter Guralnick. "After he died, that's when I really started getting into trouble. Really, I just gave up." Just a week before the plane crash that killed Otis, Huck had broken into the car of a traveling shoe salesman at a local shopping center and stolen a gun, two briefcases, and four cases of cowboy boots. Then, after the crash, he went on a burglary spree that police alleged sometimes included Bubba Howard and William Shelley (the same guy once beaten by Huck who'd escaped further injury by feigning unconsciousness). On December 22, 1967, Huck broke into an animal hospital and took an adding machine, a typewriter, and a brass clock. On December 30, he broke into a drugstore and stole several cases of watches and cigarette lighters. On January 3, he knocked a hole into the rear wall of a J. C. Penney store and stole a gun and a box of shotgun shells. The burglaries landed him a three-year prison sentence.

Then, in 1977, Huck was busted for selling heroin and cocaine;

prosecutors alleged he was responsible for a full third of the total drug traffic in the entire city of Macon. Huck struck a deal with prosecutors: He got a ten-year sentence to run concurrent with a federal prison sentence he had already received on charges that included obstructing justice and firearms violations. In return, Huck agreed to testify against his alleged drug source, Charles Shelton of Decatur, whom state and federal officials fingered as one of the state's principal drug traffickers. They also alleged that Shelton ran a $3 million–a–year numbers operation in Atlanta, and he was believed to have ties with New York crime families.

Huck later appealed his conviction from prison, arguing that his agreement with the feds was coerced. His handwritten legal brief was sometimes eloquent and sometimes pointedly blunt: "This case plainly shows that your petitioner's incarceration is because of trickery, threats of intimidation, conspiracy and discrimination and also because of your petitioner's dumbness."

Juanita Huckaby, Huck's sister, now lives in the old family home where they grew up. "Ves was smart," she said, calling her brother by his family nickname. "He had a good head on his shoulder; he just didn't use it right. Ves was very smart. He knew the Bible and he loved to read. One thing, he was afraid of dead people; it was just amazing, anybody as big as he was and as bad as he was. I remember one night, he came and knocked on the window. I let him in, and he told Momma and Daddy that he had seen a ghost in the house where he was living. He was afraid of ghosts and he sat up in Momma and Daddy's room all night until day. Momma said, 'It's not a ghost. It's the devil. You're living such a bad life, it's a devil.' I can remember him, a big and strong man sitting up there in a chair all night."

When Huck got out of prison, he went back to the old neighborhood. He was respected there, looked up to because of his relationship with Otis and his presence on the street; many people knew him as "the King of Bellevue." In 1990, he was murdered. Huck—who had once rigged up his front steps to alert him whenever someone came to his door—was gunned down, execution style, in the doorway of his house. The evidence suggested the killer knocked on Huck's door; when Huck opened it, the assailant put a gun to his right temple and fired. His body was discovered later that night by a friend. Huck was forty-nine years old. Police had no witnesses, no suspects, and no motive. One theory was that it was a mob hit, retribution for his agreement to testify against his drug supplier. Another theory popular around Bellevue is that Huck's murder was related to the spread of crack cocaine into the neighborhood. Huck had sent out the word: No crack in Bellevue. When an out-of-town drug lord staked a claim on Bellevue and began pouring the drug into the community, Huck went to confront him. Days later, Huck was dead.

His murder remains unsolved.

While Fannie Mae Redding survived her son by more than twenty years, the Reverend Otis Redding, Sr., died on March 28, 1968, just three months after the fatal plane crash. "After Otis passed, it just started looking like he was giving up," said the Reverend Moses Dumas. "He was the most pitiful person that you ever wanted to see at his son's funeral. I think he really just gave up." Not long after the funeral, Mr. Redding traveled to California to visit his daughters—asking Reverend Dumas to fill in for him at a revival in Albany while he was gone. A few weeks after he returned home, he died. "When Otis was growing up, he did just what the average parent would do, especially in that day. If you was a preacher, you had a great responsibility. There was a feeling of, 'If *my* child don't do right, then I can't tell you how to do with *yours*.' You've got to live with that pressure. The Lord blessed him; his last days were his best days. Despite all the suffering he went through, God blessed him. Let him see something and enjoy life. All in all, I think he lived a full, *full* life."

Luther Rodgers Redding began dabbling in the music business, eventually managing acts such as Johnnie Taylor and Clarence Carter (who had fired Phil Walden and accused him in a lawsuit of trying to take advantage of a blind man). "My brother may have been the smartest person I ever met," Luther Rodgers said. "It's certainly a major tribute to Otis and his music that it is as contemporary today as it was then, not only in the U.S., but throughout the world. You have to look at his body of work. It was all so damn good! His place in musical history is secure."

———

Zelma now has a shoe store in downtown Macon, which she operates with her daughter Karla. She has never remarried and still lives in the family home in Round Oak, the remains of her husband buried only a few dozen feet away from the house. "I guess it's psychological and I guess it's sentimental, but believe me, it's not being selfish," she said. "And I'm not selfish because having Otis there—God, that means so much to me."

Life without her husband has never been easy. Within two years after his death, Zelma was hospitalized three times for "nerves" and another time for surgery. She has talked of taking tranquilizers to blunt the loss. For a time she went to work as a director and vice president of Redwal Music with Phil. But there wasn't much left to do there and they sold the company—including the music publishing rights to Otis's songs—to Time Music in 1972 for $300,000. After that, she tried to break into music as a talent manager, but it didn't work out. "I was a high-school dropout," she said. "I had always depended on Otis. I doubted myself. I was nervous and afraid I would say the wrong thing. I know I'm not the world's best businesswoman, but I have good common sense and that takes me a long way."

Otis's two sons, Dexter and Otis III, grew up to be musicians, performing for a time in a group called the Reddings with their cousin, Mark Locke. While they did have a hit with a version of "Dock of the Bay," the group otherwise avoided trying to trade on their father's heritage. "People say, 'Can you sing like your father?' " Otis III said. "No, I can't. Life would be easier if I could. I admire him just like anyone else. I hear Robert Palmer or Bob Geldof talk about him, and I feel the same way they do. I think he was a genius."

For a time Dexter and Otis III even owned and operated Capricorn Studios, the same studio their father and Phil had decided to build, and which Phil later completed alone. But their brand of smooth funk never caught on and Dexter moved on to other endeavors. Otis III, however, has a studio in his home in Macon and is always at work on new songs that he hopes will jump-start his career. "Dex, personality-wise, is so much like Otis it's frightening," Zelma said. "You can't get mad with Dexter no matter what he does. Otis was a happy outgoing guy, and that's Dexter. Otis [III], the older he gets, the more serious he gets, and that's another part. And the serious side of him as a businessman and a father and an artist, that falls right back into Otis; he was so serious about everything. I'm so glad I have the kids. That's what really keeps me going. And then I have all of Otis's great memories. So that kind of keeps you going—gives you something to get up for every day."

On a brisk December day in 1987, three or four hundred people gathered in a little city park on Third Street in downtown Macon, just a couple of blocks away from the Douglass Theatre. There were as many white faces as black, maybe more, gathered for a memorial service marking the twentieth anniversary of the plane crash. But, in a greater sense, Macon was doing something else, something long overdue—the city was officially embracing Otis Redding. Hamp Swain served as the master of ceremonies. Newly inaugurated mayor Lee Robinson, a redheaded Irishman, proclaimed it Otis Redding Day and declared that Otis "represented and personified everything good about Macon." Council president pro tem Willie Hill, one of the first blacks elected to the city council since Reconstruction, recalled that his wife had taught Otis in the fourth grade. "I can't tell you how much this means to our family," Karla Redding said at the conclusion of the forty-five-minute service. "It's the most important day we've had since the death of my father."

Afterwards, the family and close friends began to line up for an automobile procession to the ranch in Round Oak for a private graveside service. Karla—only twenty-four years old and fresh out of college and newly married—climbed into the crowded backseat of a friend's car for the thirty-minute trip home. As "Respect" played on a local station over the car radio, she was flooded with memories of a father she hardly knew. "I seemed so young when my father died," she said. "And I *was* only four. But I remember everything we did." She talked about the trips to the ice-cream parlor ("His favorite flavor was chocolate") and about his love for the farm ("He got pigs and goats and cows for the farm; they were always walking up on the patio and my mother would have a fit"). There also were the sometimes too-strange-to-believe encounters with fans. The Redding kids grew up sleeping with the doors unlocked—one night, they heard noises. They got up to investigate and discovered a fan who had let himself into the house and made his way to Otis's music room, standing there as if he was visiting some holy shrine.

As Karla talked, the radio station continued to play Otis Redding song after Otis Redding song. "Respect" gave way to "Mr. Pitiful" and then "I've Been Loving You Too Long." Someone asked Karla if she sang. "No!" she exclaimed. "And I wish I could!" Her voice was playful, as if she planned to talk to someone *real soon* about why she had been left out of the family talent pool. And then she laughed with the kind of laughter that's disarming, that makes you feel instantly good when you hear it.

Before long, the short procession of cars had gone past the old Club 15 building—where her father had played so many 12:01 A.M. Sunday-night shows, where James Brown had once stormed in on a Pinetoppers gig with shotgun blazing. The procession went on toward Gray, past the barbecue joint where her father was once denied service by a woman who hadn't realized he was "Otis Redding." As everyone turned left onto the little two-lane road leading to the ranch, the haunting horn lines that introduce "Try a Little Tenderness" began playing on the radio. One by one, the conversations inside the car trailed to a halt. By the time Al Jackson began the *tick-tick* beat, someone had eased up the volume and everyone in the car was listening in reverent silence. All except one. Karla Redding was sitting in the backseat, eyes closed. Her head was slightly bowed and swaying gently to the beat. And with a voice as soft as a whisper and pretty as a woman's smile, she was singing along with her father as if they were engaged in a private communion: "You've got to try a little tenderness. . . ."

A FAN'S NOTE

Virtually the entire Otis Redding album catalog has been reissued by Rhino Records, a label that always strives to do it right and usually does. *Otis Blue* is simply one of the greatest soul albums ever recorded. Also of note is *Dictionary of Soul* and *The Soul Album*. One often-overlooked album is *Live in Europe*; the sound leaves much to be desired but there's an energy and passion in the performances that make it one of the most powerful testaments to Otis's considerable talents. Another reissue, on Stax, is an album of rare tracks called *Remember Me*, which includes fascinating alternate takes of "Dock of the Bay" and "Try a Little Tenderness."

A good introduction to Otis's music is *The Very Best of Otis Redding*, a single CD that features most of his greatest singles. If you're already a fan, you'll want the four-CD set called *The Definitive Otis Redding*. It is all the title implies, and includes an entire disc of live performances plus a well-chosen array of his studio tracks. Rhino also has released *Dreams to Remember: The Otis Redding Anthology*, which is a more budget-minded version of the four-CD set. But let's be real: If you buy the *Anthology*, you're eventually going to want everything else; you might as well start with the best—*The Definitive Otis Redding*.

There is much to see in Macon that relates to Otis Redding. In fact, the Otis Redding Bridge leads into downtown from Interstate 16. No trip to the city would be complete without a trip to the fabled Douglass Theatre and, across the street, the always fascinating Georgia Music Hall of Fame.

ACKNOWLEDGMENTS

When I arrived in Macon in 1983 to work as a rookie reporter at the *Telegraph and News*, I was excited for reasons beyond finding a job at a good newspaper. Macon was the Allman Brothers Band, Capricorn Records, the birthplace of Southern rock. I was to learn quickly that my knowledge of Macon's real place in American music history was exceedingly lacking, and what an education I was about to receive! While the music business had long ago dried up in Macon, many of the old musicians were still around town. I began to encounter them after I found myself playing guitar in an R&B combo called the Bobby O'Dea Group. Bobby was a Macon treasure—a veteran of the Motown road shows, a gifted organist and smooth-voiced singer (his chief rival on the R&B scene around town happened to be Percy Welch, still performing on the club circuit and still playing the lone hit he'd had thirty years earlier, "Back Door Man"). Bobby's band also featured Jaimoe of the Allman Brothers on drums and Robert Coleman, a former guitarist for James Brown.

Every weekend we played at a little downtown club called the Rookery; invariably the front door would open and an older black man or another carrying an old battered horn case would appear. They would walk over to the darkened corner by the stage and methodically put their horn together while we played. Then, with no ado or prompting, they would walk up on the bandstand and join in; the room was so small, no microphone was needed. When the trumpet player showed up, we'd get jazzy; with a saxophone player, we'd do a simmering slow blues or an extended jam on Marvin Gaye's "What's Goin' On?" And when we had a full horn section, it was James Brown's "I Feel Good." I didn't know who those guys were, but I knew they were masters of their craft. Afterwards, Bobby would smile: "Oh, that's Shang-a-Lang; he used to play with Otis," or, "He went out with James," or, "He used to be with Richard." Sharing a stage with them, and with Jaimoe and Coleman and Bobby, that's where I began to understand the real definition of "playing with soul." Those guys, they *had* it.

That was my introduction to the other side of the city's musical heritage. About that time, a colleague at the *Telegraph and News*— music writer Jeffrey Day—became determined to document that history because the paper had largely ignored it when it was happening. He wrote a groundbreaking series on Macon's musical roots, then a series devoted entirely to Otis. That's when some of those faces I knew from the Rookery became associated with names. And that's when I began to soak up some of the rich R&B lore of Macon.

While the Redding family declined requests to be interviewed for this book—Zelma Redding said the contract she signed for a movie project forbade her from giving interviews—the actual genesis of this book came from a conversation with Otis Redding III not long after I finished writing *Midnight Riders: The Story of the Allman Brothers Band*. I was in a little club in the alley behind Cherry Street with my friend Chank, and he introduced me to Otis III. We chatted for over an hour, until he walked out on the arms of two of the most beautiful and exotic-looking white women I'd ever seen in Macon, Georgia. "You should do your next book on my father," Otis III said before he left. "He's right," Chank chimed in. "The shame is, nobody's ever done one."

In many ways, this book is the "prequel" to the Allman Brothers book, the story of Macon before Phil Walden brought Duane Allman to town. I have talked with dozens of people who witnessed portions of the Otis Redding history and offered information and insights. I want to thank all of them for their help, their wisdom, and, often, their friendships—particularly the guys in the Pinetoppers: Johnny Jenkins, Willie "Ploonie" Bowden, Ish Mosley, Charles Davis, and Benny Davis. They each were warm and generous with their memories and most had never before told their story. Also of special note: Hewell "Chank" Middleton and Carrolle M. King, Bubba Sailor, Juanita Huckaby, Percy Welch, Jessie Hancock, Hamp Swain, Satellite Poppa, Newt Collier, and Bobby Smith, Wayne Cochran, Jaimoe, David Tharpe, Larry D. Wilder, Billy Young, Muriel Jackson and Wilton

Rocker of the Washington Library archives, and the Reverend Moses Dumas. Also: Jeffery Day; Ed Duskin of the Dawson Historical Society; Dawson mayor Robert Albritton; Nathanial James; Jack Lang; William Head, Ph.D., historian for Robins Air Force Base; Marty Willett at the Georgia Music Hall of Fame; Cheryl at the Federal Records Center and Helen Newberry at the Clerk's Office, U.S. District Court in Macon; Betsy Poore at the Douglass Theatre; John Hiscox, executive director of the Macon/Bibb County Housing Authority; Ed Johnstone at Epps Air Service; William Bell; Jerry Wexler; Duck Dunn; Steve Cropper, Estelle Axton, Phil Walden (whom I interviewed several times as a reporter in Macon—he declined to be interviewed for this book as he pursues the movie project with Zelma); Karla Redding; Otis Redding III; Earl "Speedo" Sims; Alan Walden; Bob O'Dea; Roger Cowles; Mark Pucci; Jerry Butler; Tara Murphy; and Alex Cooley.

Thanks to my friends from *Atlanta* magazine, who have given me a place to call home: Lee Walburn, Emma Edmunds, Doug Monroe, Heather Moors-Johnson, Howard Lalli, Rebecca Poyner-Burns, Jennifer McLaine, Jamie Vacca, Elaine Hightower, Darryl Moland, and Kevin Benefield. And to the guys in the band Smokestack Lightnin', who play every night with heart and verve: Tom Kessler, Neal Canis, Bill Abbott, Eric Fisher, "Picho Bill" Schultz.

For help and support beyond the call of duty through the years, special thanks to: Carolyn Lock; Ken and Alice Lyon; Virginia Schenk-Berry and William Berry; Gloria and Will Brame; Suzanne Espinosa; Susan Parker; Oby Brown; Soo Chen; Kim Payne; David and Jill Lauterborn; Paul Hemphill; Michael Pietsch; Cherie Dean; Kathy Samples; Frank White; Tinsley Ellis; Stacy Lam and for the memory of her father, Nelson Lam; Bryan Cole; Francine Reed; Edd Miller; Jimmy O'Neil; Surelle Pinkston; Mama Louise for the soul food and hugs; and my family for the love and encouragement.

Also, my deep appreciation to my agent, David Black, for seeing the vision and selling it; and thanks to Gary Morris for his crisis management and encouragement. Also, thanks to Cal Morgan at St. Martin's for believing in an Otis Redding biography and to Monique Patterson for taking it home. Also to Eric Raab and Christine Aebi for the nifty copyediting work and Steve Snider for the design.

SOURCES

Just a few weeks after completing this book, I happened to stop by the Georgia Music Hall of Fame in Macon and ran into Newt Collier. "Did you hear about Jessie Hancock?" he asked. "He died two days ago." Another link was gone.

When I met Jessie, he was running a pool hall downtown. To most people, that was his identity. But the musicians around town knew. Over and over again, people asked me, "Have you talked to Jessie?" His performing career had dried up, but he still had a little room just off his garage that was devoted to music. Inside were rows upon rows of old jazz records (Sonny Stitt was a particular favorite) and an old stereo system. Sitting reverently in the center of the room was his old saxophone. Its shine may have been stolen from years of playing on the road, but God, if that saxophone could only speak—the stories it would tell. "I haven't played in a while," Jessie said. "But I've been thinking of sitting down with it, maybe play a little around town again."

One of the challenges of this book was separating legend from the truth. In some cases, the legends *were* the truth; in many, they shadowed the truth. But the one really striking thing is that so much of the story was untold. Many of them, like Jessie, were still living in Macon and their roles in Otis's rise to fame had been lost to obscurity. It wasn't that they didn't want to talk; it was that nobody had ever asked. It is history's loss that so many died before a book on Otis Redding was written, most notably Huck, Bubba Howard, Al Jackson, Jr., Gladys Williams, and Shang-a-Lang.

Also important in the research of this book were court records. I reviewed thousands of pages of public documents, transcripts, and depositions from Memphis to Macon. There are instances in which scenes and dialogue are re-created. Those come from several sources: I witnessed a few myself; some come from court testimony; some were depicted in magazine articles; and others are based upon the remembrances of at least one person who either was present or, in a few cases, heard about an event firsthand from a participant.

As with my first book, *Midnight Riders*, the Middle Georgia Archives of the Washington Memorial Library in Macon was an important source. The library has an extensive Otis Redding collection and was a valuable source of information, especially an unpublished interview with the late Clint Brantley. So were the growing archives at the Georgia Music Hall of Fame in Macon.

ARTICLES

Alesia, Tony. "Redding Promoter Recalls Crash." Madison Newspapers, Inc., August 14, 1997.

Associated Press. "Redding Feared Dead in Crash." *Macon Telegraph*, December 11, 1967.

Bodwen, Jeff. "Thousands Pay Tribute at Otis Redding Rites." *Macon Telegraph*, December 19, 1967.

Day, Jeffrey. "Macon's Black Music Roots." *Macon Telegraph and News*, February 3, 1987.

———. "The Final Music-Making Days of Otis Redding." *Macon Telegraph and News*, December 4, 1987.

———. "The Legendary Big O." *Macon Telegraph and News*, December 4, 1987.

Fisher, Robert. "Major Drug Dealer Gets 10-Year Term." *Macon Telegraph*, June 20, 1977.

Francis, Miller. "Nothing but the Blues." *Great Speckled Bird*, September 28, 1970.

Freeman, Scott. "I Remember Everything We Did." *Macon Telegraph and News*, December 11, 1987.

———. "Macon Shows Otis 'A Little Tenderness.'" *Macon Telegraph and News*, December 11, 1987.

Hall, Andy. "Survivor Recalls Sinking in Lake." *Wisconsin State Journal*, December 6, 1992.

Hedgepath, William. "Phil Walden Reinvents Himself." *Southern*, n.d.

Hilburn, Robert. "Return of the Golden Boy." *Los Angeles Times*, August 11, 1991.

King, Jim. "Man Gets Seven Years on Pot Charges." *Macon Telegraph and News*, November 18, 1986.

Knudson, Dewey. "State Drug Ring Suspect Held in Bibb Jail." *Macon Telegraph*, June 27, 1977.

Lamb, Bob. "Macon's Own Otis Redding Returns Home." *Macon Telegraph*, July 18, 1965.

———. "Johnny Jenkins Has a Hit and a Great Sound." *Macon Telegraph*, 1965.

Maley, Dan. "Man Shot to Death in Unionville Home." *Macon Telegraph and News*, April 2, 1990.

McCready, Eldredge, Jr. "Remembering Otis Redding." *Macon Metro Times*, December 9, 1992.

Moe, Doug. "The Riddle of Otis Redding." *Madison Captial Times*, December 6, 1997.

Peters, Art. "Death of a Soul Man." *Sepia*, February 1968.

(unknown author). "Zelma Redding's Life Without Otis." *Sepia*, December 1970.

Walburn, Steve. "Phil Walden: Flip Side." *Atlanta* magazine, August 1993.

Weiler, Joseph. "Stax Records: The Dream That Died." *Memphis Commercial Appeal*, February 8, 1976.

BOOKS

Booth, Stanley. *The True Adventures of the Rolling Stones* (formerly *Dance with the Devil*). New York: Vintage Books, 1984.

———. *Rhythm Oil: A Journey Through the Music of the American South*. London: Jonathan Cape, 1991.

Bowman, Rob. *Soulsville U.S.A.* New York: Schirmer Books, 1997.

Branch, Taylor. *Parting the Waters: America in the King Years 1954–63*. New York: Simon and Schuster, 1988.

———. *Pillar of Fire: America in the King Years 1963–65*. New York: Simon and Schuster, 1998.

Charters, Samuel. *Robert Johnson*. New York: Oak Publications, 1973.

Clayman, Dr. Charles B. (medical editor). *The American Medical Association Encyclopedia of Medicine*. New York: Random House, 1989.

Comer, Harriett (editor). *History of Macon: The First 100 Years*. Macon Telegraph and News, n/d.

Daniel, Clifton. *Chronicle of America*. Liberty, Mississippi: JL International Publishing, 1961.

——— (editor). *Chronicle of the 20th Century*. New York: Dorlins Kindersley Publishing, 1987.

The editors of Rolling Stone. *Rock Almanac: The Chronicles of Rock and Roll*. New York: Rolling Stone Press/Collier Books, 1983.

Foner, Eric, and John A. Garraty (editors). *The Reader's Companion to American History*. New York: Houghton Mifflin, 1991.

Freeman, Scott. *Midnight Riders: The Story of the Allman Brothers Band*. New York: Little, Brown and Co., 1995.

Graff, Gary, Josh Freedom du Lac, and Jim McFarlin. *R&B: The Essential Album Guide*. Detroit: Visible Ink Press, 1998.

Graham, Bill, and Robert Greenfield. *Bill Graham Presents: My Life Inside Rock and Out*. New York: Doubleday, 1992.

Guralnick, Peter. *Feel like Goin' Home*. New York: Harper and Row, 1971.

———. *Lost Highway: Journeys and Arrivals of American Musicians*. Boston: David R. Godine, 1979.

———. *Sweet Soul Music: Rhythm and Blues and the Southern Dream of Freedom*. New York: Harper and Row, 1986.

———. *Searching for Robert Johnson*. New York: E. P. Dutton, 1989.

Hemphill, Paul. *The Good Old Boys*. New York: Simon and Schuster, 1974.

———. *Too Old to Cry*. New York: Viking Press, 1981.

Johnson, Paul Michael. *The Negro in Macon, Georgia, 1865–71*. Master's thesis, B.S.E.D, University of Georgia, 1968.

March, David, and John Swenson. *The New Rolling Stone Record Guide*. Random House/Rolling Stone Press, 1979.

Palmer, Robert. *Deep Blues*. New York: Viking Press, 1981.

(unknown author). *Macon's Black Heritage: The Untold Story*. Macon: Tubman African-American Museum, 1997.

Weinberg, Max, and Robert Santelli. *The Big Beat: Conversations with Rock's Great Drummers*. New York: Billboard Books, 1991.

Wexler, Jerry, and David Ritz. *Rhythm and the Blues: A Life in American Music*. New York: Knopf, 1993.

White, Charles. *The Life and Times of Little Richard*. New York: Harmony Books, 1984.

Wolf, Jaime (editorial director). *The Definitive Otis Reading*. Rhino Records, 1993.

Zalkind, Ronald. *Contemparary Music Almanac 1980–81*. New York: Schirmer Books, 1980.

COURT DOCUMENTS

U.S. District Court, Macon District

Clarence G. Carter vs. Redwal Music and Phil Walden
Claude H. Trucks vs. Phil Walden

U.S. District Court, Western Division of Tennessee

Tom Edenton vs. Sam and Dave, Phil and Alan Walden, and Walden Artists and Promotions
Estate of Otis Redding vs. Stax Records/East Memphis Music
Atlantic Records vs. Estate of Otis Redding, Stax Records, and Stax trustee A. J. Calhoun

U.S. Bankruptcy Court, Memphis

East Memphis Music/Stax Records
Isaac Hayes vs. Stax Records/East Memphis Music

Bibb County Superior Court

CIVIL:

Sam Davis vs. Phil Walden
David McGee vs. Otis Redding
Willie McGee vs. Otis Redding
Shaw Artists Corporation vs. Phil Walden

Katherine Walden vs. Phil Walden
Various incorporation papers

CRIMINAL:
   Otis Redding
   Sylvester Huckaby
   William Shelley
   Various deed and property records

Bibb County State Court

CRIMINAL:
   Otis Redding (various files)
   Sylvester Huckaby (various files)

Bibb County Probate Court
   Marriage License: Otis Redding and Zelma Atwood
   Estate of Fannie Mae Redding

Jones County (Georgia) Superior Court
   Ray Frost vs. Catherine Moore
   Various deed and property records

Jones County Probate Court
   Estate of Otis Redding, Sr.
   Estate of Otis Redding, Jr.

Federal Aviation Administration
   Crash record

INDEX